T0311839

Modernity and Malaysia

Bringing together over thirty years of detailed ethnographic research on the Menraq of Malaysia, this fascinating book analyses and documents the experience of development and modernization in tribal communities.

Descendents of hunter-gatherers who have inhabited Southeast Asia for about 40,000 years, the Menraq (also known as Semang or Negritos) were nomadic foragers until they were resettled in a Malaysian government-mandated settlement in 1972. *Modernity and Malaysia* begins with the 'Jeli Incident' in which several Menraq were alleged to have killed three Malays, members of the dominant ethnic group in the country. Alberto Gomes links this uncharacteristic violence to Menraq experiences of Malaysian-style modernity that have left them displaced, depressed, discontented, and disillusioned. Tracing the transformation of the lives of Menraq resulting from resettlement, development, and various 'civilizing projects', this book examines how the encounter with modernity has led the subsistence-oriented, relatively autonomous Menraq into a life of dependence on the state and the market.

Challenging conventional social scientific understanding of concepts such as modernity and marginalization, and providing empirical material for comparison with the experience of modernity for indigenous peoples around the world, *Modernity and Malaysia* is a valuable resource for students and scholars of anthropology, development studies and indigenous studies, as well as those with a more general interest in Asian studies.

Alberto G. Gomes is Senior Lecturer and Program Convenor of Sociology and Anthropology at La Trobe University, Australia. His books include *Looking for Money* (COAC and Trans Pacific Press, 2004) and *Malaysia and the Original People* (with R. Dentan, K. Endicott, and M. B. Hooker, Allyn and Bacon, 1997).

The Modern Anthropology of Southeast Asia

Editors
Victor T. King, University of Hull
Michael Hitchcock, London Metropolitan University

The books in this Series incorporate basic ethnographic description into a wider context of responses to development, globalisation and change. Each book embraces broadly the same concerns, but the emphasis in each differs as authors choose to concentrate on specific dimensions of change or work out particular conceptual approaches to the issues of development. Areas of concern include nation-building, technological innovations in agriculture, rural-urban migration, the expansion of industrial and commercial employ- ment, the rapid increase in cultural and ethnic tourism, the consequences of deforestation and environmental degradation, the 'modernisation of tradi- tion', ethnic identity and conflict, and the religious transformation of society.

The Modern Anthropology of Southeast Asia: An Introduction
Victor T. King & William D. Wilder

The Changing Village Environment in the Southeast
Applied anthropology and environment reclamation in the northern Philippines
Ben J. Wallace

The Changing World of Bali
Religion, society and tourism
Leo Howe

Modernity and Malaysia
Settling the Menraq forest nomads
Alberto G. Gomes

Modernity and Malaysia
Settling the Menraq forest nomads

Alberto G. Gomes

LONDON AND NEW YORK

First published 2007 by Routledge
2 Park Square, Milton Park, Abingdon, Oxon, OX14 4RN

Simultaneously published in the USA and Canada
By Routledge
270 Madison Ave, New York NY 10016

*Routledge is an imprint of the Taylor & Francis Group,
an informa business*

Transferred to Digital Printing 2010

© 2007 Alberto G. Gomes

Typeset in New Times Roman
By Graphicraft Limited, Hong Kong

All rights reserved. No part of this book may be reprinted or
reproduced or utilized in any form or by any electronic,
mechanical, or other means, now known or hereafter
invented, including photocopying and recording, or in any
information storage or retrieval system, without permission in
Writing from the publishers.

British Library Cataloguing in Publication Data
A catalogue record for this book is available from
the British Library

Library of Congress Cataloging in Publication Data
Gomes, Alberto G., 1954–
    Modernity and Malaysia : settling the Menraq forest
nomads / Alberto Gomes.
        p. cm. – (Modern anthropology of Southeast Asia series)
    Includes bibliographical references and index.
    1. Indigenous peoples–Land tenure–Malaysia–Kelantan.
2. Indigenous peoples–Malaysia–Kelantan–Social conditions.
3. Indigenous peoples–Malaysia–Kelantan–Government
relations. 4. Kelantan–Ethnic relations.   5. Kelantan–Social
conditions.   I. Title.

GN635.M4.G66 2007
306.095951–dc22
                                                    2006039594

ISBN10: 0-415-42253-1 (hbk)
ISBN10: 0-415-59620-3 (pbk)
ISBN10: 0-203-96075-0 (ebk)

ISBN13: 978-0-415-42253-6 (hbk)
ISBN13: 978-0-415-59620-6 (pbk)
ISBN13: 978-0-203-96075-2 (ebk)

Contents

Illustrations

Plates

Figures

Maps

Tables

Preface

Anyone visiting Malaysia for the first time will undoubtedly be impressed with the country's ultra-modern infrastructure and technological advancement such as the colossal and high-tech Kuala Lumpur International Airport, the extensive network of roads and highways, the automated light rail transit (LRT) in Kuala Lumpur, and the numerous skyscrapers, of which the Petronas Twin Towers, once the tallest buildings in the world, stand out. However, this image of a highly modernized and advanced nation conceals the cruel reality of people in the country living in abject poverty. The Menraq belong to this category of Malaysia's forgotten peoples. I visited the Menraq at Sungai Rual Resettlement in 1975 for the first time as a member of an undergraduate anthropology field research group. I returned to Rual several months later to investigate the demographic implications of resettlement for the Menraq people. These early field visits greatly stimulated my intellectual interest in Orang Asli studies and spurred my concern for the welfare of the people. I have visited the Menraq on several more occasions since then with the aim of studying and documenting how resettlement and the various state-sponsored development projects are transforming and affecting their lives. Drawing from these ethnographic field visits, this book focuses on Menraq experiences of Malaysian-style modernity. However, it is not just about the Menraq; it is also about Malaysian modernity and its implications for the country's tribal communities. As a case study of the effects of development on nomadic foragers, who not long ago depended almost solely on the tropical rain forest for their survival, this book provides empirical material for a comparative examination of the implications of modernity for tribal communities and indigenous peoples around the world.

For a book based on longitudinal research spanning thirty years, as one would expect I have many people and institutions to thank. First, I am immensely grateful to the Menraq of Sungai Rual for allowing me to scrutinize their lives and for narrating to me their life-stories over the many years that I have known them. I hope that this book, which reveals and documents their plight to a larger audience, will in a small measure reciprocate all the kindness, friendship, and hospitality they have afforded me in all my visits in the past thirty years. I dedicate this book to them and their fellow Orang Asli (Malaysian Aborigines).

Numerous colleagues and friends have assisted me in some way or another and I acknowledge their help with enormous gratitude. The list of names would be far too long to be included here but I would like to mention the following people for my special thanks: Bah Akeh (who accompanied me on several of my recent visits), Geoffrey Benjamin (for his crucial comments and suggestions for improving the book and for giving me permission to use an adapted version of his ethnological map (Map 2.1)), Robert Dentan (for his unwavering support and encouragement over the years), Kirk Endicott (for reading and providing good comments on an initial draft of this book), Colin Nicholas (for his support and his inspirational Orang Asli activism and scholarship), Terry Rambo (for introducing me to Menraq research thirty years ago), Diana Riboli (for sharing with me some of her field experiences at Rual), Rokeman bin Abd. Jalil (for research assistance in 1987–88), Kamal Solhaimi (for research assistance in 1999–2001 and for permitting me to use two of his photos in this book), and Bah Tony Williams-Hunt (for accompanying and assisting me on two of my visits to Rual). Several colleagues organized for me to speak about this project at their institutions and I wish to thank them for the opportunity to sharpen and improve my arguments: Karen Armstrong and Jukka Siikala (University of Helsinki), Adela Baer (Oregon State University), Robert Dentan (State University of New York, Buffalo), Alan Fix (University of California, Riverside), Signe Howell (University of Oslo), Richard Lee and Shuichi Nagata (University of Toronto).

I am grateful to the series editors of the Modern Anthropology of Southeast Asia Series, Victor King, Michael Hitchcock and, especially, William Wilder for his meticulous reading of the manuscript and his constructive comments, criticisms, and suggestions for making the book more readable. I would also like to acknowledge the helpful comments by the two anonymous readers. At Routledge/Taylor & Francis, my thanks go to Stephanie Rogers (Editor, Routledge Asian Studies), Helen Baker, Hayley Norton, Vicky Claringbull, Kathy Auger, and Lindsey Brake (copy-editor) who have all demonstrated the importance of professionalism and patience in book publishing.

I would like to acknowledge La Trobe University for funding my research visits in 1999 and 2000. I also wish to thank the staff of the School of Social Sciences at La Trobe University, particularly Bronwyn Bardsley, Barbara Matthews, Mary Reilly, Kathy Ward, and Elaine Young for their assistance, and my colleagues, especially David DeVaus, John Goldlust, Joel Kahn, Beryl Langer, Helen Lee, Wendy Mee, and John Morton for making the 'School' a superb collegial place for intellectual work.

I would also like to acknowledge the assistance given me by several members of the Malaysian Department of Aboriginal Affairs, particularly Abdullah Hassan (Pak Lah) who accompanied me on my field visits to Rual in the 1970s.

Last, but not least, I also wish to thank my family, especially Karen, my partner in life, who keeps me happy and sane with her love and support. I have also had the benefit of her marvellous typesetting skills in helping me prepare the maps and figures. I am also grateful to my amazing children Joao and Jenna, who enrich my life in countless ways.

Abbreviations

CDR	Crude Death Rate
COAC	Centre for Orang Asli Concerns
FELCRA	Federal Land Rehabilitation and Consolidation Authority
FELDA	Federal Land Development Authority
FSC	Forest Stewardship Council
ICA	Industrial Co-ordination Act 1975
IMP	Industrial Master Plan
IRRI	International Rice Research Institute
JHEOA	Jabatan Hal Ehwal Orang Asli (Department of Orang Asli Affairs)
KESEDAR	Kelatan State Development Agency
MARA	Majlis Amanah Rakyat (Council of Trust for Indigenous People)
NCP	National Culture Policy
NEP	New Economic Policy
PAS	Parti Islam (Islamic Party)
PITC	Perak Integrated Timber Complex
POASM	Persatuan Orang Asli Semananjung Malaysia (Association of Orang Asli of Peninsular Malaysia)
PPRT	Program Pembangunan Rakyat Termiskin (Development Programme for the Hardcore Poor)
RIDA	Rural and Industrial Development Authority
RISDA	Rubber Industry Smallholders' Development Authority
RPS	Rancangan Penempatan Semula/Rancangan Perkumpulan Semula (Resettlement Programme/Regroupment Programme)
RSPSP	RISDA Smallholder Plantation Limited Company
TOL	Temporary Occupation Licence
UMNO	United Malays National Organization

1 Introduction

The Jeli incident

3 killed, 2 hurt in fight with Orang Asli By Shamsul Akmar
KOTA BARU, Mon – Three men were killed and two others were injured in a fight, believed to be over land matters, with a group of Orang Asli men in Sungai Rual, Jeli, about 100km from here. Police have detained 11 Orang Asli men in connection with the killings.

(New Straits Times, 27/04/1993)

It is very seldom that Orang Asli, the aboriginal people of Malaysia, are the object of media attention. They become newsworthy only when there are reports, usually based on misconceptions or myths, about their cultural practices, deemed bizarre or exotic by the public at large, or when dignitaries visit one of their villages or when something sensational involving Orang Asli happens. In April 1993, the event of a homicide in an Orang Asli settlement achieved media prominence by making it to the front page of most of the national newspapers in the country. As in the above extract from one of the national dailies, we are told that three people were killed allegedly by a group of Orang Asli near the town of Jeli in Kelantan, close to the Malaysian-Thai border. The homicide victims were Malays, members of Malaysia's dominant ethnic group. This event, which has come to been known as 'the Jeli incident', was of more than special interest to me because the Orang Asli men came from the village, Sungai Rual (shortened to Rual hereafter), where I have carried out anthropological research since 1976 and because homicidal conflict is virtually unheard of in the community I studied. The Orang Asli of Rual belong to an ethnolinguistic group called the Semang or Negritos. I prefer calling them Menraq, a word meaning human or people in most of the languages spoken in the Rual settlement and it is a term that Rual people use to refer to themselves.[1]

The precise details of the Jeli incident are unclear as people are reluctant to elaborate what actually happened. Several months after the event I visited Rual and talked about the incident to a number of people, including the eleven men accused of killing. From these conversations and from court trial reports, I was able to piece together what had occurred. I was told that a Malay man showed up at a hamlet at Rual, demanding the people move out by the next day. He insisted that he had bought the land from the State land office and he now had legal title to it. The Menraq had just returned from a temporary settlement as their hamlet had been quarantined after a cholera outbreak that killed six villagers. The next day the man turned up with five other Malay men, reportedly brandishing machetes and speaking belligerently, to chase the Menraq away. The Menraq headman told the Malays that his people had decided not to leave their hamlet, indicating that they were residing on their ancestral land. An altercation ensued, tempers flared and the situation turned tense. The Malays abused the Menraq and physically threatened the people with their machetes. The tense situation escalated, and after a Malay man assaulted the village headman, a scuffle broke out which ended in fatalities. One Malay man succumbed to injuries purportedly inflicted by the Menraq, and two Malay men were found dead a kilometre or so away in the van they had travelled in, allegedly killed by blowpipe-propelled poisoned darts. Three Malays who bolted from the scene escaped unhurt. The incident was reported to the authorities and eleven Menraq were arrested. Subsequently nine men were charged with culpable homicide not amounting to murder. The court trial went on for months and eventually the accused were acquitted. To a question by the defence lawyers as to which one of the accused was the owner of the blowpipe believed to be the murder weapon, the police officer in court replied that he was uncertain because 'they all look alike'. With such an element of doubt, the presiding judge requested that the charges against the accused be dropped and the case was dismissed.

Anyone who is unfamiliar with the Orang Asli may think of such acts of violence as commonplace among people who are often labelled as 'savages' or 'primitives'. After all, stories of headhunting, 'tribal warfare', the use of poisoned darts, and cannibalism among tribal peoples have captured the imagination of the general public for a long time, yet rarely, except in the writings of anthropologists, are these images or portrayals ever challenged or rejected. When I was first told about what took place at Rual, I received the news with scepticism and trepidation. I was sceptical because such a display of violence was out of character for the Orang Asli. Many anthropologists have characterized Orang Asli as non-violent and non-intimidating in personal demeanour. Dentan (1979), who has written extensively on the Semai, another Orang Asli subgroup, was prompted by his observation of non-violence to title his book, *The Semai: A Non-Violent People of Malaya*. As for the Menraq, Carey (1976: 17) observes:

> The Negritos are a friendly and a peaceful people but, as might be expected, they are very shy. Being unused to outside contacts, they are suspicious of strangers and at times, a casual approach, based on curiosity and general interest, may be interpreted by them as a threat. Their

invariable response to such a threat, real or imaginary, is not one of hostility but flight.

Not once during my field research with the Menraq have I ever witnessed aggressive behaviour by the people. How then can we explain this uncharacteristic act of violence? To understand this deviant behaviour, it is necessary to follow the remarkable path of social, economic and cultural change among the Menraq. Like almost all other tribal[2] communities around the world, Rual has experienced, and is still experiencing, tremendous change. Malaysian authorities consider the Menraq traditional lifestyle of nomadic foraging to be inimical to modernity. For Malaysia to become an advanced industrialized nation, it is envisioned that all its citizens will need to be modernized. For the Menraq, modernity has in a large measure taken the form of government-directed development projects implemented to settle the nomadic forest peoples into permanent settlements and to draw them into market economies. It is believed that this will settle the perceived problem of the existence of a people considered 'out-of-place' in modern, industrialized, high-tech Malaysia. In the course of three decades of modernization, present-day life in Rual has almost nothing in common with what it used to be. But beneath this veneer of a progressive transformation of Rual lies a story of hardship. The clue to the Jeli tragedy lies in this transformation. As this book will show, these development projects have created more problems for the Menraq than they were ostensibly intended to resolve. A detailed discussion of the implications of some of these projects will demonstrate how development has operated to lead a contented group of people to misery and vulnerability, to dependence on, and exploitation by, outsiders and external forces. I hope to show how the violence of the Jeli incident is linked to the growing despair and discontentment among the Menraq, which emanates from their experiences of displacement, dispossession, and deprivation. From anthropological studies, such as Bodley (1990), Maybury-Lewis (2002), and Duncan (2004) on the experiences of modernity among tribal communities, it is possible to conclude that the Menraq situation is by no means unique. What, then, is the general picture of tribal communities in the modern world?

Tribal communities in the modern world

Tribal communities, whether referred to as aborigines, hunters and gatherers, or indigenous minorities have been drawn into the modern world in many different ways, some through violence and conquest, others more gradually and benignly. In some of the better known cases, such as the Native Americans and the Australian Aborigines, tribal communities have been forcibly annexed in the course of European colonial expansion and settlement to become outliers in territory dominated by others acting in the name of 'the Western world'. They have consequently paid a high price in displacement from their land or territory which for many of them is the spiritual basis of their social and cultural system, not to mention their source of livelihood. Some tribal communities have been enticed into the modern world through the operations of the market economy, often guided by state intervention. Social scientists, like development agencies, regard the market as central to development and modernization.

This book will, it is hoped, illustrate the experiences of modernity in tribal communities through a detailed case study of the Rual Menraq. The ethnographic evidence presented in this case study might appear familiar to readers in light of the many anthropological studies of the consequences of modernization and development for such peoples as the Rual Menraq. Anthropologists studying small-scale communities around the world have observed peoples located in what Tsing (1993) calls 'out-of-the-way' places and consider them 'the victims of progress' (Bodley 1990), forgotten minorities, or marginalized peoples. This book, however, challenges several of the propositions made in some of these studies. First, it is against the assumptions of an earlier generation of anthropologists who treated such communities as isolated and largely self-contained, having minimal or no contact with the outside world, a misconception effectively challenged and demolished in the early 1980s by anthropologists such as Eric Wolf, Sidney Mintz, and June Nash. The Orang Asli have usually been portrayed as living in remote habitats, and nomadic forest dwelling Orang Asli are considered to be people with no ties to land. These are of course myths which have been dispelled in various recent studies on the Orang Asli (see, for example, Dentan *et al.* 1997, Gomes 2004, Nicholas 2000). This book finds that Menraq are not really isolated for they live within a variety of local, national, regional and global political, economic and social contexts, and always have done so in varying degrees. They are certainly not, to use Eric Wolf's well-known phrase, 'people without history' (Wolf 1982). Furthermore, as will be outlined later, they maintain a strong sense of territorial connection and adhere to a system of land tenure. Second, contrary to popular assumptions and conventional wisdom, the marginalization of an isolated group, as the ethnographic evidence presented in this book reveals, is an outcome of their recent experience of modernity and not because they inhabit an 'out-of-the-way' place. It is a common argument that marginalization is an effect of living in areas far from economic and political centres. Hence, to draw people into the mainstream of economies and societies, governments and development agencies have advocated, implemented, and justified policies and programmes to settle or resettle people closer to the centres or in areas deemed more accessible. Paradoxically, as contended in this book, the growing marginalization of the Menraq and people like them is closely linked to their increasing involvement or entanglement with 'mainstream' Malaysian and international society. It is their immersion into the culture of global capitalism and international economics and their entrapment by the tentacles of state hegemony which have brought about their disadvantages and increased their economic and social woes. Third, while studies on tribal communities as 'victims of progress' fruitfully devoted attention to the distress such peoples have faced, and are facing, the active responses of tribal peoples to their plight have been obscured or neglected. It is my contention, as it is of many anthropologists, that people like the Menraq are not simply passive subjects in this encounter. Unlike the assumptions made in 'impact studies' of people as helpless and hapless victims, in this book the Menraq are treated as active agents who are struggling to maintain their autonomy and control of their own destiny. Their strategies, actions, and philosophies in coping with and explaining the changes which have been foisted on them are given due attention in understanding their experiences of modernity.

The violence of modernity

At a time when violent conflict, civil strife, and terrorism are making the world increasingly unsafe and insecure, it is vital to understand why people turn to violence in response to conflict or disagreements with other people or with nation-states. This book will shed light on how changing social and economic conditions emanating from modernization projects can lead to violent conflict. It has been inspired by several other studies, but two deserve mention here.

In one study, in a book provocatively titled *The Violence of the Green Revolution*, Shiva has linked the communal violence between the Sikhs and the Hindus in the Punjab, which left about 15,000 people dead between 1986 and 1991, to the adverse effects of agricultural developmental programmes, known as the 'Green Revolution', implemented by the Indian government with financial and scientific support from international agencies. Contrary to expectations and the official rhetoric proclaiming the successes of such development programmes, Shiva contends that the social, economic, and ecological changes associated with the Green Revolution have left the Punjab with 'diseased soils, pest-infested crops, water-logged deserts, and indebted and discontented farmers' (Shiva 1991: 12). This legacy, according to her, has led to a high level of frustration, anger, and discontentment among the people. Unable to contain or resolve such feelings of despair, people began to direct their anger and frustration towards members of other communities, escalating into communal strife and violence. As I discuss in greater detail later, the Green Revolution, despite success for some, has also adversely affected many farmers in Malaysia.[3] It is highly likely that the Malays who sought to evict the Rual Menraq were farmers in a similar state of economic impoverishment to their Punjabi counterparts. Rather than directing their frustration towards their neighbours in random acts of violence, these Malays' attempts to usurp land from the Menraq could be seen as their means of solving their predicament arising from the Green Revolution implemented in the rural areas of Kelantan.

Another celebrated case of conflict in rural areas is the Zapatistas' rebellion in the Chiapas region in Mexico. In her ethnography *Mayan Visions*, Nash (2001) connects the mobilization of Mayan indigenous forces into the Zapatista movement to the impoverishing effects of globalization and free trade. In 1994, peaceful demonstrations turned violent after the Mexican government attempted to crush the movement by force. In the course of armed conflict, hundreds of people have lost their lives and their property and livelihoods. Such cases underline the violence of modernity.

Modernizing Rual

Kampung Rual is a small Menraq settlement in Kelantan, a northeastern state of Peninsular Malaysia. In 2006 the settlement had 475 residents. Rual did not yet exist as a village in 1970; it was only established in 1972 as a result of a government-sponsored resettlement programme. Menraq living in the vicinity were enticed to leave their home territories and settle at the site as part of the government's modernization programme for the Orang Asli. The once nomadic hunting-and-gathering people in the area have become sedentary cultivators of cash crops and occasional wage workers. In due course they have even officially converted to Islam, although they are yet to become devout Muslims. The Menraq community, in many aspects, has become almost indistinguishable from a Malay village.

Rual itself is located in the district of Jeli (see Map 4.1). Jeli is also the name of the rural town where commercial and government services are located. With a population of about 20,000 people, it is encircled by several mainly agricultural, mainly Malay,[4] communities (*kampung*) dependent primarily on cultivation of rice and cash crops such as rubber and oil palm. In recent years, Jeli town has experienced considerable economic and population growth with the opening of the East–West Highway linking the more developed northern urban areas on the west coast of the peninsula to the less developed areas in Kelantan.

In a way then this is a book about the experience of modernity of a small-scale community – the Rual Menraq – nestled between the dwindling tropical forests they have depended upon for generations and the expanding Malay farming settlements. The primary question is, how might one describe Menraq modernity? This book will tell about the concept of modernity often and commonly associated one-dimensionally with the West but now increasingly conceptualized as pluralized and indirect. It will explore the question of how modernity in the form of capitalism and nation-state interventions has 'come to alter some of the most intimate and personal features' (Giddens 1990: 4) of the everyday lives of the Menraq in a spatially remote corner of today's Malaysia. Transcending the tendency to discuss such experiences in an abstract manner as in sociological theories of modernity, I present a more finely textured analysis.

Field research

This book is based on ethnographic data I have collected during my several field visits to Rual since 1975. I have had the privilege of meeting and living with the Orang Asli during a period spanning thirty years (1975 to 2006) but also the agony of observing in that time the dire consequences of modernity for these people. I first visited Rual Resettlement in August 1975 as an undergraduate student to fulfil an ethnographic course requirement. Together with six other students and a then university lecturer at the University of Malaya, Terry Rambo, I stayed at the resettlement for one week. My assignment was to present a photographic essay on the resettlement and the people. Imbued with a deeply romanticized perspective of the Menraq, I focused my camera lens mostly on 'exotic' aspects such as their hunting and gathering and traditional dwellings and material culture and not on what I then saw as the less exciting facets, such as the newly implemented development projects. My first encounter with a Menraq is still vivid in my mind. After walking for hours through the forest from Jeli town, our guide, a Department of Aboriginal Affairs (Jabatan Hal Ehwal Orang Asli, hereafter JHEOA) field officer, called out at the bushes on the side of the track and, suddenly, a Menraq man emerged. At the time the experience of meeting my first Menraq was almost as if one of the people described in Schebesta's book *Among the Forest Dwarfs* (first published in 1928 and the pre-fieldwork prescribed reading) had come alive.

In 1976 I visited Rual again with Terry Rambo and two other students. Each one of us focused on a topic although we collaborated in our research efforts. My topic was social demography and as part of my research tasks I carried out a detailed census and interviewed people about their attitudes and practices related to fertility, mortality, and migration. We spent a total of four weeks from April–May in the Rual Resettlement. We stayed in a house built by the JHEOA for its visiting officers. On the basis of the data I collected, I wrote a short thesis entitled 'A social demography of Jahai Negritos at Rual Post, Kelantan'.[5]

I returned to Rual in April 1978 for a two-week stay and again in April 1979 for another fortnight stay. These field visits were undertaken to update my demographic data and to conduct an economic and ecological survey. Drawing from the data collected thus far at Rual and fieldwork that I carried out in another Orang Asli community, the Temuan, I wrote a master's thesis titled 'Ecological adaptation and population change: a comparative study of Semang foragers and Temuan horticulturalists' (Gomes 1979) which formed the basis of several publications (Gomes 1982, 1983). As implied in the title, the thesis focused on the demographic implications of ecological changes resulting from resettlement. In 1988, I made a short visit to Rual to check and update demographic information that a research assistant, Rokeman Abdul Jalil (1988), had collected and used in his honours thesis. A comparative analysis of findings from 1978 and 1988 was presented in an article published in 1990 (Gomes 1990). Between 1999 and 2006, I made four short visits of a few days to a week to Rual; my last visit was in September 2006. The time depth in my field research allows for a longitudinal or diachronic analysis but the short field visits may imply a lack of ethnographic depth, as the time spent on the key anthropological research tool of participant observation is relatively short. However, for almost three decades I have carried out research among the Orang Asli at large, visiting about 100 or so villages. From 1982–84, I conducted my doctoral study on economic change among the Semai (another Orang Asli group), for which I lived for a period of fourteen months in a village as a participant observer (Gomes 2004). This book draws from my research backgrounds combined with the wealth of knowledge and information contained in several excellent studies on Menraq groups by Kirk and Karen Endicott, Razha Rashid, Shuichi Nagata, Lye Tuck Po, Csilla Dallos, and Corry van der Sluys and the numerous studies on the experiences of modernity among the Orang Asli, of which Dentan *et al.* (1997) and Nicholas (2000) stand out.

Chapter outline

The following chapter provides an ethnographic overview of the Menraq. It will address issues such as ethnicity, language, kinship and family organization, and religion and show how these various social and cultural aspects are closely connected with Menraq foraging lifestyle. In a way, Chapter 2 can be read as a 'before modernity' account of the Menraq social organization, so as to attain a fuller appreciation of the social and cultural changes resulting from modernization. Chapter 3 elaborates the various understandings of concepts – development, modernity, and indigeneity – used in this book. It also traces the development of Malaysian modernity and outlines Malaysia's development policies for the Orang Asli in general. The focus of Chapter 4 is on the state policy of Orang Asli resettlement. After discussing this policy in general, I provide a description of the history, demography, settlement pattern, and administrative structure of the Rual Resettlement. Chapter 5 is concerned with the Menraq economy before resettlement. It outlines the various subsistence-oriented activities of the Menraq that have made them renowned as a hunting and gathering people. As will be shown, with the disappearance of forests and the pressure to participate in government-mandated development projects, Menraq have had to cease hunting, fishing, and gathering and this raises questions as to what the decline in foraging means for social practices, such as generalized reciprocity, closely associated with it. Chapter 6 outlines the various government-mandated economic development projects carried out in Rual since resettlement in 1972, while Chapter 7 focuses on the social programmes such as formal education and Islamization that the Malaysian government and its agencies have implemented to 'integrate' Menraq into the 'mainstream of society'. Both these chapters discuss how these 'civilizing projects' have affected the social,

political, and cultural lives of the Menraq. These effects include the development of incipient social differentiation in a community which values
egalitarianism, growing dependency on outsiders for their livelihood and
future survival, displacement and alienation from their cultural history, poor
nutritional status and increased morbidity and mortality, and curtailment of
their self-determination and cultural rights. The final chapter summarizes
the main ethnographic findings of this study and returns to the question of
the Jeli violence of 1993: why did the Menraq respond in an uncharacteristic
violent manner?

2 Social and cultural milieu

The ethnographic outline presented here looks at the Menraq as they were before the full effects of changes due to their resettlement and their involvement in development projects made themselves felt. This description is in part derived from my field research, but a considerable part of it is gleaned from several detailed ethnographic studies on the traditional life of the people. What constitutes traditional culture is a tricky question since many elements or traits anthropologists consider as traditional are arguably borrowed from other cultures. This question is particularly poignant in the case of the Menraq. Through their longstanding interaction with a plethora of other peoples, but mainly with other Orang Asli and Malays, Menraq have adopted traits that anthropologists have deemed as traditional to Menraq culture. Debating what is traditional serves little purpose here. Instead, in this chapter I focus on the question of how the Menraq lived, subsisted, organized themselves into groups, and thought about the world and the afterlife before they were resettled, modernized, and converted to Islam. First, however, because the Menraq are one of several tribal peoples inhabiting Peninsular Malaysia, and because they are all in some measure subject to the same pressures of modernity, it is useful to give a profile of the Orang Asli presence as we know it in the Malay Peninsula.

The peoples of the Malayan forests have become known as Orang Asli only recently, but their societies and cultures began to be known to, and reported by, Europeans more than 150 years earlier, around the beginning of the nineteenth century. The fascination for these early writers was the idea that these forest dwellers descended from an ancient 'tribe' or 'race'. Skeat and Bladgen's two-volume compendium entitled *Pagan Races of the Malay Peninsula*, first published in 1906, summarized most of the early literature, consisting of mainly travelogues and reports by colonial administrators and a few scholarly journal articles. Much of this literature is marred by several deficiencies. As Hamilton (2001: 90) notes, they 'are often difficult to interpret, their texts being constructed largely in an evolutionary framework with little attention to historical factors on the relations between Orang Asli and others'. Furthermore, these writings drew heavily on interviews with Malay villagers about the Orang Asli rather than on primary anthropologically oriented research. Nevertheless, despite the lack of attention to historical factors, these accounts do provide evidence about how the Orang Asli lived during the time of the writing.

As for the Menraq, important twentieth-century researches are by Schebesta (1928, 1954) and Evans (1937) whose work is referred to below. More recent researches, by Dallos, Kirk and Karen Endicott, Lye, Shuichi Nagata, Razha and, van der Sluys (see bibliography), have added considerably to knowledge of Menraq social organization, economy, and religion. Most of this modern research is focused on the Batek and Kintaq groups.

'Layer cake versus marble cake': ethnic classification

King and Wilder (2003: 193) note how difficult it is to establish clear identification of ethnic groups in Southeast Asia. This problem, they argue, stems from the observed fluidity of ethnic categories and the ongoing processes of ethnic group fission, fusion, and ethnogenesis in the region. Consequently, the typologies and criteria of ethnic categorization for many groups in Southeast Asia are simply incongruous with the peoples' self-identification or subjectivities. Furthermore, as King and Wilder observe, 'the various criteria used to delineate groupings often do not coincide or demonstrate sufficiently marked discontinuities to establish clear ethnic boundaries' (2003: 193). The Orang Asli are a case in point as Benjamin (2002: 21) indicates:

> The degree of correlation between language, cultural tradition, conscious identity and population genetics within the Malay World is at best partial. The interflow of genes, ideas and languages has often been so intensive and multidirectional as to render futile any attempt to delineate the various 'peoples' in terms of completely distinct bundles of geographical, linguistic, biological, or culture-historical features.

Nonetheless, this has not discouraged anthropologists (particularly in the past) and the Malaysian government from identifying and dividing Orang Asli into ethnic categories. Imbued with a goal, if not an obsession, to locate Malaysia's diverse peoples into neat and fixed ethnic categories, anthropologists and government officials have produced various ethnic typologies and ethnographic maps for the Orang Asli. Such mapping exercises are by no means a recent undertaking. In fact, the categorization of the Orang Asli into three subgroups was first established in the early 1900s during the colonial administration. The tripartite model was presented in Skeat and Blagden's monumental work on the Orang Asli (1906) and subsequently refined by Schebesta (1926).[1] The objective and exercise of categorizing people during the colonial period are associated primarily with the facilitation of administration, surveillance, control, and domination. The significance of ethnic identification today is, however, spurred by an additional factor: the importance of ethnicity in a multi-ethnic society. In Malaysia, ethnicity is a significant aspect of everyday life. Judith Nagata's observation made about three decades ago is still applicable to contemporary Malaysia:

> One of the most salient features of modern Malaysian society is its poly-ethnic character which pervades most of the institutions, activities, and attitudes of the population in all spheres of life. All Malaysians are, first and foremost, members of one of the three major 'races,' Malay, Chinese, or Indian, and are only secondarily 'Malaysians.' It is virtually impossible to be ethnically 'neutral' by claiming no intervening ethnic status at all. Identity cards (carried by every member of the population over the age of twelve) classify the bearer's 'race,' as do all official records, from educational institutions at all levels, to labor exchanges and the registry of births, marriages, and deaths. Most political activity is carried out from ethnic-based parties.
>
> (1974: 333–4)

Ethnic-based economic and social policies since the 1970s have further deepened cleavages among the different ethnic groups in the country leading to severe ethnic polarization and inter-ethnic cultural contestation (see, for example, Gomes 1999a). It must therefore be borne in mind that policies of integration and assimilation are drawing Orang Asli into a deeply ethnicized and ethnicly polarized society.

Orang Asli, together with the various native peoples of Sabah and Sarawak and the Malaysian Malays, are considered to form a broader ethnic category of Malaysians known, in a recent coinage, as *Bumiputera* or 'princes or sons of the soil'[2] (Nagata 1974: 334). The Orang Asli population of 147, 239 in 2004, comprising 0.5 per cent of Malaysia's population of 25 million, of which roughly 80 per cent reside on the Malay Peninsula,[3] is officially divided into three main groups – Negrito (Menraq), Senoi, and Melayu Asli (Aboriginal Malays or Proto-Malays) – which are further subdivided into eighteen 'tribes' (*sukubangsa*). This division is deemed to be empirically straightforward as Carey (1976: 13) asserts, 'language, culture and physical appearance make it plain that there are, in fact, three separate ethnic groups; each group includes a number of related tribes who speak similar languages and who follow a similar way of life'. Benjamin (1976: 44) echoes the views of many Orang Asli specialists in his contention that 'the official classification is rather too cavalier with ethnic divisions that the Orang Asli themselves consider to be significant'. For example, in the official classification, the 'Negrito' category is subdivided into six groups, namely Kensiu, Kintaq, Jahai, Lanoh, Mendriq, and Batek; Benjamin (1976: 45–8) identifies eleven subgroups of 'Negritos'[4] and just within the Batek category, Kirk Endicott (1979a: 3–5) found five linguistic subgroups.[5]

Implicit in this tripartite classificatory scheme is the 'migratory wave' theory of the origins of the people and their settlement on the Malay Peninsula. This theory has been discredited in many anthropological studies on the weight of new linguistic and archaeological evidence. Nevertheless, it is still commonly recited in some scholarly work, in the media, and in official discourse as evidenced in the following passage from the Malaysian Department of Aboriginal Affairs website (cited 'unedited' in Benjamin 2002: 18):

> According to historical researchers the Negritos are descendants of the prehistorical man known as Australia-Melanesians that migrated to south east from China 7,000 to 10,000 years ago. However, there are also ancient historical records that suggest that they have been in this area much earlier.
>
> The Senois and Proto-Malays are descendants from the pre-historical man known as Austranesian (Malayo-Polynesian) which is believed to have gradually migrated in small numbers from southern China and Taiwan to South East Asia up to the east approximately 3,000 to 5,000 years ago. Nevertheless there were evidence of intermarriage and assimilation between these two groups of historical men. Historian also concludes that the present Malays, Indonesian and Filipinos are of Proto-Malays descent after intermarriage with the Chinese during the Chao Dynasty, Indians from Bengal and Dacca together with the Arabs and Thais.

Benjamin (2002) has aptly referred to the 'migratory wave' theory as '*kuih lapis* (layer cake) folk-scholarly ethnology'. It resembles the way the popular Malaysian layer cake is made, layer by layer.[6] According to this theory as epitomized in the above quotation, each successive wave of people is perceived to have pushed the earlier settlers into the interior. There is also a cultural evolutionist perspective inherent in this theory; each successive group of people is seen to be culturally more advanced than the preceding group. As Benjamin observed, this kind of race-based evolutionary theory is found in textbooks used in Malaysian schools. In one such book, Benjamin (2002: 19) noted that the readers were told that 'the Senoi are *lebih berakal* (cleverer, more capable) than the Negritos, and that the Proto-Malays are in turn more *berakal* than the Senoi'.

The alternative model of the origin of the Orang Asli, which I have labelled 'marble cake', can also be considered as evolutionist in perspective. The focus, however, is on diversification rather than progressivism in evolutionary theory. According to this theory, inspired predominantly by historical linguistic studies (Benjamin 1976, 2001a, Diffloth 1979) and supported by archaeological (Bellwood 1997, Bulbeck 2003, 2004) and human biological (Fix 2002) research, the ethnic diversity of the Orang Asli is considered to be a product of 6,000 years or so of *in situ* diversification from a single ancestral population or cultural matrix, a proto-Orang Asli population. From the extensive lexical borrowings discernible in the various Aslian languages, linguists have contended that these languages have diverged from a common proto-Aslian language. This implies that there must have been one speech community, from which others evolved through diversification as a result of dispersal and cultural exchange on the Peninsula and on Mainland Southeast Asia. In the case of one group, the Northern Aslian speakers (see below for classification), the discovery of a high degree of lexical borrowing between the languages has prompted linguists to conclude that the people 'have from early times maintained a continuous mesh of communication with each other extending from Isthmian Thailand right down to central Pahang' (Benjamin 1985: 234), a mesh like the colours in a marble cake.

Recent linguistic studies have not only served to challenge the *kuih lapis* theory; they have also inspired new ethnic classificatory models. Benjamin provides an ethnic typology based on linguistic affiliations that clearly avoids the embedded racist assumptions in the official classification. Table 2.1 on population numbers according to subgroup divisions is adapted from Benjamin's tabulation (2002: 22)[7] and Map 2.1, adapted from a map provided in Benjamin (1985), indicates the historically known maximal distributions of the various Orang Asli ethnolinguistic groups. Classifying people by linguistic affiliation is a sensible method as it is apparent that people differentiate themselves on the basis of the dialect they speak or their native language. Two-thirds of Orang Asli, including all Menraq, speak distinctive languages belonging to the Mon-Khmer language family (named after the two main languages in the group) and linguists have labelled these languages as 'Aslian' languages, 'because they are spoken *only* by Orang Asli' (Benjamin 2001a: 101). The Mon-Khmer language family, according to linguists, is a branch

Table 2.1 Orang Asli population by linguistic affiliation (2004)[1,2]

Mon-Khmer							Austronesian	
Northern Aslian		Central Aslian		Southern Aslian			Malayic	
Kensiu	232	Lanoh	350	Semaq Beri	3,345		Temuan	21,512
Kentaq	187	Temiar	25,590	Semelai	7,198		Orang Hulu	27,448
Jahai	1,843	Semai	43,927	Besisi	2,856		Orang Kanaq	83
Mendriq	154	Jah Hut	5,194				Orang Seletar	1,407
Batek	1,283						Orang Kuala	4,066
Chewong	564							
Sub-totals	4,263		75,061		13,399			54,516

Source: Adapted from Benjamin 2002: 22, Table 2.1

Notes
1   Population figures were obtained from the JHEOA head office in Kuala Lumpur.
2   The language names differ from the official ethnic names: Besisi is Mah Meri, Chewong is Che Wong, Orang Hulu is Jakun. Benjamin (1985) refers to the Orang Kuala language as 'Duano' but I have used the official name instead to refer to the language, as 'Duano' is not commonly used among Orang Asli specialists.

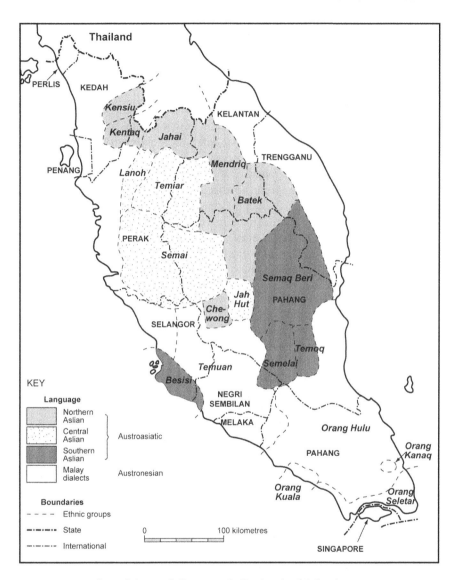

Map 2.1 Location of Orang Asli groups in Peninsular Malaysia
Source: Adapted from Benjamin 1985: Fig. 10.1

of the Austroasiatic stock (Benjamin 1976, Diffloth 1979). Aslian languages are further subdivided into Northern, Central and Southern on the basis of the geographical location of the speech communities. The other Orang Asli peoples speak Austronesian languages which are related to the Malay language. Many of the indigenous peoples of mainland Southeast Asia speak Austroasiatic languages while Austronesian languages are found mostly among native communities in insular Southeast Asia. Geographically located between mainland and insular Southeast Asia, it should not be surprising that the two language families are found on the Malay Peninsula.

The question of identity: who are the Orang Asli?

For most Orang Asli, establishing a common ethnic name or identity has not gained the sort of importance it has for anthropologists studying them. Within their communities, Orang Asli refer to themselves by vernacular renditions of the term for humans or people. These names have been deemed as being far too open-ended, generalized, and imprecise for anthropologists and for Malaysian government authorities as they are common rather than proper nouns.[8] What to call the people they are studying is a question that has drawn considerable attention from anthropologists, particularly the early researchers. This scholarly endeavour, however, has been marred by confusion over names and ambiguities in ethnic identification as Benjamin (1966: 9–10) has noted and explained:

> Yet we are faced with the fact that these tribal names (essentially as first worked out by Schebesta in the 1920s) were obtained as Aborigines' replies to such questions as, 'What people are you here?' Ambiguous questions posed often enough necessarily produce ambiguous replies; and this must be what happened. The tribal names obtained by these means over the years are a mixed lot. Some are innocuous Malay terms such as Orang Darat, Orang Ulu, Orang Hutan, Orang Pangan (respectively, 'men of the Interior, the Headwaters, the Forest, the Scrubland'). Others, still Malay, are less innocuous, such as the well-known Sakai ('serf, dependent' in archaic Malay). Yet others incorporate place names: Orang Seletar, 'Men of the Seletar creeks' (a group of sea nomads on the south coast of the Peninsula). These terms all fail to delimit unambiguously Aborigines from non-Aborigines, leave alone one Aboriginal tribe from another.

Before the 1950s, the British used the term 'Sakai', a former label for the subgroup of people now called 'Senoi', to refer to the Orang Asli in general. This name, however, was dropped from official usage upon recognition that it is a derogatory label, meaning 'serf' and is held to be invidious by the Orang Asli. 'Sakai' was replaced with the epithet 'Aborigines' in the latter years of the British colonial administration. However, this term was also deemed inappropriate and was changed to 'Orang Asli' in the early 1960s. Carey (1976: 3), the Commissioner for Orang Asli Affairs in the 1960s, offers the following reason for this change:

> The Malaysian Government, some years ago, felt that the word 'aborigines' had certain pejorative connotations; it was associated with concepts such as backwardness, under-development and primitiveness.

Benjamin (2002: 12, emphasis in original), however, rightly contends:

> Social labels are not usually *inherently* offensive; normally, they simply *become* offensive when used by those who despise the people referred to. The solution is not to constantly re-make our lexicon, but to mend our attitudes.

Today, the ethnic label 'Orang Asli' refers to all the indigenous non-Malay peoples of Peninsular Malaysia. It is commonly interpreted as 'Original People' (Dentan *et al.* 1997); 'orang' is the Malay word for people or humans and 'asli' as used here means 'original'. However, as Benjamin (2002: 17) indicates, 'asli' means 'genuine, authentic, natural (as in *getah asli* "natural rubber")' and as such, the literal translation of the epithet 'Orang Asli' should be 'natural people'. Nevertheless, as Carey (1976: 3) suggests, the term 'asli' originates from 'the Arabic word "asali", meaning "original", "well-born" or "aristocratic" '. The actual Malay term for 'original peoples' is 'orang asal' where 'asal' literally means 'original' but the government did not adopt this label as an ethnonym as it was first coined and used by the outlawed Malayan Communist Party in reference to Orang Asli in the early 1950s (Nicholas 2000: 6). 'Orang Asal' is now used as an inclusive autonym by indigenous communities to refer to the non-dominant indigenes in Peninsular Malaysia, Sabah, and Sarawak (Nicholas 2000: 204).

With the wide acceptance of the ethnonym 'Orang Asli' among anthropologists and the people it refers to, the knotty problem of nomenclature for the non-Malay indigenous peoples in the Malay Peninsula appears to get closer to resolution but the question of how to define such peoples remains vexatious. The Aboriginal Peoples Act, 1954 (revised in 1974) legally defines an Orang Asli as:

(a) any person whose male parent is or was, a member of an aboriginal ethnic group, who speaks an aboriginal language and habitually follows an aboriginal way of life, aboriginal customs and beliefs, and includes a descendant through males of such persons;

(b) any person of any race adopted when an infant by aborigines who has been brought up as an aborigine, habitually speaks an aboriginal language, habitually follows an aboriginal way of life and aboriginal customs and beliefs and is a member of an aboriginal community;

(c) the child of any union between an aboriginal female and male of another race, provided that such child habitually speaks an aboriginal language, habitually follows an aboriginal way of life and aboriginal customs and beliefs and remains a member of an aboriginal community.

Modelled on the constitutional definition of 'Malay',[9] this definition is fraught with ambiguities and false assumptions. Consequently it obfuscates, rather than clarifies, ethnic identification of the Orang Asli. First, the words 'aborigines' and 'aboriginal' are vague. It is not clear how aboriginality is defined. Is it defined on the basis of pre-existence in relation to other residents of the land? Or, is it reckoned on the grounds of specific and unique cultural features that separate such peoples from others who have settled in the area? There is an a priori assumption of the existence of a people deemed to be aboriginal without clarifying the criteria for such aboriginal status. Second, there is a presumption of patrilateral affiliation, which is clearly an aspect of Islamic Malay culture, but not common to many of the Orang Asli communities. Third, the terms 'way of life' and 'race' are problematic: the former is too open-ended while the latter has been rejected in conventional social science as a valid way of defining humans even though it is used in Malaysia to mean ethnicity (Nagata 1974: 347).

What used to be one of the key defining characteristics of the Orang Asli people is religion, the fact that they are non-Muslims or 'people without a religion' ('Pagan' in the early anthropological literature and *Orang Tak Beragama* in Malay). In emic terms, Orang Asli do not see themselves in this way, but do regard the religion of others, particularly the Malays, as an important aspect of ethnic differentiation; Muslim Malays are commonly looked upon as a significant other by Orang Asli. I have often heard Orang Asli describe themselves in oppositional terms to Malays. The focus tends to be on certain Islamic practices such as circumcision and pig taboo. Writing about one of the Orang Asli groups, the Semai, Dentan (1975: 48) observes: 'Semai normally identify themselves as the opposite of Malays along the lines of "we do this, Malays do that"'. In other words, Semai maintained their ethnic boundaries on the basis of their assumptions or perceptions of Malay identity. According to this view, advocated in Dentan's article entitled 'If there were no Malays, who would the Semai be', Semai (and for that matter, Orang Asli) ethnicity is predicated on their perceptions of and interactions with Malays. However, such oppositional identification has become less significant for a growing number of Orang Asli people who have become Muslims as a result of active and persistent government-sponsored Islamization programmes carried out in Orang Asli communities. In the process these Orang Asli are said to have *masuk Melayu*, literally 'entering Malay' or 'Malaydom' but effectively meaning 'becoming Malay'.

In any case, the relatively impoverished status of a large majority of Orang Asli peoples vis à vis the other citizens of Malaysia does make the Orang Asli stand out. It would not be wrong to say that most Orang Asli live below the poverty line, however it is defined. Their relative poverty, lack of access to economic opportunities, and weak political position have defined their marginality, which has, ironically, become for them an important form of identity that sets them apart from the other peoples of Malaysia.

Who are the Menraq?

There has been much written and debated about the origins of the Menraq, their ethnic identification, and what might be the most appropriate ethnonym for them. The Menraq are believed to be descendants of an ancient people who inhabited the region (Sundaland), part of which is now submerged by seawater leaving a string of islands, comprising the nation-states of Malaysia, Indonesia, and the Philippines (Bellwood 1997, 1999, Bulbeck 2003, 2004). As Bellwood (1997: 128) asserts 'the Negritos and their traditional hunting and gathering lifestyle must be considered as autochthonous to the Indo-Malaysian Archipelago'. On the basis of a review of archaeological record, Bulbeck (2004) states that hunter-gatherers have occupied the Malay Penin-sula continuously throughout the Holocene and essentially from at least 40,000 years ago.

Today there are people labelled by anthropologists as 'Negritos' living in the northern parts of the Malay Peninsula, Southern Thailand, in various parts of the Philippines, and in the Andaman Islands in the Indian Ocean. Malaysian 'Negritos' share considerable linguistic and cultural traits with their counterparts in Thailand. It is apparent that they are the same group of people divided by national boundaries and historical experiences. In con-trast, apart from physiognomy and a foraging lifestyle, there is little that Malaysian 'Negritos' have in common with 'Negritos' in the Philippines and the Andaman Islands.

Anyone familiar with the early literature on the Menraq may well be surprised that such people continue to exist today. Many of the early writers forecasted the demise of the Menraq as a people. Schebesta, who studied them in the 1920s, predicted that the Menraq are 'dying out' (Schebesta [1928] 1973: 16). Robinson and Kloss (1913) and Evans (1937) also made similar assertions. Evans (1937: 12) reported the following observation:

> To one who likes the Negritos as much as I do, it is painful to have to acknowledge that these little people are decreasing. Districts that knew them formerly, even since the coming of the British, know them no longer, and where they are still found there is only too good a reason to believe that it is, in some cases, in sadly depleted numbers.

Why was the Menraq population in decline? The forecasters of Menraq demise offered several reasons. Schebesta ([1928] 1973: 16) maintained:

> A great dearth of women is making itself felt in their ranks and the vices of the cultured races are gaining a hold on them, especially opium-smoking. Syphilis is, as far as I know, unknown among them. European civilisation is digging the grave of the dwarfs of Malaya as it presses further into the interior, thrusting the Malays before it and crowding the nomadic Semang into an area too confined for them where they are being economically smothered.

In a similar vein, Evans (1937: 13) attributed the Menraq drop in popula-tion to epidemic diseases and 'the reduction in the area occupied by the Negritos' resulting from 'the opening up of the country', a process which grew in pace rapidly with the British colonial economic expansion in Malaya in the late nineteenth century. There is no question in respect to Schebesta's contention about European civilization (a significant aspect of the experience of modernity) 'digging the grave of the dwarfs of Malaya' but his prediction of the Menraq 'dying out' is absolutely off the mark as the current Menraq population in the Malay Peninsula rather than disappearing altogether has in fact doubled to about 4,000.

The Menraq are renowned in anthropological circles as a tropical forest hunting and gathering people. Even though Menraq no longer practise hunting and gathering (for reasons to be discussed later), these activities are still symbolically significant in their identity formation and self-characterization. Another criterion in their identification or differentiation from other people in Malaysia is their phenotype. They are described as short, dark-skinned, woolly haired people with broad noses and thick lips and as such, they have been called 'Negritos'. Writers in the nineteenth and early twentieth centuries, it seems, were sufficiently preoccupied and obsessed with the physiological appearance of the Menraq peoples to warrant labels such as 'negritos' and 'forest dwarfs'. Schebesta ([1928] 1973: 277), for example, labelled them as 'true dwarf tribes'. Such a portrayal was widely circulated in the anthropological literature of the time. For example, Murdock, in his book *Our Primitive Contemporaries*, first published in 1934, described Menraq as 'a race of true pygmies, descended probably from the earliest inhabitants of the land' (1934: 86). However, Orang Asli specialists have discredited labels based on phenotypical features not just because of their racial overtones but also because of their incommensurability with reality. As Fix (2002: 192) contends, 'these traditional "racial markers" are not neatly apportioned among actual populations of Semang, Senoi, and Melayu Asli'. The Rual population exemplifies this; the residents display great individual variation in height, skin pigmentation, hair form, and facial features. There are tall as well as short people at Rual; there are dark almost black-skinned people to brown-skinned individuals; and there are people with woolly hair as well as with wavy hair. Some are even physically indistinguishable from Malays, making any ethnic classification on the basis of phenotype contentious, problematic, and of little descriptive value. Nevertheless, the label 'Negrito' is still used in official documents, suggesting that phenotype may still be an important consideration in the minds of government administrators. However, the continued use of this term may also be due to the reluctance or recalcitrance on the part of the government officials to change a long-standing ethnic categorization.

Another issue of ethnic identification is whether to refer to people as 'Negritos' or 'Semang'. Kirk Endicott (1979a: 1) used the ethnic name 'Negrito'[10] in his earlier publications and as he explains:

> I retain the term Negrito, which means 'little black' in Spanish, because it has gained general acceptance in the anthropological literature and

because it has none of the pejorative connotations of the Malay terms for the people. The Negritos are called Semang in the western half of the Peninsula, which is roughly equivalent to the English term 'savage'. In Kelantan they are generally termed Pangan, which means, among other things, 'people who live like animals and eat their food raw'.

Nicholas (2000: 14) states that he prefers the ethnonym 'Negrito' to 'Semang' as the latter term in his view 'carries a negative connotation when used by some of the Senoi groups'. He appears to have accepted Wilkinson's (1910: 9) contention:

The word *Semang* is a term applied by the Malays of Kedah to the negrito aborigines who live in their country. Like most names given by a dominant to a subject people it has come to be regarded as contemptuous, so that no wild tribesmen will answer to it. 'We are not Semang,' say the negritoes of Ijok, 'we are Sakai of the Swamps; if you want Semang you will find them in the hills behind us.' 'Not so', say the negritoes of the hills, 'we also are not Semang, but if you cross the valley of the Perak to the main range of the Peninsula you will find Semang on the heights behind the rivers Piah and Plus.' ... A name that is rejected or misapplied in this way is a fruitful source of error and confusion, especially among anthropologists of the excursionist type who accept uncritically everything that they hear.

Several Orang Asli researchers, notably Dentan (1997) and Benjamin (2002), have indicated that the term 'Semang' is a descriptive label. In an etymological analysis of the term, Dentan (1997: 112–13) notes:

The Malay term 'Semang' comes from Aslian words for person generally written as *smak'* for Lanoh, Semoq Beri, Semelai, and Temoq (Benjamin 1976: 113, Skeat and Blagden 1906 I: 21, II: 653; Wilkinson n.d. II: 418). It occurs in such Malaysian ethnonyms as 'Semoq Beri' and 'Mah Meri', both meaning 'jungle folk'. In the days of the 'Hikayat' it seems to have referred to hill foragers of Kedah and Northern Perak ... Like other native ethnonyms, eg. 'polack' or 'yid' in English, 'Semang' has a derogatory connotation in Malay, so that some writers prefer the inaccurate and racist term 'Negrito' ... As a status term, *semang* referred to debt-slaves, bond servants, dependents who worked for their room and board without other pay.

Benjamin (2002: 64) rightly indicates that the epithet 'Semang' is a 'culture-type label' and not an ethnonym as 'no Orang Asli population calls itself by this name, although the word has been applied to some of them in the past by Malays'.

While this debate on nomenclature remains unresolved, the subjects of this debate, however, appear to be certain about how to refer to themselves. As mentioned, they generally use terms such as *Menraq, Menri'* or *Batek* as autonyms. Derivatives of *Menri'* exist as ethnic labels: Mendriq, one of the subgroups in the ethnic category of 'Negritos' in Malaysia, and Menik or Maniq, a 'Negrito' people found in Southern Thailand (Porath 2001, Hamilton 2001). *Batek* is an autonym used by related peoples found in Southern Kelantan and in Pahang (Endicott 1997, Lye 1997). These autonyms mean 'human' or 'people' in their respective Northern Aslian languages. Interestingly, my informants define *Menraq* as humans who 'consume pork and are uncircumcized'. As noted earlier, they, like the Semai, described in Dentan (1975) and Gomes (1994b), define their ethnicity in oppositional terms to Muslim Malays. This definition would now be inappropriate or inapplicable and would require rethinking in light of the fact that the Rual people converted to Islam in 1994. If racial features and religion are problematic or inappropriate criteria for ethnic identification, the question is what might be an acceptable way of identifying and categorizing the Menraq. The answer is of course language but this also poses several problems as I will show.

Some researchers have hypothesized the existence of an ancient Menraq language that has been replaced by their current languages. As Endicott (1979: 2) notes:

> Although the grammar of the Negrito languages fits the Mon-Khmer pattern and many Negrito words have cognates, there are a number of common Negrito words that cannot be traced to either a Mon-Khmer or Austronesian source . . . Presumably these are the residue of a more ancient language which was somehow superseded by one or more Mon-Khmer languages.

Brandt (1961) makes a similar assertion from his study of the 'Negritos' in Southern Thailand. It is hypothesized that this ancient 'Negrito' language or languages was slowly replaced with the present languages as an outcome of culture contact with Austroasiatic speakers. As Endicott (1979: 3) maintains:

> The present evidence seems to suggest that the Negritos took over, probably gradually, the language or languages of the Austroasiatic speaking Senoi who must have come into the Peninsula several thousand years ago.

It has also been postulated that 'Negritos' in Malaysia and Southern Thailand shared this pre-Austroasiatic language with 'Negritos' in the Philippines and Andaman Islands. This has been labelled by several researchers as 'Proto-Negrito Hypothesis' (Burenhult 2001: 78) and Kirk Endicott (1979: 3) appears to lend support to this view with his observation that 'the name for the thunder-god of the Negritos of the northern Camarines in the Philippines, "Kayai" . . . is cognate with the most common name given the thunder-god by Malaysian Negritos, "Karei" '. However, Endicott (1979: 3) concedes that '[t]he connection between the languages of the Malaysian Negritos and those of the Andamans and Philippines is so ancient as to be virtually undemonstrable'. Furthermore, as Burenhult (2001: 78) indicates, 'the number of similar lexical items [between the Malaysian and Southern Thai Negritos and other Negritos] has not been significant enough to warrant a clear genetic connection . . . and some researchers, notably Diffloth, have argued that much of the supposed substratum vocabulary is indeed of Austroasiatic origin, so the "Proto-Negrito Hypothesis" must be regarded as highly uncertain'.

The 'Semang' or 'Negrito' ethnic category is not altogether meaningful to many of the Rual people, although they do point out similarities between themselves and 'those Jahai from Perak and Siam (Thailand)'. Furthermore, they seem to have adopted the Malay term *bangsa*, which means 'race' or 'ethnicity', to refer to their group of fellow 'Semang' or 'Negrito'. This is also the case with the Batek as Kirk Endicott (1997: 35) observes:

> The Batek seem to conceive of *bansa?* as groups of persons habitually speaking a common dialect and living together, at any given time, in specifiable places within the Batek home range. They speak of *bansa?* as having come from certain river watersheds, as moving to other areas, as splitting, converging, expanding, and contracting.

This form of identification is nonetheless flexible at Rual. With the mixing of people from different Menraq groups as a result of resettlement and intermarriage, any attempt to establish clear social boundaries of a *bansa?* will be superfluous. As Endicott (1997: 36) notes:

> The apparent concreteness of these *bansa?* as groups dissolves, however, when they are examined in terms of their individual members. In principle, it should be possible to specify to which *bansa?* a person belongs to by the 'dialect' he or she speaks. But, in practice, most Batek know and use several dialects according to circumstances, and people may change dialects several times during their lifetimes as they move from group to group and spouse to spouse.

At Rual, I have heard people use the term *bansa?* to refer to the whole Orang Asli population. But what appears to be missing or lacking is a clear sense of group membership, not only to the Menraq group but also to the Orang Asli group. This is, however, changing as over the years I have heard people speak about being Orang Asli and about having connections with other Orang Asli people. Some use the Malay term *saudara* (brother- or sister-hood), to refer to their 'fellow' Orang Asli. Nevertheless, the ethnic divisions are still prevalent and apparently meaningful to the people, as Nicholas (2000: 125) has found:

> when meeting with the Jahais in Perak and Kelantan in 1993, the Jahais of Banun (Perak) emphatically denied that those in Jeli (Kelantan) were also Jahais. Similarly, the Jeli Jahais strongly insist that they were the real Jahais. This is despite both groups having similar physical features and linguistic affiliations.

Over the years of my research visits to Rual, I have come to appreciate first-hand the ambiguity of ethnicity among the Menraq. On the ethno-linguistic map, Rual falls into Jahai 'territory'. Hence, one would expect people at Rual to be Jahai speakers and on such basis the resettlement was officially called 'Sungai Rual Jahai Post' (Pos Jahai Sungai Rual) at the time of its establishment. When I first visited Rual in 1975, most people unequivocally and predictably told me in response to my question about their ethnicity (*bansa?*) that they were Jahai. A few, however, conceded that they were Mendriq and one, who interestingly was the headman of one of the bands, revealed that he was by origin a Temiar, that is, from one of the Senoi (Central Aslian) subgroups. The few families of Mendriq heritage, however, did not openly acknowledge that they were *not* Jahai. This could have been because of the government's designation of the resettlement as Jahai and because, as I will discuss later, the land they were settled on is considered to be the traditional homeland of two Jahai bands. The Jahai privately assert that the Mendriq are *Orang Luar* (outsiders). During my subsequent visits I learned that there were actually only two 'pure' Jahai bands while the others were mixed groups of Mendriq and Batek. In my visits in 1999 and 2000, I was told that there are as many Batek speakers in the resettlement as there are Jahai. Nonetheless, over the years with life together in a common village setting people appear to communicate with one another with ease. They may still speak in their 'native' dialect with members of their own group but they have learnt to speak in the other dialects. Benjamin (2001a: 102) relates an interesting case which illustrates such multilingualism among the Menraq:

> I am thinking of a Kensiw (Northern Aslian) man I once worked with in Kedah who, though completely non-literate, spoke excellent Kensiw, Jahai (also Northern Aslian), Temiar (Central Aslian), Malay and Southern Thai (spanning three linguistic phyla), and who tried hard to get me to teach him some English (from a fourth phylum).

The mixing of people from different dialect groups in a common locality, as in the case of Rual, as well as population mobility, has led to increased 'mutual comprehensibility' (Benjamin 1976: 74). Schebesta (1928), who claimed to speak Jahai fluently, reveals that there are only very minor differences in the dialects. This seems to be consistent with the views of several of the Rual people whom I asked about dialectical differences. With increased communication with other people, there is of course a possibility of language change. As Kirk Endicott (1997: 45) notes, 'the Batek language is constantly changing. In the mere nineteen years I have worked with the Batek, I have seen many Malay words replace Batek words in everyday conversation, and there are even hints that Batek syntax is being affected by Malay.' Given my limited linguistic ability in Northern Aslian languages, it is hard to tell whether the Jahai spoken by the people in 1975, when I first visited them, has changed over the years due to borrowing from the other dialects and languages. However, most Rual people, with the exception of a few women, are fluent Malay speakers. While many are able to converse in standard Malay with outsiders, most use the Kelantan Malay dialect. But there is still extensive use of Northern Aslian languages within the community and this fact certainly sets them apart language-wise from outsiders and continues to be an important source and substance of their identity.

The 'Semang' social pattern

Benjamin (1985) has noted an isomorphism of ecology, economy, and social organization inherent in what he labels as the 'Semang pattern'. According to him, this pattern has three main components: 'the maintenance of a widespread low-density population, a minimalist social organization that allows them to break into conjugal-family groups at almost a moment's notice, and an avoidance of a long-term commitment to sedentism' (Benjamin 2002: 34). In an earlier publication, Benjamin (1985: 228) describes this pattern as:

> an inclusive network, the nodes of which are individuals or conjugal families (nothing bigger), constantly realigning their relations with each other so that no bounded or corporate groupings are formed and their focus of attention remains on the detachable here-and-now of the present moment. Local aggregations are constantly in flux, and no core-groups are found, because no one person or group is felt to have a better claim of attachment to a particular place than anyone else.

Further to this, Benjamin (1985) has also noted the prohibition of marriage between kin, both consanguineal and affinal, and wide-ranging exogamy. All these aspects of the 'Semang pattern' tie in well with the demands of small-group nomadism, which in turn is an adaptation to a foraging lifestyle in the tropical forest environment.

Menraq traditionally lived in small bands, which people refer to as *puak*[11] (band), and numbering between 15 and 50 people per band. Lee and Daly (1999: 826) define the band among hunting and gathering peoples as 'a small-scale nomadic group of 15–50 people related by kinship' and note that it is 'the basic unit of social organization of most (but not all) hunting and gathering peoples'. Schebesta ([1928] 1973: 279) correctly observed that, 'the Semang cannot live together except in small groups, as it is impossible for the forest to feed large masses of human beings' and points out that that is why they are found 'living in family groups without any strict tribal organization'. They do not have corporate kin groups such as lineages and clans. At Rual, even though people are living in a village situation with a distinct administrative and social structure, the band form of social organization is still prominent. As I shall outline later, Rual Resettlement is divided into three hamlets and each hamlet is further subdivided into bands. The houses of members of a puak are typically clustered together within the hamlet, in a way resembling the traditional camp organization.

While membership of a *puak* is gained initially by birth, it is not strictly permanent. People change bands when they marry and sometimes they, particularly adolescents and young unmarried adults, may even voluntarily join another *puak* after obtaining an implicit approval from the other band members. With such impermanence in band membership, the composition of the *puak* is in constant flux. The members of a *puak* cooperate in economic and social activities but such cooperation is voluntary rather than socially prescribed. The *puak* is also a sharing unit; surpluses from economic production are often distributed among its members. It is this sharing which serves to cement social relations within the *puak*.[12] As Kirk Endicott (1988: 116) writes:

> Yet even when food is abundant, the sharing goes on according to the same principles, thus taking on a ritualized aspect as each family gives portions of its excess food to other families and receives portions – sometimes of the same kind of food – in turn. This apparently unnecessary distribution confirms that sharing of food is a dominant value in Batek culture.

Kinship and affinal ties strengthen the solidarity of the *puak*. Menraq adhere to a bilateral or cognatic kinship system where individuals trace their ancestry or descent through both males and female. There is, however, a discernible patri-bias as Benjamin (1985: 255) notes:

> They ['Semang'] do exhibit 'patrifocal' tendencies in, for example, the patrilaterally skewed shapes of their personal genealogical memories or the statistical predominance of patri-virilocal residence in their local-group organization.

Kirk Endicott (1974: 219) declares that there is no residence rule among the Batek and points out that there 'would be no way to enforce it if there were'. He does, however, note that 'there is a tendency in first marriages, however, for the couple to spend the first few months in the camp of the girl's parents' (Endicott 1974: 219). In my analysis of post-marital residence among the Rual people in 1979, I found that 19 out of the 27 (70.4 per cent) band exogamous marriages were patrilocal, where the wife left her *puak* to join her husband's *puak*, and eight cases (29.6 per cent) were matrilocal, with husbands living together with their spouses' relatives (Gomes 1982: 6). Considered by anthropologists (see, for example, Rambo 1985) as adaptive to a hunting ecology, patrilocal residence ensures that most males of the *puak* remain together. Growing up together and knowing their territory intimately, the men are better able to engage in cooperative production activities and thus increase their chances of being productive in activities such as hunting (Rambo 1979). However, Endicott (1974: 220) also states that '[t]here is no particular economic advantage to it [patrilocal residence] because all areas have roughly the same resources, and they are freely available everywhere'.

I have observed that most Menraq marry before turning 20. In 1979, I found that only one out of the 50 individuals between the ages of 15 to 29 was unmarried (Gomes 1979: 91). Of the 95 Menraq above the age of 15, two (2.1 per cent) had never been married, 93 (97.9 per cent) had been married at least once, ten were widowed and three divorced. Menraq are mostly monogamous but there is no rule against polygamy. I have come across three polygamous unions at Rual. Most of the married couples in Rual have remained married to one another since my first census in 1976 with about 10 per cent ending in divorce.[13]

Carey (1976: 51) found that 'Among all of the Negrito tribes, marriage is an informal arrangement and it is not marked by any special ceremony.' Menraq marriage is usually instituted when a couple sleep together and begin to function as a conjugal family. The word for marriage in Batek, as Endicott (1974: 215) indicates, is *tek*, which means 'to sleep' (with someone). There are signs today that marriage is becoming a more elaborate and formal affair. As Endicott (1974: 216–17) reports, a new practice among the Batek is the presentation of store-bought gifts from the bridegroom to his in-laws and a small feast to celebrate marriages, practices that he suggests are 'obviously influenced by Malay customs'. One can say that marriage is the central institution in Menraq social organization in that it is the necessary step to the formation of the conjugal family, and because it engenders, when a child is born, a definite change in a person's social identity.

Now, as then, the basic social structural unit is the conjugal family, consisting of a couple and their young children normally occupying an individual dwelling, and referred to by Menraq speakers as *kelamin*, a Malay loan word for 'marital pair'.[14] It is common for a grown child or several grown children to set up a household close to their parent's house. The Menraq conjugal family is responsible for social reproduction, that is, producing children, and through socialization inculcating in them the basic cultural values of the group. The conjugal family is also the day-to-day economic production unit among the Menraq where productive activities and products

1 Traditional Menraq lean-to shelter (1976) Photo: A. Gomes

2 Manok Hamlet at Rual Resettlement (1979) Photo: A. Gomes

are shared among the members of the family. Traditionally, the abode of the Menraq conjugal family with young children had the form of a lean-to or windscreen, which was easily constructed with two poles holding up a thatched roof leaning at a 45-degree angle. Such dwellings were temporary residences adaptable to a foraging lifestyle. Today in the Rual Resettlement, Menraq live in Malay-type houses constructed of timber and roofed with corrugated iron sheets and some, the village leaders, reside in more elaborate government-allocated houses with concrete walls and floor.

The focus on the conjugal family reflects what Benjamin (2002: 34) has identified as a minimalist social organization in the 'Semang pattern'. Such minimalism is well suited to a nomadic lifestyle as 'the conjugal family can take off autonomously at a moment's notice, without putting the wider social network at risk' (Benjamin 2001b: 140). One of the ways this minimalism is sustained is through kinship avoidance rules as Benjamin (2001b: 140) explains:

> the minimalism is locked into place by a set of taboos that impose avoidance relations between precisely those opposite-set adults whose relationships sit astride the boundary between the conjugal family and the rest of kin network. These are (1) adult brother and sister, (2) brother-in-law and sister-in-law, (3) mother-in-law and son-in-law, or father-in-law and daughter-in-law. The three avoidance rules . . . serve to picture the most desirable form of society as one constituted of easily detachable conjugal-family groups, linked together through marriage between men and women who are previously related either by consanguinity or affinity.

Another social rule in the 'Semang pattern' that engenders the observed social minimalism is the prohibition of marriages between traceable consanguines and affines. Concomitantly, as Benjamin (2001b: 140) indicates, 'they marry at relatively great social and geographical distances, thereby maintaining a very wide-ranging spatial network of social relations'. Like the cross-sex avoidances, this leads to a 'randomness of consociation' (Benjamin 1985: 257). In my survey conducted in 1979, I found that out of a total of 41 married couples in Rual, 27 (66 per cent) had taken their partners from other *puak* while the remaining 14 (34 per cent) had married within their *puak* (Gomes 1982: 6). The fact that two out of every three marriages are band exogamous lends only weak support to the feature of wide-ranging exogamy in the 'Semang pattern'. The situation at Rual in the 1970s may have hindered the practice of wide-ranging exogamy. First, due to the intensive government military operations against communist insurgents in the vicinity of Rual, Menraq were unwilling to take the risk of travelling to other areas. Second, the establishment of resettlement projects at Rual and in the other Menraq areas has restricted peoples' movements which are closely monitored by government officials.

Egalitarianism, personal autonomy, and headmanship

Menraq fit well with Woodburn's characterization of 'immediate-return' foraging societies, which are 'societies that do not store food or engage in protracted production processes' (quoted in Endicott 1988: 121). Woodburn (1982: 435) observed that immediate-return foraging groups tend to be egalitarian primarily because of their nomadism, which allows people 'to move away without difficulty and at a moment's notice from constraint which others may seek to impose on them' and because of the relative personal autonomy of individuals who are not dependent on others for basic survival:

> Whatever the system of territorial rights, in practice in their own areas and in other areas with which they have ties, people have free and equal access to wild foods and water; to all the various raw materials they need for making shelters, tools, weapons and ornaments; to whatever wild resources they use, processed or unprocessed, for trade.
>
> (Woodburn 1982: 437)

As is common in egalitarian foraging societies, no individual or a group of individuals in Menraq society possesses the power or authority to control or manipulate consensus. Individuals may make decisions, whether political, economic, or jural, through consultations, deliberations, and negotiations with other members of the *puak*. The opinions and ideas of older, usually male, members are given more weight but not without some open discussion. Deciding on where to forage or set camp is a good and intriguing example of this process. Instead of people getting together to talk about this matter, they remain in their respective shelters and simply loudly call out prospective sites and reasons for the choice. The *puak* members present arrive at a decision upon weighing the pros and cons of the various suggestions. Women do take part in this consultative process but they play their role in a rather inconspicuous manner.[15] They express their views, sometimes in whispers, to their husbands who will then repeat them loudly for the benefit of the others in the camp. The male spouse, it appears, acts on these occasions as a spokesperson for the conjugal family. Any form of coercion or physical threatening is viewed with disdain and Menraq would simply avoid such confrontations by flight. Furthermore, as van der Sluys (1999: 310) notes, Menraq strongly believe that forcing someone to do one's bidding will raise 'hot' emotions and in the process weaken the person's *ruway* (soul) causing him or her to fall ill or even die. But obviously such a direct decision-making process can be carried out only in a camp-like situation where shelters are arranged in a semi-circle allowing for the people to communicate in the manner described above. The modern arrangement of houses that are separate and well spaced out from one another makes such communication difficult, if not impossible.

While strong egalitarianism within the band may suggest an absence of political leadership, in reality Menraq do adhere to a system of headmanship which appears to be partly adopted from the Malays, especially in reference to the title of the leader, *penghulu* (Malay: village headman).[16] As Kirk Endicott (1974: 245) has suggested, this system of headmanship may have existed for a long time in 'Semang' society. However, the roles of the headmen, which in the past may have been loosely defined, have become more important or authoritative; they are primarily facilitated by state officials' insistence on arranging matters through an acknowledged leader. The official selects an individual from the *puak* to assume the role of *penghulu*, although the selection is usually legitimized locally by a presumption that the *puak* members have elected their own headman. An important criterion for headmanship is a good ability to converse and negotiate in Malay (*Bahasa Malaysia*), the national language of Malaysia, as his primary duty is to act as a go-between for the state officials and agencies, particularly the JHEOA. Endicott (1974: 245) has also noted this criterion in his study of the Batek:

> In fact, the main duty of a *penghulu* is to deal with outsiders, including government agencies. He acts as a kind of foreign minister for his group, a spokesman and communicator of information from outside. What little authority he has internally, qua *penghulu*, is derived from his role as intermediary between the J.O.A. and the Batek.

Headmen also often assume the role of mediator in commercial exchanges between Menraq and traders. In arranging for the supply of forest products, traders contact the band headmen and place orders for specific products. The traders also negotiate with the headmen the terms of trading such as the price of the products and time and place of the eventual commercial exchange. Headmen then pass this information on to the members of their band. Previously, the headmen did not receive any payment or gratuities for this role but these days they demand a payment from the trader. They refer to this payment as their 'cut' or commission.

It is not always easy for headmen to secure overwhelming support from their *puak* members who generally value their personal autonomy and independence. This is in spite of the headman's position being government-authorized; he is provided with an official letter of appointment and a nominal salary. In the early years of the Rual Resettlement, only the headmen of the respective *puak* were given special timber houses as a mark of their headmanship. The government's act of installing and recognizing a headman and establishing a rather elaborate system of leadership among the Menraq has certainly sown seeds of inequality in a community noted for its egalitarianism.[17]

'We people' versus 'strangers': interpersonal relations

In a recent personal communication (2005), Riboli, an anthropologist currently researching the Rual Menraq, reported:

> In the beginning it was not easy to be accepted by the people of the
> three villages in the Sungai Rual area. Everybody was afraid I could
> have been something like a spy . . . After a few days everything changed.

Riboli proceeds to relate her experience of a warm, open, and happy relationship with the people. This should not be surprising as research participants
usually become affable as soon as the researcher gains the trust of the people
and builds a good rapport with them. However, in this case, similar to what
I experienced in my first field visit to Rual, the change in the behaviour and
attitude of the Menraq towards an outsider is a reflection of the acceptance
of the outsider into their 'known world'[18] or 'internal culture'.[19] The Rual
Menraq, like many other tribal communities in Southeast Asia, observe
what Sellato (1994: 210) in the context of his study on the Punan, a hunting-
gathering people of Borneo, called 'double life'. The people adhere to a set
of rules and norms in their intra-community interactions but present a different face to outsiders. The salient features of Rual Menraq internal culture
include (1) an egalitarian outlook, (2) high value placed on personal autonomy,
(3) gregariousness towards each other with the exception of encounters
with people implicated in cross-sex avoidances, and (4) non-aggressive or
aggrandizing behaviour towards fellow community members. The 'external
face' of the Menraq (which as mentioned earlier means 'human' or 'people')
is one of shyness, timidity, subservience, and fearfulness of outsiders whom
they refer to as *gob* (strangers). Menraq xenophobia has been widely noted
and explained in many scholarly writings and I will discuss these explanations later. First, we will look at how Menraq 'double life' in interpersonal
relations between outsiders and themselves is reflected in the Menraq naming
practice.

In Menraq society, individuals have several personal names. A person
receives his or her 'real' name at the time of birth and, as Endicott (1974:
200) observes, 'The name chosen is normally the name of the place where
the birth took place (the side-stream) or the name of some kind of plant or
animal that was noticed about the time of birth.' A personal name is a
symbol of one's social personhood as McKinley (1976: 118) elaborates:

> Personal names and recognized faces are truly the most intimate expres-
> sions of social identity. While they present us to society, they also present
> us as our own unique selves and not some stereotyped social category.

In Rual, the 'real' name is the name used within the *puak* or among fellow
Menraq, the internal culture. But, teknonymy is also common. When a
Menraq marries and has a child, he or she is addressed as and referred to by
teknonym, a cognomen combining the name of the oldest living child with
the kinship term for father or mother. Teknonymy assumes prior knowledge
of the genealogical relations in the village, something that strangers are not
privy to. To outsiders, a person is known by another name. Usually this

name is either a Malay translation of the 'real' name or a common Malay name. These days children are given Malay Muslim names in keeping with their birth as Muslims. Nevertheless, my informants have told me that they still give 'traditional' names to their children at birth although the children are officially registered with their Malay-Muslim names. Hence, it appears that Menraq individuals are known by different names according to the context of their interactions. Within the community, Muslim Menraq are addressed by their 'real' name and by their Muslim name to outsiders, reflecting two different social identities, one in relation to the internal culture and the other, an 'external face'.

To return to the issue of Menraq xenophobia, the explanation for this can be found in the past experiences of the people in their interactions with outsiders. What seems to have left an indelible mark on the people is the traumatic episode of slave-raiding carried out against them and their fellow Orang Asli by outsiders, especially Indonesian immigrants to the Malay Peninsula in the 1800s and early 1900s. Skeat and Blagden (1906: 532–3) narrate this sad event in the lives of the Orang Asli:

> Hunted by the Malays, who stole their children, they were forced to leave their dwellings and fly hither and thither, passing the night in caves or in huts ('pondok') which they burnt on their departure. 'In those days' they say, 'we never walked in the beaten tracks lest the print of our footsteps in the mud should betray us.' For wherever the Malay perceived any indication of their presence, he would build himself a small shelter, and never leave it until he had discovered the place of retreat where they generally spent the night. Accompanied by a few accomplices, he would then repair to the spot at nightfall, and the party, concealing themselves until dark, would wait until the 'Hill-men' were asleep. The Malays would then fire several rifle shots, spreading terror and confusion in every family, whose breaking up made them an easy prey to their assailants, who would promptly rush to the spot where they heard the shrieks of women and children. The girls were, as a rule, at once knocked on the head, and the boys were carried off and sold as slaves. There is hardly a family that has not its own especial calamity to relate, the result being the profound aversion that they avowedly cherish for the Malay . . . Any act of vengeance, moreover, would be fatal to them, in view of their insignificant numbers and lack of means of defence. They prefer therefore to sacrifice the part for the whole, and this is certainly the only possible course open to them.

Kirk Endicott (1983) maintains that slave-raiding had enduring effects, of which one was the fear of encounter with strangers. Slave-raiding is remembered in oral traditions which serve to 'shape and justify a world view in which outsiders, especially Malays, are pictured as dangerous and untrustworthy' (Endicott 1983: 237). Orang Asli children are often taught to fear and distrust outsiders. Illustrative of the Orang Asli fear of outsiders, in this case Malays, is an incident related by Nagata (1995: 103) which took place in a 'Semang' resettlement in Kedah:

> One night in November 1991, there was a *kenduri* [feast] and *ceramah* (lecture) in Kampung Memali, about two miles from Legong village, to commemorate the Memali incident of 1985, in which the people of Memali [not Orang Asli] and the police had clashed and some women and children were killed in the skirmish. On the night in question, a lot of people were converging on Memali village by motorcycles and cars, which created a considerable commotion on the streets. Suddenly a group of Orang Asli emerged from the darkness of the night, men carrying babies on their back, wearing *parangs* [machetes] and carrying bamboo blowpipes, and women leading older children and carrying sleeping mats and pots and pans. An old man then approached me to go with them to take refuge on the hilltop as the Malays were going to kill them. So saying, he pointed to a stream of headlights heading to Kampung Memali. I pointed out that since a public meeting has to have a police permit, the police would be there to prevent any trouble from breaking out. I was then countered by the son-in-law of the old man who said that they could not feel safe since the police were Malays.

Orang Asli xenophobia could also be a reaction to Malay prejudice and discrimination towards the Orang Asli (see, for example, Dentan 1997). Many Menraq have told me that Malays typically treat them condescendingly and sometimes with contempt. Some Malays I have talked to in Jeli have expressed negative stereotypes of Menraq. The common statements I have heard are: 'They are unkempt', 'They live like animals', 'They have *kurap* (skin sores) and lice', 'They cannot be trusted'. At a coffee shop once, a Malay man enquired with a puzzled look, 'How come you are staying with the *Orang Hutan* (Jungle people)?'

Such negative views, however, do not seem to have hampered interactions between Menraq and Malays. These relations expectedly have been unequal, with Menraq being subservient to the Malays, as Schebesta observed in the 1920s:

> Wherever I encountered a group, I discovered that they had made some sort of pact with a Malay. To him they brought from time to time the products of the forest, which they exchanged for rice, iron knives, or cloth. The Malay in this way exercises a certain degree of protectorship in regard to the forest dwarfs, whom, it goes without saying, he does not always treat honourably, so often reaps great personal profit from this arrangement. If he requires them to work for him, he fetches them out of the forest and often rewards them most inadequately for their hard labour.
>
> (Schebesta [1928] 1973: 32)

Despite some minor changes, I have found that such form of Malay–Menraq relations still prevails (see, for example, Dentan 1997). Carey (1976: 50), however, speaks of this relationship not as one of dependence of the Menraq on the Malays nor exploitative in nature but as a 'symbiotic relationship'. He notes that Menraq 'settle down near villages for a limited period, *helping* with the rice harvest and with other occasional or seasonal work' (Carey 1976: 50, emphasis added). I have often heard Abdullah Hassan, the JHEOA field officer in the 1970s and early 1980s, claiming that his relationship with the Rual people is one of *tolong menolong* (mutual help). It is of course a matter of interpretation as to what 'help' really means. Today, the Menraq are subservient to, and dependent on, a (predominantly) Malay bureaucracy rather than the Malay trader.

Gender relations

A common finding of studies on gender relations in Orang Asli communities (see Karen Endicott 1979, 1999, Howell 1983, Nowak 1986, Karim 1995, Thambiah 1999) is that such relations tend to be complementary. Men tend to dominate in public arenas and trading and women in the domestic sphere. The dichotomization of public and domestic arenas in the performance of gender roles is, however, not fixed and rigid as there is some degree of flexibility where women may engage in trading and buying things from traders or shopping in the market towns. Karen Endicott (1999: 411) found that 'Batek men and women are free to decide their own movements, activities, and relationships, and neither gender holds an economic, religious, or social advantage over the other.' In traditional subsistence pursuits, there appears to be a division of labour where men do the hunting and women the gathering of vegetable food. However, this division of labour is not rigid; women do occasionally procure small game while men often gather tubers and vegetables. This flexibility is also evident in the carrying out of domestic tasks, such as house cleaning, cooking, and laundry. Menraq regard these activities as women's work but men are not averse to performing them, as I have observed men on numerous occasions taking on such tasks. One could say that in theory there is sex-typing of some activities in Menraq society but this is not strictly followed in reality.

As noted earlier, Menraq gender ideology and practice does generally preclude women from making decisions of a 'public' nature. There are of course exceptions to the rule. Kirk Endicott (personal communication) indicates that Batek women are not excluded from the public domain. He notes that the recognized 'headman' of the group he lived with in 1975–76 was a woman. Nevertheless, Menraq experiences of modernity, particularly the introduction of male-dominated forms of social organization via resettlement and Malay-Muslim gender models have led to changes in gender ideologies in the Rual village. I shall discuss the implications of these changes in more depth in Chapter 7.

Spatialized consciousness

There is no clear consensus among anthropologists about Menraq conceptions of land rights and ownership. Some, like Schebesta (1954: 209), observe
that Menraq do have a sense of territory:

> Every tribe has its own territory, in which are found the foraging areas
> of the groups or family kin-groups . . . No one oversteps its boundaries
> unless groups related by marriage live on either side. Every family group
> claims a clearly defined forest tract as its own in which they wander and
> from which they get their livelihood by gathering plants and honey and
> by hunting and fishing.

Carey, on the other hand, gives the impression that the Menraq have only
weak links to land, an aspect which is considered to be congruent with a
foraging lifestyle. A statement by one of Carey's informants, recorded in
1957, on concepts of territory is worth repeating here:

> We, the Jahai, have never stayed in a place for more than three or four
> days. We cannot stay for a longer period, otherwise, our children will
> go hungry. So we are always on the move and we cover long distances.
> My group is often in Perak [western Peninsular Malaysia], but we have
> also been to Kelantan and Thailand. But wherever we go, it is our
> country (*tempat*), the place of the Jahai. The villages belong to the
> Malays, and the towns to the Chinese, but the jungle is ours – it belongs
> to us. We do not go to the hills which are the country of the Temiars
> but we stay in the *belukar* [secondary forest]. We meet the Mendrik in
> Kuala Krai. They are our relatives and friends, but they have another
> country. We will always stay in the country of the Jahai. Of course, the
> Mendrik will not like it if we take their fruit, and we do not want them
> to take ours also. They are our relatives, but they are different from us.
> They speak another language.
>
> (Carey 1976: 37)

While being constantly on the move may imply a weak link to land, the
informant's reference to having a 'country', referred to by the Malay word
tempat, 'place', reveals that Menraq do have a sense of 'place'. Interestingly,
they maintain connections to this place by moving about rather than simply
staying put. So, what are the principles of Menraq traditional land rights
and ownership?

Traditionally, a *puak* occupies a specific territory defined by natural boundaries such as streams and hills. This territory is referred to as *sakaq*, a term
most likely derived from the Malay word *pusaka*, meaning inheritance or
heritage. The members of the *puak*, irrespective of age and sex, possess
equal usufruct rights over the land they occupy. While every member of the
puak has equal rights to the resources available in their *sakaq*, individuals

may 'own' some fruit trees, such as *durian*, *petai*, and *kerdas*, and the *ipoh* tree (from which poison for the blowpipe dart is obtained). The ownership of these trees is generally inheritable, passing from parent to all his or her children. Individuals are entitled to claim ownership of any trees they themselves have planted. Menraq on most occasions hunt and forage within their *sakaq* but may collect forest products from outside their 'home territory'.

The reference to their *sakaq* as 'home territory' is interesting as it challenges conceptions of nomadic people as 'homeless'. Tsing's contention in respect of Meratus Dayak she studied is also applicable to the Menraq:

> Hiking through forests and across mountains may seem more like primitive wandering than the transnational mobility associated with modern travel. Yet the traveling politics I describe is not nomadic. The *nomad* is defined as one who has no home. Meratus travel both expands social spaces and shapes political communities; it is not a practice of homelessness.
>
> (Tsing 1993: 150)

It is important to note that Menraq connection to 'territory' is not only resource related; it is also of immense symbolic significance or value. Menraq often define themselves in association with the material world such as the forest, hills, and rivers. In other words, they take on an ecocentric identity that is principally embodied in toponymy. When asked to identify themselves or others familiar to them, they would say 'we are Lubuk Bungor (a place-name) people' or 'they are Grik (name of a town) people'. A *puak* is also sometimes referred to by its place of origin. For example, *Puak Teras* (see Chapter 4 for details about the different bands at Rual) are also addressed as 'Menraq Long', 'people from Long', where 'Long' is the name of the main river flowing through Teras' *sakaq*.

The *sakaq* also conveys memories that connect Menraq with their individual and collective past. This form of social memory is by no means unique to the Menraq. In his ethnographic research among the Ilongot of the Philippines, Renato Rosaldo discovered that people told stories about the past always in relation to the places significant to the tales rather than when they took place (the dates). As Rosaldo (1980: 15–16) puts it:

> Stories usually are a series of relatively autonomous episodes that are united, like beads on a string, by winding thread of continuous movement through space, rather than by a rising plot line that points towards its own resolution in a climax. At their most elemental, Ilongot stories may simply list a lifetime of place names where people have gardened or erected their houseposts. More elaborate stories, often about oratory, fishing, hunting, and headhunting, begin at home, move in gradual step-by-step fashion toward their destinations, and conclude with a quick return to the place of origin.

Menraq, as most other Orang Asli people, also tell stories of the past in relation to where, rather than when, the events took place. Their historical consciousness or reconstructions of the past do not follow the conventional method of temporal determination or giving importance to time. This means that the 'events' in people's history are inscribed in the landscape. To put it another way, Menraq historical consciousness, just as in the case of the Ilongot, is spatialized rather than temporalized as in the narratives of Western or modern historiography. Walking through the forest with Menraq was often also a 'journey' into their past. Menraq would point to particular sites or landmarks and then tell stories of past events which occurred there. This raises several questions: if the connection to land is immensely significant as a bearer of identity and history as well as a source of Menraq livelihood, what happens then if the people are resettled or displaced from their traditional land? Would this be tantamount to an erasure of their history? These are issues that I shall return to later in the book.

Deities, shamans, and the supernatural realm: Menraq religion

On the basis of numerous studies (Amran 1991, Benjamin 1967, 1979, Endicott 1979, Hood 1978, Howell 1989, Karim 1981, Laird 1978, and Roseman 1991) on religions of the various Orang Asli groups, it appears to me that the traditional religious beliefs and practices of the Rual Menraq have much in common with those of the other Orang Asli. These religions are certainly syncretic in character and are flexible interpretatively. It makes it difficult and even superfluous to provide a standard description of Menraq religion given the extent of individual interpretations and understandings, not to mention the possibilities of considerable cultural borrowing and diffusion. Nonetheless, it is possible to provide a generalized depiction of Menraq religion based on the studies of other 'Semang' groups (Endicott 1979, Evans 1937, Schebesta 1928 and Van der Sluys 1999, 2000) and the statements from my respondents to my enquiries about their traditional religious beliefs and practices.

In his book *Among the Forest Dwarfs*, Schebesta ([1928] 1973: 184) notes that Menraq throughout Peninsular Malaysia fear three phenomena of nature: thunder, flood, and storm. One of their principal deities, *Karey*, is believed to be the thunder god. According to Rual Menraq, *Karey* creates thunder and lightning by spinning his top; the lightning is believed to represent the string that spins the top while the thunder is said to be the crashing sound produced when the top makes contact with the ground. Van der Sluys (1999: 310) reports that the Menraq she studied believed that *Karey* was once a human who had become 'a giant long haired monkey' and that he 'exemplifies the dangers of "anger out-of-control"'. *Karey* is strongly disliked but greatly revered because of his wrath and wickedness, exhibited in his punishment afflicted on humans who anger him by breaking certain taboos. In this way *Karey* serves an important moral function in Menraq society. *Karey* punishes, as one would expect, through lightning but also through his pet wild animals, causing personal injury, illness, and even death to taboo violators. Some of these taboos are related to ecological and population control strategies such as the prohibition of postpartum sexual intercourse. Other infringements believed to attract the wrath of *Karey* include having sex during the day in the open, engaging in incestuous relations, showing disrespect to one's elders, torturing or mistreating a captured animal (especially snakes, leeches, and snails which are believed to be *Karey*'s pets), or not instantly killing without pain any game injured by one's blowpipe. Endicott (1979a) who provides a thorough ethnographic understanding of Menraq religion in his book *Batek Negrito Religion* surmises in another publication that:

> It is tempting to view the alleged power of the thundergod and the earth deity as a Durkheimian personification of the power of society over the individual and to suggest that the need for such a mystical means of enforcement lies in the absence of sufficient power in the secular political system.
>
> (Endicott 1988: 124)

There are, however, some aspects of human behaviour that attract the wrath of *Karey* which do not appear to have moral implications. One such case is the exposing of shiny metal or other objects that reflect the sun's rays upwards to the sky which is believed to be *Karey's* abode. On one occasion during a severe thunderstorm, several Menraq, who appeared to be overwhelmed with fear, approached us and demanded we remove several metal rain gauges which we had placed in the open to record rainfall. They felt that the reflection from metal containers angered *Karey* and the only way he could be appeased was the removal of the metal objects, as these were the source of his irritation. They said that several people in the settlement had already tried to appease the thunder god through the blood sacrifice ritual. This ritual involves the drawing of blood from the outer side of the right leg near the shinbone and throwing it into the rain as an offering to *Karey* (Evans 1937: 171, Needham 1964). The women often initiate this sacrifice.

The thunder god is not the only deity in Menraq traditional religion. Rual people also believe in the existence of a supreme creator god called *Ta Pedn*, a deity referred to as *Tohan* among the Batek (Endicott 1979a). The forests, according to Menraq beliefs, are populated with tiny elf-like helpers of *Ta Pedn* called *cenoi*. Some people who are believed to have special spiritual powers are regarded as shamans. These shamans, known as *halaq*, have the dual function of officiating at rituals and performing magical rites as well as serving as traditional medicine practitioners who provide herbal and spiritual cures for sickness. There is no clear consensus of the process of becoming, and who can become, a *halaq*. As Endicott (1979a: 134) observes:

According to the Lebir Batek, any person who has sufficient ability and interest can become a shaman. To do so, he must learn shamanistic songs and spells and must acquire the clear blood of the *hala'*. The Aring Batek, on the other hand, believe that only persons who are descended from shamans have the potential to become shamans themselves. They claim that the clear blood cannot be acquired; it can only be inherited from a shaman parent.

The pertinent question which needs to be asked now is what are the implications, if any, of the conversion of the Rual Menraq to Islam for their traditional beliefs and practices? Has this religious conversion led to the demise of their traditional religious beliefs and practices? Or has it simply resulted in the formation of yet another layer in the complex religious system of the people? These are questions I address later when discussing the social implications of modernity for the Rual people.

Conclusion

The Menraq social organization outlined in this chapter fits neatly into the common social pattern of foraging societies described by Leacock and Lee (1982: 7–8) as having the following salient features:

> egalitarian patterns of sharing; strong anti-authoritarianism; an emphasis on the importance of cooperation in conjunction with greater respect for individuality; marked flexibility in band membership and living arrangements generally; and common techniques for handling problems of conflict and reinforcing group cohesion, such as often-merciless teasing and joking, endless talking, and the ritualization of potential antagonisms.

These aspects superbly accommodate group mobility which is a necessary precondition for foraging in areas such as forests and deserts with dispersed resources. Even their religious beliefs seem to tie in very well with a forest-dependent foraging existence. The economic changes following resettlement and modernization programmes have resulted in a new type of economy which has brought about changes in the social and political organization and this is bound to have deeper social and cultural implications for the Menraq. Is the Rual community likely to remain egalitarian with a strong sharing ethic in the face of modernity? Will their religion, which is closely linked to the forest and nature in general, lose its cultural significance as their connections with the fast disappearing forest are severed or as their conversion to Islam takes full effect? These are questions the following chapters will take up.

3 Modernity, development, and tribal communities

What is modernity? What is development? How are tribal communities affected by modernization, the process that initiates and establishes modernity? These are the questions I intend to address in this chapter. I will first outline some of the theories that have inspired and guided development plans and projects in Malaysia, particularly for its tribal minorities like the Menraq. I will then provide an overview of Malaysia's development policies and programmes and its economic transformation from a producer of primary products to a semi-industrialized nation. This overview will give a broad national context to the analysis of Menraq encounter with modernity to be presented in the following chapters; it will also help to elucidate relevant concepts such as modernity, development, and the 'Green Revolution' to be met with in my analysis.

Like many of the newly independent nations in Asia and Africa, Malaysia's transformation intensified at the twilight of colonialism and during the early period of decolonization (1957 to 1965). In the context of Southeast Asia, King and Wilder (2003: 158), drawing from several anthropological studies of such transformations, outline the changes in rural communities in the region as:

> one of increasingly commercialized agriculture and other economic activities, the expansion of markets in land, labour and agricultural and other rural products, the opening up of opportunities for social and physical mobility with the availability of work outside agriculture, especially in towns, improvements in educational provision, the development of infrastructure, particularly road and rail transport, the introduction of technological innovations, and the incorporation of rural communities, and their leaders, into state-wide bureaucratic systems.

While some of these changes are due to the growing involvement and interactions of these communities with the capitalist-oriented market economy and the state bureaucracy, most of the transformations stem from 'top-down' forms of social and economic intervention commonly referred to as development or modernization.

Modernity

Defining the concept of modernity is not a straightforward task. Like so many other concepts, there is no particular agreement among social scientists about the defining elements of the concept of modernity. While modernity has no fixed defining features, it is not vacuous or descriptively invalid. Knauft (2002a: 18) defines modernity 'as the images and institutions associated with Western-style progress and development in a contemporary world'. In the broadest sense, modernity refers to the conditions of being modern, a word that is sometimes used interchangeably with adjectives like new or up-to-date. There is a range of theoretical analyses and empirical instances of the 'modern condition'. To most social theorists, modernity essentially refers to the conditions laid down by the institutions of capitalism and the nation-state. These conditions are the outcome of a chain of processes – industrialization, urbanization, rationalization, bureaucratization – associated with the ascendancy of capitalism, the spread of ideas such as individualism and achievement motivation, and the affirmation of reason and science in the West from the sixteenth century onwards. Such processes have resulted in significant historical developments and transformations in the social, political, economic, cultural, and ideological conditions in the West and continue to have an impact on the whole world through the globalization of modernity. As many social scientists, particularly radical Marxist-inspired ones, have revealed, the experience of modernity tends to be fraught with contradictions: growth and disintegration, progress and deterioration, freedom and domination, hope and despair. Nevertheless, the quest to achieve modernity is ever-appealing as is evident in the fact that people are generally willing to make considerable sacrifices to fulfil their aspirations to be 'modern'. Some forsake their own cultural traditions, often viewed as inimical to modernity, to join the ranks of the 'modern' populace, but many have been involuntarily drawn into modernity through diverse means and strategies, some subtle and subliminal such as the enticing appeal of consumerism and others, such as government-sponsored development and commoditization projects, more blatant.

As several anthropologists (for example, Appadurai 1996, Kahn 2001, Knauft 2002a) have noted, while modernity is modelled on Western institutions and images it is reconfigured to suit local or national conditions. Faced with the diversity of experiences and visions associated with the 'modern', some social scientists now tend to speak about modernity as pluralized, recognizing the existence of 'alternative modernities'. In such conceptualizations, modernity has been detached from its Western origins and bias and it is now no longer considered improper to speak about an Islamic modernity or a Chinese modernity or a Malaysian modernity, each with its culturally-mediated processes of industrialization, urbanization, rationalization, and bureaucratization. As this case study will show, the Menraq experience is of a Malaysian modernity that promotes Islam as a significant aspect of the modernization programme called 'spiritual development'. This development goes against the grain of the conventional understanding of modernization that advocates, among other things, secularization.

Development

As with the concept of modernity, there is a lack of consensus about the meaning of development, primarily due to the considerable range of different, often opposing, theories and ideas that shape and inform the various development policies and practices.[1] While development, as a concept, emerged after the Second World War as a programme for planned economic and social change, policies and practices which could be defined as developmental have a much longer history. There were certainly aspects of development thinking in colonial interventions into the lives of its subjects. The various paternalistically oriented policies and programmes for Orang Asli welfare during the British colonial administration, particularly in the 1930s and during the Emergency (1948–60) certainly fit into this category. In the aftermath of the Second World War, the concept of development was advocated and carried out in a range of initiatives born in the United States, such as the Truman Doctrine, the Marshall Plan, and the Point Four Doctrine in the European Recovery Program, and became a key objective of the several agencies, such as the United Nations (UN), the World Bank, and the International Monetary Fund (IMF), which were established during the period.

During the 1950s and 1960s, developed nations proposed and implemented development policies and programmes explicitly with the aim of improving the welfare of people in the Third World, especially in the rural sectors. These programmes of social change were guided by social science theories and approaches referred to collectively as the modernization model. There are many versions of this model, some economically oriented, some focused on social and cultural aspects of development in 'new nations'. Embraced as the solution to the perceived problems of poverty, illiteracy, and disease, believed to be associated with 'backwardness', 'underdevelopment', and outmoded traditions, these models were popular in the 1950s and 1960s. Most of these models are dualistic, depicting the existence of two diametrically opposed sectors: traditional and modern. The 'traditional' is often defined not on the basis of its essences but on the lack or absence of the various features found in the modern condition. Modernization theorists view 'Third World' countries and 'Fourth World' communities (indigenous peoples in settler nations) as 'backward' or 'late-starters' and the solution to the problem of 'backwardness' to them is straightforward and uncomplicated. They propose a diffusion of modernity, mainly attributes from the developed West. This process called modernization is simply the transformation of traditional society into modern society. Rostow's *The Stages of Economic Growth* provides arguably one of the best-known modernization theories and it is worth noting that it is singled out as the influencing model in the

JHEOA's developmental thinking. In fact, as Nicholas (2000: 43) rightly points out:

> Much of the rationale for governmental approaches to Orang Asli development has its roots in the development theories of the 1960s and 1970s. Even today, the basic philosophy underlying the current develop-ment strategies remains the same, although the specific programmes may differ.

In Rostow's model, as in most other modernization models, development is envisaged as a movement along a continuum of historical change on which all societies can be positioned according to several, mainly economic, indices, such as gross national product (GNP), per capita income, the level of international trade, and the status of economic institutions. For Rostow, all developing societies had to pass through five stages: (1) traditional; (2) pre-takeoff society; (3) takeoff; (4) the drive to maturity; and (5) mass consumption society. Modernization theorists have advocated or promoted changes seen as necessary for development (or 'takeoff' in Rostow's words) at several levels. Some of these include the establishment of capitalist-oriented enterprises, banking and financial institutions, and modern bureau-cracy and a professional class, the promotion of mass education directed towards producing labour for manufacturing industries, and the better facilitation of international trading of commodities.

In the late 1950s several scholars (such as Paul Baran, André Gunder Frank, Samir Amin, Fernando Henrique Cardoso, and Immanuel Wallerstein), mostly Latin American specialists, formulated new approaches to under-standing development. They used Marxist perspectives and concepts such as surplus accumulation, exploitation, imperialism, and dialectical reasoning in their analyses of such Third World economic problems as development failures, unemployment, and debt crisis. They opposed modernization the-orists by arguing that capitalism, rather than solving the problems of per-ceived 'backwardness', actually exacerbates poverty and social inequality. Their main contention is that underdevelopment and economic stagnation in much of the developing world stem from colonialism in the past and from modernization since the 1950s, which has turned out to be a form of neo-colonialism. In true Marxist fashion, they assert that the expansion of capitalism leads to increased accumulation of surplus through exploitation or the appropriation of part of a producer's labour or product by a non-producer on the basis of ownership and control of the means of production. Surplus is also accumulated through monopolistic control of markets and production systems worldwide.

In the 1950s and 1960s, governments and development agencies, following modernization models, advocated intervention in the lives of peoples seen as less fortunate to solve the problems of poverty, illiteracy, food shortage, and health. In the 1960s and 1970s, the dependency and other Marxist theorists opposed such interventions, arguing that these interventions made matters worse by exacerbating the very problems that they were designed to solve. They promoted import substitution, local industries, and the curtailment of unequal international trade. As if such criticisms were having an effect, governments and development agencies in the 1980s and 1990s advocated seemingly non-interventionist policies and programmes, labelled as neo-liberalism. Neoliberal policies included the reduction of government spending, privatizing state enterprises, eliminating state subsidies and protectionism, liberalizing markets and trade, and a shift to export-oriented production. They have been promoted as structural adjustment policies (SAPs) by multilateral agencies such as the IMF and the World Bank to address rising debt problems and economic stagnation in developing nations. However, this has not sounded the death knell for development programmes. The eradication of poverty, among other developmental concerns, is still very much in the sights of multilateral agencies and governments. One of the goals stated in the United Nations Millennium Declaration (2000: 4)[2] is:

> We will spare no effort to free our fellow men, women and children from the abject and dehumanizing conditions of extreme poverty, to which more than a billion of them are currently subjected. We are committed to making the right to development a reality for everyone and to freeing the entire human race from want.

The 1950s vision of development is still held by the United States. The US government-managed Millennium Challenge Corporation (MCC), established in 2002, directs an aid package called the millennium challenge account (MCA) with one of its key principles being:

> Reduce Poverty through Economic Growth: The MCC will focus specifically on promoting sustainable economic growth that reduces poverty through investments in areas such as agriculture, education, private sector development, and capacity building.[3]

The promotion of 'investments' to eradicate poverty can be interpreted as a reinstatement of an interventionist form of development. What is also poignant in this statement is the adherence to the strategy of economic growth as a solution, which effectively means the expansion of capitalist-oriented development and as such a return to the goals of modernization with one major amendment: the reduction in the role of the state in developing nations and concomitantly the greater involvement of the private sector. We turn to how these changes in development thinking and policies have played out in the context of Malaysia.

Malaysian modernity

The history of modernity in the Malay Peninsula in a way coincided with the advent of European colonialism in the region. European colonialism commenced with the conquest of Melaka in 1511 by the Portuguese who were followed about a century later by the Dutch. While these European powers maintained a strong grip on the maritime trade passing through the port of Melaka, they did not establish a broad and effective colonial bureaucracy or structure, as did the British who replaced the Dutch as colonial masters of the Malay Peninsula in the 1800s. From the early 1800s the British steadily spread their tentacles of power and dominion in the Malay Peninsula and by the end of the nineteenth century had consolidated their control over much of the Peninsula and even over parts of Borneo (which became the Malaysian states of Sabah and Sarawak after 1963).[4] As Andaya and Andaya (1982: 205) note, 'By 1919 the entire Malay peninsula had come under some kind of British control.' Guided by a modernist philosophy of rationalism, progressivism, supremacy of the nation-state, and technological mastery of nature, the British colonial administration gradually instituted radical changes in the society and economy of the Malay Peninsula. Among other things, it facilitated the growth of the tin mining industry, the establishment of rubber estates, the improvement of roads and railways and other infrastructure, and the expansion of the population of the Malay Peninsula through a migration programme which brought into the country many Chinese, Indians, and Indonesians to meet the rising labour demand in the tin mining and rubber industries. One could say that the Orang Asli began their encounter with modernity as these social, political, and economic transformations spread into the hinterland of the Malay Peninsula.

At the end of British rule in 1957, Peninsular Malaysia (known then as the Federation of Malaya) inherited 'an economy largely shaped by British colonial business interests, built around the export of tin and rubber' (Gomez and Jomo 1997: 10). Malaya was faced with a dilemma of modernizing the nation without compromising the delicate ethnic balance of the plural society. Malaysia, especially since its enlargement to include the Borneo states in 1963, is a multicultural nation comprising several ethnic groups, namely Malays, who form the majority of close to 50 per cent of the population, Chinese, Indians, Ibans, Kadazans, and several other minorities, including the Orang Asli in Peninsular Malaysia. At the time of independence in 1957, the country was governed by an alliance of three ethnically-aligned political parties: the United Malays National Organization (UMNO), Malayan (later changed to Malaysian) Chinese Association (MCA), and Malayan (Malaysian after 1963) Indian Congress (MIC). The party itself was called the Alliance (*Perikatan* in Malay), with a traditional image of a sailboat (*kapal layar*) as its political symbol. During the first few years of independence the economy was generally smooth sailing although the struggle against communist insurgents, which began soon after the end of the Second World War, continued until 1960. With the economy doing reasonably well as a result of good rubber and tin markets and with the euphoria of independence, Malayans (as they were called then) upheld the *merdeka* (Malay: independence or freedom) 'bargain', the tacit agreement between the elites of a quid pro quo of Malay political hegemony for unhindered Chinese and Indian economic freedom. In the early years of economic planning in the form of the five-year plans – First Malayan Plan (1956–60), Second Malayan Plan (1961–65), and the First Malaysian Plan (1966–70) the focus was on import-substituting manufacturing, designed to reduce Malaysia's foreign trade deficits, and on the development of infrastructure such as transport, power, and communication, and credit facilities. As Gomez and Jomo (1997: 16) have noted, half of Malaysia's total public development expenditure was allocated to infrastructure development. While on the surface things looked calm, there were undercurrents of inter-ethnic animosities that eventually rocked the boat and culminated in the 13 May 1969 race riots which shook the very foundations of the nation.

The 13 May riots were a result of the breakdown of the *merdeka* bargain. In the 1960s, although foreign ownership (mainly British) of capital was still high, estimated at about 60 per cent, the Chinese were able to consolidate further their hold on the economy. However, they also began to gain more political ground as evidenced in the 1969 General Elections where the non-Malay opposition parties denied the government a two-thirds majority in parliament for the first time. In the case of the Malays, the *laissez-faire* economy of the new nation left many of them, particularly in the rural areas, disgruntled at what they saw as government inertia and lack of support in eradicating rural poverty and exploitation. This mood had grown despite development programmes favouring Malays, such as the Rural and Industrial Development Authority (RIDA, established in 1951) which in 1966 became MARA (Majlis Amanah Rakyat, Council of Trust for Indigenous People) designed to promote commerce and industry for Malays. Another Malay-targeted programme was the implementation of integrated land development schemes by FELDA (Federal Land Development Authority) which involved the clearing of forest areas and the establishment of infrastructure, housing and, cash crop (rubber and oil palm) holdings essentially for rural Malay communities. In 1965, the government sponsored the first Bumiputera Economic Congress, which led to the establishment of the first Malay commercial bank, Bank Bumiputera, to provide easier access to credit facilities for Malay entrepreneurs. These programmes did not help to maintain the delicate 'ethnic balance' as they were perceived by non-Malays as pandering to the increasingly vociferous Malay lobby for greater share of the economic cake through more state invention and preferential policies for Malays. On the other hand, the indispensable role of the Malaysian Chinese in the economy of the country left aspiring Malay capitalists feeling marginalized. As Searle (1999: 38) notes:

Growing inequality within the Malay community corresponded with the observation that Chinese movement into modern well-paid activities was more rapid and broadly based than that of the Malays (or Indians). By contrast, the great majority of Malays remained in poorly paid occupations such as rice cultivation, rubber smallholding and fishing.

Ethnic harmony was shattered with the race riots of 13 May 1969, which traumatized the government. The underlying cause of this shocking expression of ethnic animosities and violent conflict was generally perceived as emanating from economic and social disparities. In order to restore national wellbeing, the government focused on resolving ethnic problems. It introduced a number of policies, notably the New Economic Policy (NEP) and the National Culture Policy (NCP), and made several constitutional amendments in 1971 aimed, it claimed, to foster ethnic peace and social justice in the country. The two-pronged objectives of the NEP were outlined in the Second Malaysian Plan (1971–75):

> The first prong is to reduce and eventually eradicate poverty, by raising income levels and increasing employment opportunities for all Malaysians, irrespective of race. The second program aims at accelerating the process of restructuring Malaysian society to correct economic imbalance, so as to reduce and eventually eliminate the identification of race with economic function.

To achieve the second objective, the government introduced several programmes to provide Malays with privileged access to education, employment, and economic ventures with a target for Malay control of 30 per cent of capital ownership, industry, and commerce by 1990. In effect, the privileging of a group on the basis of ethnicity served to accentuate ethnic differentiation by ethnicizing almost every facet of life in Malaysia rather than removing identification of race with economic function.

During the NEP period (1970 to 1990), the Malaysian government intensified its intervention in the economy and took a more active role in fiscal regulation and pro-Malay development efforts. With the NEP policies, as Searle (1999: 45) notes:

> the *laissez-faire* Alliance state was replaced by one that was more interventionist and avowedly pro-Malay in its orientation, particularly where increasing Malay ownership of the economy and the fostering of Malay capitalism were concerned. In concert with these developments, decision making, particularly with regard to national economic management, became increasingly centralised and concentrated in a few key bureaucratic and technocratic state agencies.

Several new initiatives, especially the Industrial Co-ordination Act (ICA) of 1975, were instituted as part of this more interventionist economic strategy.

These enabled the government to control the rapidly expanding manufacturing sector and in the process provide greater opportunities for Malay investors in this sector. As was intended, Malays, particularly those who were politically well-connected, benefited from these preferential policies and economic initiatives, but the Orang Asli did not figure at all in such programmes and were generally overlooked. In fact, the Orang Asli in many instances were looked upon as being too far behind in the Rostowian 'stages of growth' to be able to achieve 'takeoff' in such programmes. They were at best perceived as candidates for the positions that upwardly mobile Malays, particularly in the agricultural sector, had vacated.

After 1985, Malaysia embarked on an economic course radically different from the one charted in the early years of the nation. In contrast to the 1960s which was a period characterized by import substitution strategies and appropriate technological developments, the post-1985 neo-liberal inspired economic policies were steered by export orientation and capital intensive manufactures. In the framework of economic nationalism, import substitution is inward-looking while export orientation with its emphasis on foreign trade and investment is outward-looking and competitive. This radical economic shift was manifested in Malaysia's policy change from interventionist to market- or private sector-led economic development; it was instituted in former Prime Minister Mahathir's 'Malaysia Incorporated' policy, which encouraged privatization of government enterprises mainly to Malay capitalists. In his speech announcing the Malaysia Incorporated concept, Mahathir (1984: 2) related this policy to the 'the task of nation-building' where the 'private and public sectors see themselves as sharing the same fate and destiny as partners, shareholders and workers within the same "corporation", which in this case is the Nation'.

A second important policy introduced in 1985 was the Industrial Master Plan (IMP), which resulted in the development of heavy industries such as the national car (Proton) project, steel and cement enterprises, and the construction of 'megaprojects' such as the Kuala Lumpur International Airport (KLIA), the administrative capital of Putrajaya, the Petronas Twin Towers (until recently the world's tallest buildings), and the Multimedia Super Corridor. The economic and technological advances have led to much euphoria and a heightened sense of confidence among Malaysians. In his analysis of Malaysia's economic performance up to the 1990s, Halim Salleh (1999: 188–9) observed that:

> there was general satisfaction and happiness in the air. There was full employment, money to be made on the stock market and in business in general, and the Malays in particular saw the rise of a new class of rentier capitalist who gained from the 30 per cent Malay quota on all new share issues, particularly the privatized projects. Many Malaysians in the mid-1990s saw nothing else but wealth. The middle class and the rich talked only about the share market. In general, social perceptions

of wealth, power and the good life suddenly took a new turn: traditional dependence on the government gave way to the material gains promised by the private sector. Private employment and business ventures acquired a new sense of elevated social status.

This economic boom in turn sparked a kind of hyper-consumerism, once again as Halim Salleh (1999: 190) noted:

> With higher incomes, lifestyles also changed, giving rise to new shopping and recreational complexes, mega malls, hypermarkets, as well as tourist complexes. Malaysians entered into consumerism at a level never before seen in the country. The new fetishes of the rich followed the footsteps of the rich and famous of the world. The middle class competed against one another with status symbols, including the holding of blue chip shares, expensive houses, motor-cars, membership of golf clubs, household consumer durables, and the omnipresent cellular phones. The working class as well as the rural population were similarly caught in the new wave of consumerism, but tended to stay at the lower end of the market, thus encouraging the growth of the motor-cycle industry, imitation products, black markets, and the informal sector.

This push to transform Malaysia into a fully modern economy was made explicit in the government's national policy directive called Vision 2020 with a goal of turning Malaysia into a fully industrialized country with a truly united *Bangsa Malaysia* (Malaysian 'race'). As Sloane (1999: 110–11) indicates:

> 'Vision 2020' became a clarion call and catchy, futuristic-sounding slogan supporting a somewhat vague set of norms and programmes that would bring Malaysians into the future by replicating traditional-style social relations in an increasingly sophisticated, highly technical, enterprise-based economy. Key to Prime Minister Mahathir's vision was a concept of civil society that leaned heavily on a rhetoric of 'family', 'local', '*kampung*', and 'Asian' values in contrast to decayed and decadent Western ones.

What is extolled in this vision is a Malaysian brand of modernity that does not forgo traditions but in fact promotes neo-traditionalism focusing on Malay *kampong* (village) values and Islamic ideals. Hence, one can conclude that Orang Asli are being incorporated into a Malaysian modernity where neoliberalism, industrialization, and Islamic neo-traditionalism are combined and envisaged in national goals such as Vision 2020. Yet much of the rural sector in the country is still coming to terms with agricultural modernization, to which I will now turn my attention.

Agricultural modernization

In the 1960s many newly independent nations, like Malaysia, considered the improvement of agricultural systems a priority in plans for rural development. Agricultural policies and programmes were directed towards increasing food production and transforming subsistence-oriented farming into commercial agriculture involving the cultivation of Hevea rubber, oil palm, cocoa, and coconut. Inspired by the 'Green Revolution' technology[5] associated with the use of scientifically developed, high-yielding crop varieties, food production was perceived to be an important developmental issue. In Malaysia, a higher agricultural productivity was deemed necessary to relieve dependence on rice imports, estimated to be around 35 to 40 per cent of total supply of rice in the 1960s and costing about US$50 million (Gibbons *et al.* 1979: 4). It was also believed to be politically vital for the government to eradicate poverty among the mainly Malay rural farmers who were electorally the most important group for the ruling elite. Appeasing Malays through 'modernizing' projects in farming, especially rice, was regarded by the authorities as a strategy towards consolidating political influence in rural Malaysia. With funding and expertise from such international agencies as the Colombo Plan and the World Bank, Malaysia, like so many other developing countries, implemented Green Revolution programmes in several rice growing areas.

Apart from the introduction of high-yielding varieties of rice, development agencies also promoted the use of chemical fertilizers and pesticides that these crops required, and, through credit facilities for the purchase of machines, promoted farm mechanization. High-yielding crops grew faster and could be double-cropped requiring more efficient ploughing and harvesting beyond the capacity of human labour. Hence, machines like tractors and combine harvesters were needed to keep to the hectic farming schedule. With improved production efficiency and greater use of fertilizers, farmers expectedly harvested more grain for sale, but there were costs, some direct and most hidden.

Like rubber and oil palm small-holders, rice farmers in due course became entrenched in agricultural commodity markets (Scott 1985, see also Gupta 1998 and Shiva 1991) and this was at the expense of subsistence enterprises and concomitantly, food security (see, for example, Nash 2001). Furthermore, increased mechanization and the use of chemical fertilizers and pesticides in all forms of commercialized agriculture have thrown people into growing and greater dependence on transnational corporations for supplies of chemical inputs, financial institutions for loans to buy machines and agro-chemicals, and external agricultural expertise. This has in turn compounded indebtedness, leading to a widening gap between rich farmers who have been able to take advantage of their position to accumulate surpluses by buying more land and agricultural inputs and poor farmers who have simply accumulated more debts and fallen into misery, eventually losing their land, their primary source of livelihood. Several studies of the effects of agricultural modernization, such as Conway and Barbier (1990), Gibbons *et al.* (1979), Gupta (1998), Scott (1985), and Shiva (1991), have reported increasing landlessness, unemployment, and growing social inequality as outcomes of such development. There was also an ecological cost; as Shiva (1991), among other researchers, has noted, chemical inputs into agricultural systems have resulted in environmental pollution.

All in all, many researchers and development agencies consider the Green Revolution, rather than being a success story, as a social and ecological disaster. The high level of discontentment which Shiva (1991) opined as the underlying cause of communal violence in Punjab in the 1980s could very much also have been a factor in the tension and hostilities that culminated in the Jeli tragedy. The rural landscape in Kelantan where the Menraq are found has been radically transformed, leading to considerable disillusionment and discontentment among the people with the government developmental efforts in the State. This level of dissatisfaction with the central government and its style and form of development planning and implementation is certainly one of the factors instrumental in the State being ruled by an Islamic-based opposition party, Partai Islam (PAS). The people's support for what is regarded as an anti-modernist party could very much be interpreted as a form of resistance and rejection of Malaysia's modernist government.

Modernity and tribal communities

As Benjamin (2002: 12) notes, 'People sometimes find the word "tribal" offensive.' He argues that the term 'tribal' is not 'inherently offensive', but has 'become offensive when used by those who despise the people referred to' (2002: 12). I concur with his view that the appellation 'tribal' is appropriate, particularly in the context of Malaysia as I discuss below, 'precisely because it refers to a characteristic way of life and of social organization for which no other unambiguous label exists' (Benjamin 2002: 13). In current official classifications and in academic literature, tribal people are often referred to as indigenous people. While most, if not all, tribal peoples easily fit the label 'indigenous', not all indigenous people are tribal, like the Menraq, in terms of social organization and economic and political status.

Much attention has been given to the perplexing and deeply politicized issue of how to define 'indigenous people'.[6] Howitt *et al.* (1996: 11) warn, 'What is encompassed by any definition will inevitably depend upon who is doing the defining, and for what purpose(s)'. A widely accepted definition for indigenous peoples is the one provided in a United Nations' report entitled *Study of the Problem of Discrimination Against Indigenous Populations*:

> Indigenous communities, peoples and nations are those which, having a historical continuity with pre-invasion and pre-colonial societies that developed on their territories, consider themselves distinct from

other sectors of societies now prevailing in those territories, or parts of them. They form at present non-dominant sectors of societies and are determined to preserve, develop, and transmit to future generations their ancestral territories, and their ethnic identity, as the basis of their continued existence as peoples, in accordance with their own cultural patterns, social institutions and legal systems.

(José Martínez-Cobo 1987: 48, cited in Niezen 2003: 20)

Discernible from this statement are four elements in the definition of indigenous peoples: pre-existence, non-dominance, cultural difference, and self-identification as indigenous. This definition has been contested on the basis of several ambiguities and its incongruence with certain empirical situations. As Niezen (2003: 20) indicates, 'Comprehensive and durable as Martínez Cobo's definition is, it does not apply unfailingly to all situations in which people claim indigenous status and protections.' For example, not all the peoples defined as indigenous would fulfil the requirement of pre-existence in the context of contemporary nation-states. The Hmong in Thailand are a case in point. They are viewed by Thai officials as 'migrants' from the North. Compared to other hill peoples in Thailand, the Hmong may have arrived recently in the area now part of the nation-state of Thailand but in the context of the region they are undoubtedly autochthonous to the mountain areas which have been carved into sections each belonging to China, Laos, Vietnam, and Thailand.

Formal definitions for a socially and historically diverse group of people will always be problematic and contested. A rigorous definition may exclude a group which sees itself as indigenous, while a loose definition will be too open-ended for situations requiring a precise identification of an indigenous group, such as providing access to redress for past and current injustices. Niezen reveals the prevalence of an unwritten or unexpressed 'definition' held by people belonging to the indigenous collectivity:

there is an attachment that all participants [of an international indigenous meeting] share to some form of subsistence economy, to a territory or homeland that predates the arrival of settlers and surveyors, to a spiritual system that predates the arrival of missionaries, and to a language that expresses everything that is important and distinct about their place in the universe. Most importantly, they share the destruction and loss of these things. Their cultural markers gain self-conscious significance the more they are diminished by outside forces. They also share the corresponding commitment to find stability and restorative justice – even if it means using the very tools of literacy and law that, in other hands, are responsible for their oppression.

(Niezen 2003: 23)

Indigenous minorities are referred to by various labels – 'tribal', 'aborigines', 'natives', 'highlanders', 'mountain people', 'forest people'. In Malaysia, including Sabah and Sarawak, the official ethnonyms for these peoples are Orang Asli (Aborigines) in Peninsular Malaysia, and Pribumi (natives) or Dayak in East Malaysia. Typical of governmental or bureaucratic definitions of indigenous communities is Indonesia's definition of what it referred to as *suku suku terasing* ('isolated communities') during the Suharto regime:

> People who are isolated and have a limited capacity to communicate with other more advanced groups, resulting in their having backward attitudes, and being left behind in the economic, political, socio-cultural, religious and ideological development process.
>
> (*Down in Earth*, No 12, February 1991, cited in Colchester, 1994)

Since 1993, indigenous communities in Indonesia are referred to as *masyarakat adat*, or communities that adhere to customary ways (*adat*) (Li 2001: 645), emphasizing the perceived connection of such peoples to traditional cultures. However, as in the case of other countries in the region, what is missing in this official ethnonym is the vernacular term for 'indigenous'. This relates to the controversy surrounding the question of indigeneity in the region. In contrast to the immigrant-conscious United States, Canada, or Australia, in most countries of Southeast Asia the dominant ethnic groups who usually reside in the urban centres or occupy the lowlands or coastal areas claim to be indigenous to the country. For example, as discussed in the previous chapter, Malays in Malaysia assert *bumiputera* ('sons or princes of the soil') status even though a category of people called *Orang Asli* ('original people') is legally recognized.

Indigeneity is a thorny issue in Malaysia and there are legal edicts in the Malaysian Constitution prohibiting public discussion of this issue, particularly pertaining to Malay claims to indigenous status.[7] How is the Malaysian conundrum relating to indigeneity resolved? Several Malay leaders have justified Malay indigeneity on the basis of political and demographic supremacy. This is epitomized in the former prime minister's opinion on this matter:

> The first conclusion from the study of other countries is that the presence of aborigines prior to settlement by other races does not mean that the country is internationally recognised as belonging to the aborigines. Aborigines are found in Australia, Taiwan and Japan, to name a few, but nowhere are they regarded as the definitive people of the country concerned. The definitive people are those who set up the first governments and these governments were the ones with which other countries did official business and had diplomatic relations. There is another condition. The people who form the first effective Government and their legal successors must at all times outnumber the original tribes found in a given country ... In Malaya, the Malays without doubt formed the first effective governments ... The *Orang Melayu* or Malays have

always been the definitive people of the Malay Peninsula. The aborigines were never accorded any such recognition. There was no known aborigine government or aborigine state. Above all, at no time did they outnumber the Malays.

(Mahathir 1970: 126–7)

Tribal communities are often seen as 'traditional'. In fact, this is typically the way by which people in such communities generally see themselves: peoples who are connected deeply to traditions 'from time immemorial' (Perry 1996, Wilmer 1993) in a particular 'place'. In the parlance of the modernization approach, traditional is the logical opposite to modernity and as discussed earlier, modernization is viewed as a process of transformation from traditional to modern. Apart from 'modernization', governments have employed a range of rhetorical concepts such as 'economic growth', 'nation-building', 'poverty alleviation', and more recently 'sustainable development' to justify and legitimize intervention in the lives of tribal communities. Many tribal communities, as in the case of the Orang Asli, have been most directly affected by state programmes designed to 'uplift' them or 'integrate them into the mainstream of society'. In the context of China, Harrell (1995: 4) has aptly referred to such interventions as 'civilizing projects' defined as

a kind of interaction between peoples, in which one group, the civilizing center, interacts with other groups (the peripheral peoples) in terms of a particular kind of inequality. In this interaction, the inequality between the civilizing center and the peripheral peoples has its ideological basis in the center's claim to a superior degree of civilization, along with a commitment to raise the peripheral people's civilization to the level of the center, or at least closer to that level.

As I will discuss in the following chapter, civilizing projects for tribal communities generally take the form of resettlement, advocated by policy-makers who consider the purported 'unsettled lifestyles' of the beneficiaries to be uncivilized or inimical to modernity.

Not all such interventions in the lives of tribal communities are driven by the objective to civilize the people. Tribal communities have also been affected by development projects such as the construction of large-scale dams and other infrastructures, land development schemes, plantations, and conservation parks which largely benefit non-tribal minorities (Dentan *et al.* 1997).[8] Anderson (1987: 11) has summed up this situation for tribal communities in Southeast Asia:

In most cases their humble wish is simply to be left alone, or to make quiet, slow adaptations to the outside world. But this outside world – not merely the nation-state, but more importantly the great engines of planetary power – will not leave them be. They may sit on valuable mineral or forest resources coveted by the outside; their subsistence agriculture may be regarded as ecologically destructive by international bureaucrats and national planners; demographic pressures may push lowlanders up into their mountain retreats; and they may be unlucky enough to live on sensitive borders between rival nations or rival world blocs.

Governments and some international agencies rarely acknowledge the fact that tribal communities have become marginalized as a result of economic and political incorporation. Instead the marginalized status is typically blamed on the physical, historical, and social location of the people or on some essentialized characteristics of the people considered to be inimical to modernity. This is implied in the World Bank's definition of 'indigenous peoples' which includes tribal communities:

> Despite their historical and cultural differences, they often have a *limited capacity* to participate in the national development process because of *cultural barriers* or low social and political status.
>
> (World Bank 1990: 1, emphasis added)

The experience of modernity for tribal peoples, however, is not just a straightforward process of economic and social transformation as a result of penetration of capitalism or nationalist ideology. It also involves cultural articulations as people attempt to localize the experience of modernity. Pred and Watts (1992: xiii) note that these articulations:

> are likely to assume some form of symbolic discontent, some form of cultural contestation, some form of struggle over meaning deriving from experience of new material circumstances and new power-relation-embedded rules, from the experience of disjunction and discontinuity, from the experience of the 'modern' shockingly displacing the 'traditional', in a word, from the experience of modernity.

In other words, tribal peoples develop forms of cultural expressions in their attempts to come to terms with the incursions of modernity into their everyday lives. They also resist domination through a range of strategies which June Nash (2001) has aptly labelled 'indigenous counterplots'.

Development for the Orang Asli, then and now

Government policies in respect of Orang Asli in Peninsular Malaysia were formulated and passed as a statute, the Aboriginal Peoples Act 1954, by the colonial administration during the height of the Emergency (1948–60, Communist Insurgency). In 1955, the Department of Aboriginal Affairs (JHEOA) was set up primarily as a tool of the security forces engaged in armed battle with the communist insurgents. Some Orang Asli were suspected of providing food and logistical information to the communists, who operated mainly from remote bases in the forests. To win over the Orang Asli communist sympathizers to its side, the colonial administration provided welfare services to Orang Asli and resettled Orang Asli living in 'communist areas' to safer sites.[9] The newly established JHEOA was given the task of implementing these programmes. It is worth noting that, as Nicholas (2000: 107) contends:

> The department was modelled along the lines of the United States Bureau of Indian Affairs and the Australian Department of Aborigines, not just in terms of administrative structure, but also in rationale: to 'protect' a class of people deemed to be 'wards of the state'. The policy of establishing Orang Asli reserves is an example of policy similarities.

Upon independence in 1957, the new government continued with these policies but with more vigour and a different emphasis. In addition to security protection measures, it aimed to integrate the Orang Asli into 'the mainstream of society'. As stated in an official document (Government of Malaysia 1961: 2):

> The social, economic and cultural development of the aborigines should be promoted with the ultimate objective of natural integration as opposed to artificial assimilation. The primary objective should be the fostering of individual usefulness and initiative.

Analysing the language or rhetoric used in these official documents can produce interesting insights into the policies for the Orang Asli. I will analyse the 'discourses' of development for the Orang Asli as implicated in the official statements, documents, and speeches but given spatial constraints, the discussion presented here is by no means comprehensive.[10] However, it will provide a deeper and more nuanced perspective of government policies for the Orang Asli while the following chapters will focus on the practical implications of these policies as they are implemented and applied in Orang Asli communities.

The JHEOA has been located in different government ministries over the years, and this constant shifting of the department is a reflection of the changing emphasis of state policies towards the Orang Asli. When it was first established, it was under the Ministry of Home Affairs (which is a ministry concerned with the internal security of the country, among other things) from 1955 to 1956, and then it was located briefly under the Ministry of Education (1956–59) before it returned to the Ministry of Home Affairs from 1959 to 1964, and again from 1974 to 1990. Interestingly, the periods that the JHEOA was under the Ministry of Home Affairs almost perfectly tally with the periods associated with heightened communist guerrilla activity in forest areas. The Department was moved to the Ministry of Land and Mines in 1964 where it remained till 1970 when it came under the Ministry of Agriculture and Land. From 1971 to 1974, it became part of the Ministry of National and Rural Development and it returned to this ministry, which was revamped into the Ministry of Rural Development, in 1990. Since 1994, the JHEOA has been under the Ministry of National Unity and Social Development. This constant relocation of the JHEOA nicely maps the Malaysian state's shifting agenda for the Orang Asli, from security concerns to resource extraction to rural development and, finally, to national unity and social development.

In its early policy statements, the government's paternalistic attitude, a legacy of the colonial administration, of 'protecting' the Orang Asli, was evident, as the following assertion reveals:

> The aborigines, being one of the ethnic minorities of the Federation must be allowed to benefit on an equal footing from the rights and opportunities which the law grants to the other sections of community. In so far as their social, economic and cultural conditions prevent them from enjoying the benefits of the laws of the country, special measures should be adopted for the protection of the institutions, customs, modes of life, person, and property and labour of the aborigine people. However, such measures of protection should not be used as a means of creating or prolonging a state of segregation and should be continued only so long as there is need for special protection and only to the extent that protection is necessary.
>
> (Government of Malaysia 1961: 4)

The Aboriginal Peoples Act 1954 (1974) gave the JHEOA the power to exclude any person or 'class of persons' from entering an Orang Asli area. In theory, therefore, the JHEOA acquired some control over the external relations of the Orang Asli. This view continued to be expressed openly in the 1980s as we can see from a 1983 development report by Jimin (1983: 35–6), who was then Director-General of the JHEOA; he justified his department's intervention in the economy of the villages and control of the marketing of village products as a measure in preventing Orang Asli from being grossly 'exploited' by outsiders. This official goal of 'protecting' the Orang Asli is often invoked when state officials are keen to control the affairs of the Orang Asli or to maintain control of access to Orang Asli peoples by, for instance, prohibiting missionaries other than Islamic ones from visiting Orang Asli villages or disallowing activists from contacting Orang Asli.

In a 1976 publication, Carey (1976: 300), who was the Head of the JHEOA in the 1960s, stated that the JHEOA performs three main tasks, namely 'the provision of medical treatment, education, and rural development'. JHEOA rural development projects include (a) the resettlement of Orang Asli into 'pattern settlements' where they are housed in new Malay-style dwellings, provided with a piped water supply, encouraged to cultivate cash crops such as rubber, oil palm, and trees in specially designated plots of land, and provided with facilities such as a school, community hall, health clinic, and sanitary conveniences; (b) the promotion of cash crops; and (c) the provision of agricultural skills and knowledge to previously non-settled Orang Asli. Clearly, these rural development programmes are planned and operate to incorporate the Orang Asli more fully into the market economy and the Malaysian state. In the 1983 official document (Jimin 1983: 550) we are told the source of inspiration for these development policies. The document states:

> The 'modernization model', subscribing to the 'stages of growth' theory as expounded by W. W. Rostow *et al.*, is still being pursued by the department with respect of those Orang Asli groups who are living within the rural fringe areas.

Interestingly, as Nicholas (2000: 94) has pointed out, 'the primacy of "development" in the earlier policy statements was replaced by integration, with socio-economic development being the *means* rather than the end of Orang Asli progress and advancement'. Also, as the 1983 document revealed, 'development' was viewed as 'growth plus change', a policy which is 'not only seeking an increase in the Orang Asli's productive capacity, but also the transformation of their productive capacity' (Jimin 1983: 114, in Nicholas 2000: 51).

The JHEOA carried out various development tasks on its own until the mid-1990s when it began to collaborate with other government ministries and agencies, such as the Ministry of Education and Health and the Federal Land Rehabilitation and Consolidation Authority (FELCRA) and the Rubber Industry Smallholders' Development Authority (RISDA), in implementing development projects in Orang Asli settlements (Nicholas 2000: 96). In 1993 the JHEOA announced a '10-point strategy' with the overarching objective to 'place the Orang Asli firmly on the path of development in a way that is non-compulsive [sic] in nature and allows them to set their own pace' (JHEOA 1993: 5). Nicholas (2000: 96–8) has listed these ten strategies as delineated in the English language version of the *Programme Summary* of the JHEOA's 1993 publication and it is worth repeating them here:

1. Modernising their way of life and living conditions, by introducing modern agricultural methods and other economic activities like commerce and industry.
2. Upgrading medical and health services, including having better-equipped clinics in interior areas, to bring about a healthy and energetic Orang Asli community.
3. Improving educational and skill development facilities, including programmes to provide better hostel facilities for both primary and secondary students.

4. Inculcating the desire among Orang Asli youth to become success-ful entrepreneurs by showing and sometimes opening doors of opportunity for them.
5. Getting Orang Asli interior areas to accept Regrouping Schemes (sic) as an effective means of improving their living standards and turning their settlements into economically viable units.
6. Encouraging the development of growth centres through the restructuring of forest-fringe Orang Asli kampungs, including the establishment of institutions such as Area Farmers Organisation and co-operatives.
7. Gearing up Orang Asli culture and arts, not only to preserve their traditions, but also as tourist attractions.
8. Eradicating poverty, or at least reducing the number of hardcore poor among the Orang Asli.
9. Introducing privatisation as a tool in the development of Orang Asli areas.
10. Ascertaining a more effective form of development management in line with the direction in which the Orang Asli community is progressing.

Nicholas (2000: 96) indicates that a striking difference in this policy state-ment from the preceding declarations is the reference to privatization as a development strategy. This is certainly in keeping with the neo-liberalist development thinking of the 1990s that promotes and advocates privatiza-tion as a means of reducing government intervention in, and expenditure on, development programmes and in the process, facilitating greater 'free market' involvement. Nicholas also notes a discrepancy between the English language and Malay language versions of the policy strategies. The Malay language version contained another strategy: 'to increase efforts at intro-ducing a value system based on Islam for the integration of the Orang Asli with the wider society in general and the Malays in particular' (Nicholas 2000: 98) and this is a policy direction that implicates the government's assimilation policy towards the Orang Asli, a policy aimed at turning Orang Asli into Malay Muslims. Such a policy was tacitly adhered to in the early days of the state's intervention in the lives of the Orang Asli but since 1993 there appears to be open admittance of the objective to convert the Orang Asli to Islam, especially with the establishment of a special *dakwah* (Islamic missionary) unit sometime in the 1980s to fulfil the goal declared in the 1983 JHEOA document of 'the Islamisation of the whole Orang Asli community' (Nicholas 2000: 98, Dentan *et al.* 1997: 144). This is, however, not just a policy to facilitate religious conversion; it is also implicitly a policy to pre-vent Orang Asli from converting to another religion. What has been dubbed as the 'Srigala Incident' exemplifies this insidious aspect of the conversion policy. Dentan *et al.* (1997: 68) provide a succinct description of the Srigala Incident:

At the urging of a Christian missionary and using funds he supplied, the thirty Christians in the forty-person Semai settlement of Teiw Srigala' (Malay *Sungai Srigala*) in Selangor began in August, 1990, to build a M$16,000 church, which was also to serve as a kindergarten. On orders from the Malay District Officer, they applied for a building permit on September 2. On September 14 the D.O. denied their application on grounds that 'certain' relevant laws forbade it. The D.O. circulated several copies of this letter, including one to the Selangor Department of Religious Affairs. The Semai unsuccessfully appealed the decision. The D.O. ordered them to destroy the building and accused the Christians, particularly their leader Bah Supeh, of illegally occupying government land. But Bah Supeh remained defiant . . . On November 27, officials from the District Office, armed policemen, and Federal Reservists armed with batons, machetes, and M-16s invaded Teiw Srigala'. With the help of two bulldozers from the Public Works Department (JKR), they levelled the church.

In December 2005, a Christian church in another Orang Asli village, Kampung Orang Laut Masai, in the southern state of Johor was similarly demolished (*New Straits Times*, 18 December 2005).

Having development schemes is one thing, but successfully implementing them is another and the JHEOA and the Malaysian government have not been altogether successful in their development efforts for the Orang Asli. The blame for this lack of progress is usually levelled at the Orang Asli themselves as people reluctant to change. As our Menraq case study will show, people's reluctance or lack of motivation can be interpreted as strategies of resistance or 'indigenous counterplots' (Nash 2001). In his doctoral dissertation titled 'An examination of development planning among the rural Orang Asli of West Malaysia', Mohd. Tap, a former high-ranking officer of the JHEOA, outlined reasons for what he saw as the failure of his former department's developmental efforts. He indicated that the highly centralized planning structure of the JHEOA and its predominantly unmotivated and disinterested staff resulted in poorly implemented programmes for the Orang Asli that were ill suited to the needs of the people and lacked adequate follow-up support (see also Nicholas 2000: 52). To these we can add the factor that the policies aimed at the Orang Asli are often based on misconceptions or popular mythology such as their being 'backward', 'people without history', nomadic, and 'remote dwellers'. They are also viewed as people without a religion.

Summary

Tribal communities around the world have received attention from national governments and development agencies to solve the perceived problem of their 'backwardness', isolation, and poverty. In the Malaysian context, as we have seen in this chapter, policies have been in place to civilize the Orang Asli. These policies can be interpreted as attempts to assimilate or integrate these minorities into the politically dominant Muslim Malay community. In the early days of independent Malaysia, the sudden attention devoted to the forest-dwelling Orang Asli was bound up with the government's military and security strategies directed at fighting the communist insurgents operating from forest bases. Later, the focus was on development and modernization programmes. This was not just confined to economic transformation but included 'spiritual development', a designation for Islamic conversion. In general, the implications of development, both economic and 'spiritual', for the Orang Asli people include increased impoverishment and dependence on external agencies, the loss of autonomy, and habitat displacement. The following chapters will provide a more detailed ethnographic account of these implications as well as the tribal counterplots in the context of the Menraq community at Rual.

4   Rual Resettlement

As a common government strategy for 'settling' the perceived problems of non-sedentary peoples, resettlement or 'regroupment' schemes[1] have been carried out for a large number of Orang Asli and almost all Menraq. Relocation is often the first stage in the modernization programme, followed by a range of 'civilizing projects'. In the following chapters, the effects of such projects for the Orang Asli will be examined. We will look at why resettlement policies are popular among governments and development agencies before discussing such policies in the context of the whole Orang Asli population and outlining specific data on the history, demography, settlement patterns, and social organization of the Rual Resettlement village in Kelantan, which I have studied at first-hand. This outline provides a background for my analysis of the effects of resettlement – economic, ecological, social, and cultural – on the recently established community of Rual Menraq to be covered in Chapters 6 and 7.

States and sedentarization

To most governments and development agencies, the existence of a group of people following a nomadic lifestyle is unsettling. Since they 'do not go to school, cannot easily be reached by state medical services, and are "lawless", but worst of all they may regard tribal loyalties above national loyalties', nomadic peoples are considered by national governments to be a 'stigma, an affront to national pride' (Bodley 1990: 58). Their lifestyle is deemed incompatible with the goals of the nation, be they economic development or national security. States and their development agencies commonly view mobility as a hindrance to the implementation of civilizing projects and see it as easier to carry out such projects in sedentary communities. In other words, nomadism is often perceived to be inimical to modernity, a view illuminated in Carey's statement in reference to the Semang/Negritos (1976: 66):

> There is, however, a much more valid and acceptable reason for encouraging the Negritos to settle down. This arises from the consideration that an entire lifetime spent in the gathering of roots and fruits in the

Malayan jungles is rather a poor way to live. There are hardly any opportunities for learning, or for acquiring knowledge of the outside world, and the individual is in this sense impoverished. He is denied the opportunity of enriching his personality, and of realizing his mental and psychological potential.

The association of nomadism with simplicity, primitivity, or naivety is by no means a recent view. Skeat and Blagden's statement about the Semang in the early 1900s ([1906] 1966: 167) is illustrative of this perspective:

We have as yet no record of the use of 'high places' or shrines among the pure Negritos, and perhaps naturally so, since the idea of regarding a specific locality as sacred could only grow up with the greatest difficulty among tribes who are so essentially nomadic that they never stay more than four or five nights in a single spot.

Nomadic peoples are also likely to inhabit or occupy places coveted for other purposes by more politically dominant populations in the country or they may move regularly into national security sensitive areas. Settling such populations into villages serves to free resources or land for other uses or activities, such as mining, logging, dams, plantations, land schemes for other people, military and security operations, or even golf courses. Governments are keen on settling nomadic peoples also because the policy of resettlement is viewed favourably by a range of interested parties, as Nicholas (2000: 66) outlines:

For politicians, land settlement schemes can be used to legitimate those who hold power by demonstrating, in a highly visible fashion, that something is being done to alleviate rural problems. For bureaucrats, such schemes are attractive because they can be planned and developed in 'project units' that are amenable to the algebra of conventional cost-benefit calculations. For donor agencies, land schemes are an 'off-the-shelf' project type that can be speedily planned and funded on a large scale. Finally, commercial interests favour such projects because of their high dependence on external expertise and supplies, opening up profitable opportunities for business.

Resettlement, however, is not popular among the Orang Asli. For quite some time, so-called nomadic Orang Asli in Malaysia have resisted settling down. Such disinclination has even been ridiculously linked to the people's biological predisposition, as Carey (1976: 65) comments:

The reluctance of the Negritos to settle down has puzzled many people, particularly government officials, some of whom are under the impression that these people have a nomadic instinct, of a biological kind, and which presumably is transmitted from one generation to the next.

Peoples' own (various and individual) views are of course very different; resettlement projects are not well liked among the Orang Asli because of the various problems such projects have created for the beneficiaries. Let us now look at how resettlement policies have been carried out among the Orang Asli.

Orang Asli resettlement

In the mid-1930s, H. D. (Pat) Noone, a colonial administrator appointed to the newly created position of Protector of Aborigines in 1939 for the state of Perak, advocated setting up what he called 'pattern settlements' for the Orang Asli. Noone (1936: 63) proposed:

> that in each district, a Pattern Settlement be instituted among the border aboriginal population, where culture contact is inevitable, for purpose of controlling the contact and for dissemination of agricultural knowledge and health measures to the group.

He referred to these as 'controlled reservations', apparently modelled on the notorious Indian reservation programmes implemented for Native Americans in the United States in the 1800s. While a stated objective of such 'reservations' was to establish control over the Orang Asli, it was also clear that Noone envisaged these projects as a means of facilitating agricultural modernization. As he asserted:

> A 'Pattern settlement' would mean the permanent settling of a group depending on cultivation of dry crops on the five-field system selected as a base for propaganda. Such a settlement situated down river would be easily accessible to the various officers of the district who could visit it during their rounds . . . The pattern settlement would be the means of getting in touch with all the inhabitants of a river valley and propaganda would spread from it.
>
> (Noone 1936: 69)

It is interesting to note that Noone used the word 'propaganda' to refer to the spread of development.[2] Nevertheless, given his generally favourable attitude towards the Orang Asli, his intentions of setting up reservations for the people were likely to have been steered by a genuine concern for the welfare of the Orang Asli, particularly for the Temiar, with whom he was most familiar.

Noone's proposal was shelved for almost twenty years as in 1941 Japanese forces drove the British out of the Malay Peninsula, and the programme could not be implemented. It was only in the aftermath of the Second World War and during the period of communist insurgency in the 1950s that the authorities reconsidered the policy. However, it was at that time executed not as a strategy for development, but as a tool of national security. Government intelligence reported that the communist insurgents operating from their jungle bases were using Orang Asli as guides and as purveyors of information and food. To deny the communists such support, the government implemented an ambitious resettlement programme referred to as the Briggs Plan.[3] Thousands of Orang Asli were herded from their forest abodes into settlements in populated areas to facilitate surveillance and control. The settlements were fenced by barbed wire and were under constant military guard. These settlements appeared more like internment camps than the 'patterned settlements' that Noone had envisaged. The housing and sanitary facilities were poor and food supply was irregular. Orang Asli were cramped into densely populated settlements, many of them with more than a thousand people, more than ten times the size of a large traditional Orang Asli village. With crowded conditions and malnutrition, disease was rife and many people died. Some estimates put the total death toll among the Orang Asli in resettlement as high as 7,000 people (Jimin 1983: 60). In one large camp the death rate in 1951 reached 204 per thousand and the authorities expressed concern that, unchecked, mortalities at this rate could lead to the complete demise of the group concerned (Jones 1968: 297).

The experience of resettlement, combined with rough, or at best insensitive treatment, of the Orang Asli by the security forces, left an indelible mark on Orang Asli perceptions of government intervention in general and resettlement in particular. Many Orang Asli escaped from the camps and returned to their forest habitat. The authorities soon realized the follies of the resettlement strategy. It became clear that this plan had backfired and it was summarily abandoned. In its place, the authorities established what were called 'jungle forts' close to Orang Asli villages in the forest. About fifteen such forts were created in the mid-1950s. Unlike the previous disastrous attempt to safeguard national security, this programme was designed to win the 'hearts and minds' of the people through the provision of educational and health services to Orang Asli living nearby. They were also treated in a more humane manner than before.

The policy of resettlement was, however, not completely discarded. Policy-makers remained adamant about relocating people from forest areas by any means, voluntary or involuntary. In the 1961 official publication entitled 'Statement of Policy regarding the Administration of the Aborigine [sic] Peoples of the Federation of Malaya' discussed in the previous chapter, it is stated:

> The nomadic Negritos are traditionally accustomed to a way of life involving a purely hunting and collecting economy. Their methods or practices therefore often conflict with the policy of forest conservation. During the Emergency a number of attempts were made to settle some of these groups but these always failed. It would in fact be quite impossible to change their habits except by application of totally undemocratic and indefensible methods.

Revealed in this statement is yet another agenda in plans to relocate or settle Menraq: forest conservation. It is also an acknowledgment that the government might need to use 'undemocratic and indefensible' methods to carry out this policy. In other words, it might need to resettle people involuntarily, particularly since resettlement had gained such a bad reputation among the Orang Asli. From the late 1950s to the early 1970s, the Malaysian government, through the JHEOA, implemented a number of resettlement projects for the Orang Asli, and the Rual project was one of these. Inspired by the 'jungle forts' concept, these projects were located in the vicinity of the original homesteads of the beneficiaries. However, to remove the military emphasis of the earlier projects, these settlements were referred to as 'posts' rather than 'forts'. Furthermore, the focus of these 'posts' was ostensibly on development projects such as cash crop plantations and animal husbandry, although the regular visits of military and police personnel would suggest that the security agenda was still firmly on the minds of the government sponsors.

One of the earliest attempts at resettling the Menraq was carried out in 1956 among people living in Ulu Lebir area in Kelantan. Carey (1976: 118), who, as mentioned earlier, was the first Commissioner of the Department of Aborigines and was anthropologically trained with a PhD based on work in West Africa on 'development'-type issues, provides an account of this resettlement:

> Negritos agreed readily to settle down on hearing that the government would provide free rations, especially rice, for a year and during this period they would also be given an opportunity to grow their own crops. The Negritos thus settled down and cleared a patch of jungle for the cultivation of tapioca, maize and other crops. The government supplied them with large quantities of rice and other foodstuffs weekly. This proved to be an extremely costly undertaking, since the rations had to be sent to them over long distances by motor-boat. After a year, it was found that the crops which were grown by the settlers were insufficient for their needs, and a further period of rationing, for about six months or so, was agreed upon. At the end of this period the state government decided that no further funds could be spared, especially since, at least in theory, the Negritos were by now expected to be self-sufficient, and to be able to rely upon their own crops . . . On the day when the entire group, involving some four hundred people or so, was officially told that no further rations would be supplied, the members abandoned their camp immediately, divided themselves into various original bands and resumed their nomadic way of life.

Carey (1976: 118) was candid in his appraisal of this project:

> The experiment was in fact a resounding failure. It proved that it was easy to induce the nomadic Negritos to settle down, as long as free rice

and other foodstuffs were provided . . . Their efforts at cultivation were half-hearted, largely a camouflage and a kind of encouragement for the government to keep on sending the rice and other foodstuffs to them. Once it had become clear that no further rations would be supplied, it seemed entirely natural for these people to abandon the settlement and to resume their traditional way of life.

Carey (1976: 119) mentions another attempt at resettlement, which interestingly was an initiative of a Malay villager in the state of Kelantan rather than the government. Details of this 'project' are sketchy but it seems that the impetus was religious. The Malay man converted the twenty-five or so Menraq adults to Islam and asked them to settle near a Malay village so that as Muslims they could have easy access to the village mosque. This scheme was short-lived, however, as the Menraq soon gave up being Muslims and returned to their forest camps.

In the late 1960s the JHEOA resettled 130 people from different 'tribes' – Kensiu, Kintak Bong, and Jahai – into a single village called Kampong Lalang, located near Baling, Kedah. To the government sponsors, the project was considered unsatisfactory for several reasons. As Carey (1976: 120) indicates, one of the problems was the semi-permanent nature of the 'village':

> the people have come to regard their village as a sort of general headquarters, rather than as a permanent settlement. They live there for only two or three weeks, after which all the able-bodied men and women would go into the jungle for a number of weeks in order to collect rotan [rattan] and other jungle produce which would later be sold to Chinese middlemen at Baling.

For Carey (1976: 121), Kampong Lalang 'presented an untidy appearance at all times'. Tidiness is certainly subjective and relative. Carey may be comparing Kampong Lalang to relatively tidy Malay villages he had visited. What is interesting, however, is that he blames this untidiness on the people's nomadic attitude and existence where 'an accumulation of dirt and refuse does not matter in the least' (Carey 1976: 121). He reasons:

> After all, nomads only live in a particular place for a few days before they move on again. There is therefore no tradition of village cleanliness, and habits which make good sense in nomadic existence are carried on under conditions in which they are no longer appropriate.
>
> (Carey 1976: 121)

In the mid-1970s the communist threat re-emerged. Increasing guerrilla activity in various parts of Peninsular Malaysia, particularly in the northern regions close to the border with Thailand, once again drew the government's attention to the Orang Asli living in these areas. Ostensibly to protect the forest dwelling or mobile populations from getting caught up in the guerrilla warfare between the security forces and the militant communists, the Malaysian government embarked on a grand programme of resettlement, which was also designed as part of a modernization plan for the Orang Asli. As mentioned earlier, instead of referring to the removals as resettlement projects (Rancangan Penempatan Semula or RPS) they were called 'regroupment' programmes (Rancangan Perkumpulan Semula, referred to by the identical acronym RPS). While the acronym in reference to these two programmes conveniently remained the same, the use of the term 'regroupment' (*Perkumpulan*) rather than 'resettlement' (*Penempatan*) can be seen as an attempt to soften the perceived effects of the government's actions. Regroupment is, as a concept, more innocuous than resettlement, a word which implies displacement from traditional homelands. It shifts the focus from spatial discontinuity to social realignment, a more positive notion involving the enlargement of the village community and social milieu.

The JHEOA provided four objectives of the regroupment schemes, namely 'to eradicate poverty or to reduce the number of hardcore poor among the Orang Asli'; 'to modernise their way of life through provision of social services and basic facilities such as education, health, housing, water and electricity supply, etc.'; 'to regroup and reorganise (*menyusun*) Orang Asli in suitable centres in their traditional areas'; and finally, 'to guarantee the security of the Orang Asli from subversive and anti-national elements' (JHEOA 1992: Lampiran [Appendix] A, cited in Nicholas 2000: 113). The underlying rationale is that grouping small and widely dispersed villages into a larger settlement facilitates the implementation of development programmes. Some of the projects require considerable amounts of regular and reliable labour that a small village would be hard pressed to supply. Furthermore it is easier and more efficient to supply provisions and development goods to a few locations than to many inaccessible and dispersed villages. The relocations, however, are justified on a falsehood that people do not have strong links to their homelands. As Endicott (1997: 33) points out:

> When pressed to justify summarily evicting the Batek from their homeland, officials claim – contrary to all evidence – that, because the Batek and similar Orang Asli groups are nomadic, they have no attachment to particular places and can just as happily live on a resettlement project somewhere else.

In 1979, the government proposed to create twenty-five regroupment schemes to be implemented within ten to fifteen years, costing an estimated RM260 million (US$68.4 million at the 1979 exchange rate) (Nicholas 2000: 95). In these schemes large tracts of forest areas would be cleared and developed into cash crop plantations and settlements. Logging companies holding concessions in the areas were requested to clear the forests and construct dirt tracks and roads. This was not just cost-effective; it helped to raise additional revenue for the government through the taxes and levies on the timber extracted. Following the practice on land development schemes for Malays, several prefabricated Malay-type timber houses with corrugated iron roofs were built for the settlers. However, unlike housing in the Malay land development schemes, not all the settlers were provided with houses; many were expected to construct their own traditional style dwellings – bamboo wall and flooring and a thatched palm roof. The schemes also included the building of a school and a community hall incorporating a prayer room, usually centrally located. The houses were arranged in clusters representing hamlets formed out of the original settlements. The areas around the hamlets were planted with cash crops, mainly rubber and oil palm. Government departments and agencies specializing in agricultural development, such as RISDA (Rubber Industry Smallholders' Development Authority) and FELCRA (Federal Land Consolidation and Rehabilitation Authority) were drawn in to facilitate the development.

By the late 1990s, eighteen schemes were set up, involving roughly 10,700 people living in slightly more than 2,500 households. The total area devoted to these schemes was 33,427 hectares, ranging from 4,148 hectares in RPS Kemar [Perak] to 469 hectares for 161 people in RPS Tonggang [Perak] (Nicholas 2000: 115). The schemes are currently in different stages of implementation and economic transformation. In some of the early established projects, people have been earning secure and regular cash income from rubber and oil palm plantations, wage labour, and rural enterprises since the early 1990s. In others, however, people are still greatly dependent on traditional subsistence-oriented pursuits such as the collection of forest products.

It is apparent that a large number of these resettlement schemes, if not all, have been implemented with other agendas in mind. Many villages have been resettled for a variety of reasons, to make way, for example, for commercial logging, land schemes for Malays, agribusiness plantations, golf courses, and the construction of roads and dams (Dentan *et al.* 1997, Endicott 1979, Nicholas 2000). Some Orang Asli have been removed to provide land for the building of a university in Bangi and the Kuala Lumpur International Airport in Sepang (Dentan *et al.* 1997: 103–10). A group of Menraq, living in an area about 50 kilometres west of Rual, were moved twice. In the mid-1970s, thirteen bands of Menraq were resettled at a place called Pulau Tujuh in response to reports that communist insurgents, who were attempting to disrupt the construction of the cross-peninsular East–West Highway (see Map 4.1), were exploiting the Menraq living in the vicinity. A few years later, in 1979, the people were again asked to move, this time into a newly established regroupment scheme, RPS Banun, as it became evident that the construction of the 127 metres high Temenggor Dam was going to result in the flooding of some 15,200 hectares of mainly forest land, including Pulau Tujuh, and displacing in the process 1,500 Orang Asli. As well as the Menraq of Pulau Tujuh, 700 other Orang Asli affected by the dam were relocated to RPS Banun. The new settlers of RPS Banun were offered access to 2,529 hectares of state land but an application to the State government to designate the area as an Orang Asli reserve was rejected, leaving the people with no security of tenure or secure access to the land (Nicholas 2000: 116).

With poor economic opportunities and general hardship at RPS Banun, many people left the scheme. In 2003, one group of people from RPS Banun set up a new village at Sungai Selaur near a logging camp in their traditional homeland. They settled there to take advantage of opportunities offered by a timber company, Perak Integrated Timber Complex (PITC).[4] Government officials consider this new village as temporary, indicating that the people's permanent 'home' is RPS Banun where most of their kin live. However, the residents of Sungai Selaur see it differently. They say that there are more opportunities available at their present location than at RPS Banun. Apart from what they see as a reliable and fairly lucrative source of income from PITC, the Sungei Selaur villagers also engage in collecting rattan, *gaharu* (agarwood or eaglewood), and bamboo for sale, and some have even planted swiddens.

This case raises several interesting points. First, in the past two decades or so the mobility of the Sungai Selaur community was due to government initiative rather than the dictates of a foraging economy. Second, the reasons for relocating the people had more to do with other agendas, such as the military and security priorities in the 1970s, the construction of the dam in the late 1970s, and commercial considerations such as timber extraction, than development specifically for the Orang Asli. Third, as demonstrated by the establishment of Sungai Seluar, people are likely to leave regroupment schemes for places affording them better economic opportunities. In this case, the job opportunities that PITC offered enticed the people to set up a new village close to the logging camp. All in all, as these cases and the Rual case that I will turn to now exemplify that regroupment programmes, as Dentan *et al.* (1997: 131) contend, are instituted 'to obfuscate dislocation, dispossession, and the destruction of real property'.

The Rual Resettlement

Rual is easily accessible by road today but at the time of its initial establishment in 1972 the only way to the settlement was by foot through the forest or by helicopter. It is approximately 8 kilometres from the Malay village of Kampong Jeli and about 14 kilometres from Jeli town and 11.2 kilometres from Batu Melintang (see Map 4.1 for the location of the Rual Resettlement). Engulfed within a circle of small Malay kampungs, the resettlement is divided into three separate hamlets named after the main rivers or streams running close to them: Sungai Rual, Sungai Manok, and Sungai Kalok. Sungei Rual is the main settlement where the school and official quarters are located.

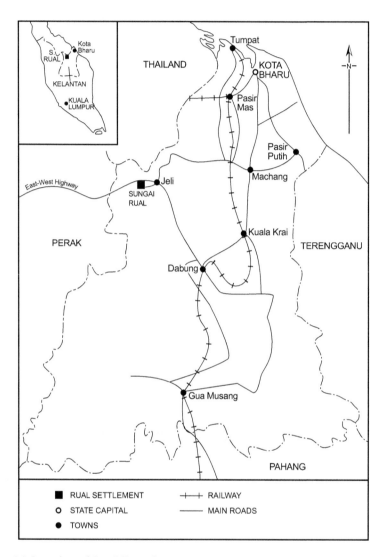

Map 4.1 Location of Rual Resettlement

Persuading the Menraq in the vicinity of Jeli to settle down evidently took several years. Beginning in the late 1960s, officers from the JHEOA attempted to talk people into joining a resettlement project planned for the Jeli Orang Asli. They were promised a better future and more comfortable living but what they were not told was that the resettlement was a military design to remove people from the so-called 'sensitive' areas, places notorious for communist activity. Abdullah Hassan, a JHEOA field officer, told me in an interview in 1976 that the Menraq were initially wary of the promises of a better life which his department made to the people. He claimed that he used his personal influence, having been friendly with several Menraq since childhood, to persuade them to accept the government's offer. As a form of inducement, people were promised houses and rations while they engaged in the various agricultural projects planned as part of the resettlement. Even though he was on the payroll of the JHEOA, Abdullah claimed that he saw his role more as an intermediary between the government and the Menraq. Speaking about his Menraq friends, he expressed his desire 'to help them because they were poor and disadvantaged'. Abdullah told me that it was his 'duty as a good Muslim' to assist the less fortunate Menraq.

In about 1970, the Menraq were given a choice of two possible sites for their new settlement, one close to the Malay village in Jeli and the other about 9 kilometres further away along the Rual River (see Map 4.1). The Menraq picked the more distant Rual site as the area close to Jeli village was within the *sakaq* of two bands, raising the potential of conflict over rights to resources. In contrast, much of the Rual site, with the exception of a small part claimed by one of the *puak*, did not 'belong' to any of the Menraq bands. The site was surveyed and mapped and a total area of 1,630 hectares was set aside for land development. The Menraq provided much of the labour for land clearing and construction work. They were 'paid' with rations of food and medicines airdropped regularly to ensure constant supply. A health clinic managed by a trained medical assistant was built along with a two-classroom school staffed by two teachers, and there was a radio telephone at

3 The main section of Rual Resettlement in 1975 Photo: A. Gomes

4 Rual Resettlement in 1978 Photo: A. Gomes

5 Rual Resettlement in 1979 Photo: A. Gomes

6 Menraq taking advantage of the relative coolness under a house (1979) Photo: A. Gomes

7 A section of Rual Resettlement in 1987 Photo: A. Gomes

8 A section of Rual Resettlement in 2006 Photo: A. Gomes

the clinic to contact the main JHEOA branch for any emergencies or other communications, a hut for storing food supplies, teachers' quarters, and a helicopter landing pad. The buildings were made out of forest timber as the framework, bamboo for the walls and flooring, and corrugated iron as roofing. The Menraq men assisted several JHEOA builders in the construction of the school, store, and clinic and four houses allocated to the headmen residing at the main settlement. The other settlers built their own houses. An area of about 22 hectares was allocated for the actual settlement sites.

When I first visited Rual in 1975, five Menraq bands were living in the resettlement, namely Mat Din, Macang, Meraju, Pusu (now Langsat, who took over the position from his deceased brother), and Lanas.[5] *Puak* Puteh (now under Teras, his son) were still 'camping' in their *sakaq* until the death of the headman soon afterwards, and even after that the band was still nomadic as compared to the other bands at Rual. During my one-month fieldwork in 1976, *Puak* Teras stayed for only seven days at the settlement and spent the rest of the time in foraging camps in the forest. Furthermore, unlike the dwellings of their fellow residents, the houses of *Puak* Teras were rather rudimentary and seemed temporary. Abdullah Hassan, the JHEOA field officer, referred to members of *Puak* Teras as obstinate and 'backward' compared to the other Menraq. There were also rumours that they were under the influence of the communist insurgents operating in the area and that they served the communists as forest guides and food suppliers. *Puak* Bernas, which joined in the 1980s, is believed to be from the neighbouring state, Perak. Map 4.2 shows the places of origin of the various bands (with the exception of *Puak* Bernas) with an estimate of the population contribution to Rual resettlement at the time of its establishment in 1972.

In 1978, the teachers' and JHEOA officers' quarters were replaced with more sturdy timber houses. The school building was also rebuilt and no longer looked like a makeshift structure. There were also proper desks and other educational paraphernalia in the school. The people in the main settlement, with the exception of the headmen, still lived in dilapidated houses made out of bamboo and palm thatched roofs. In 1982, the JHEOA built six wooden, Malay-style houses for the headmen. The preferential allocation of houses to the headmen is an example of the government's attempt to impose the Malay inspired village political system on the Menraq. As I discuss in Chapter 7,

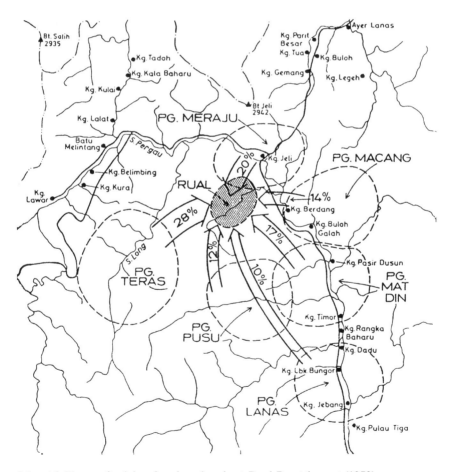

Map 4.2 Places of origin of various bands at Rual Resettlement (1972)

this new hierarchy tends to accentuate intra-village social differentiation, which in turn is likely to be socially disruptive, particularly in a strongly egalitarian social setting such as the Menraq community.

In 1986 and 1987, a further 22 Malay-type houses were built for the people at the resettlement. Following the design of PPRT[6] prefabricated dwellings, these houses had three rooms: a bedroom, a family room, and a kitchen. When I visited Rual in 1988, much of the area around the settlements had been cleared of forest, primarily due to intense logging, which was well under way in 1976. The school building had been improved and expanded, and there was now a soccer playing field in front of the building and a concrete floor volleyball court (which doubled as a *sepak takraw*[7]) near by. The wooden houses and the buildings were erected on concrete slabs. There was a piped water supply to the timber houses. Menraq men and women called these houses 'government houses' (*rumah kerajaan*). The much-improved infrastructure in the village and the grander wooden houses made the settlement look more mature and permanent than it was in 1978. Nevertheless, fifteen years after its foundation, many residents of the village still lived in huts made out of bamboo and thatched roof. At first glance, this looks like hidden poverty, which to an extent is correct. Yet there is more to these old-style dwelling-huts than at first appears. Some of the owners of the more lavish wooden houses had such huts erected next-door to them. Indeed, during my visits to Rual, I observed that Menraq tend to spend more time in the huts, especially at the heat of the day, than in their 'government houses' which are uncomfortably hot during the day because of the corrugated iron roofs and the lack of ventilation in the houses. It was apparent to me that the Menraq used their 'government houses' more as places for entertaining guests and storing personal items and household goods than as living quarters. It seemed clear to me that their traditional huts are better suited than the new ones for day-to-day living in Rual. The walls and flooring, which are made out of loose-woven split bamboo, allow air movement through the huts and the palm leaf thatched roof does not transfer heat as do the corrugated iron sheets used as roofing in the 'government houses'. Also, the noise of rain on tin roofs is deafening, even if it keeps the house dryer.

In the 1990s more infrastructural development was carried out. With the conversion of a majority of the Rual Menraq to Islam in 1994, two concrete structured prayer houses (*surau*) were built. In 1995, all the timber houses were electrified. A community hall (*balai*) was completed in 1997. Today, with public buildings such as the prayer houses and the community hall and with electric power poles and cables crisscrossing the site, Rual Resettlement resembles a typical rural Malay village. It now has a metalled road linking the three hamlets and a road connecting it to the Malay village at Sungai Long.[8] When I visited Rual settlement in 1999, there were 74 government-built houses in its three hamlets, seven official quarters (five for the teachers and two for visiting JHEOA officers), a four-classroom school, a rural health clinic, a community hall, and a *sepak tekraw* court. In my most recent visit in September 2006, I noticed more concrete buildings and structures in the settlement. The government built eight concrete houses for the headmen and their assistants, three concrete officers' quarters, a larger community hall, and a bridge over Rual River linking newly constructed houses across the river to the main settlement centre. In the span of slightly more than three decades since its founding, the Menraq resettlement at Rual has been transformed from a makeshift settlement with traditional huts resembling a typical temporary Orang Asli village into a permanent and well-serviced settlement akin to a Malay *kampung*.

The environs around the settlement have also undergone a transformation. In the 1970s we had to walk through the lush green forests to reach the settlement, crossing the swift flowing and clear Rual River several times. Now we approach the settlement by car through the Malay village at Sungai Long (originally a small homestead that has grown into a large Malay *kampung*, primarily as the result of a nearby government-sponsored land development scheme). The lush green forest has all but gone due to commercial logging and clearing by Malay settlers. One could say that Rual is now more accessible as one no longer needs to traverse thick forest to get to the settlement. The settlement is a fifteen- or twenty-minute drive from the intersection between the Sungai Long Road and the ultra-modern East–West Highway (Map 4.1). It appears that expansion and accessibility, while generally welcome, have been achieved at a cost: deforestation, clouding and silting of rivers and streams, with their negative implications for the Rual Menraq who have yet to enter fully into mainstream Malaysian society. Such are some of the visible environmental changes at Rual I have observed. We will look at the implications of these changes in Chapters 6 and 7.

Settlement pattern and spatial organization

In 1976, I described Rual Resettlement in the following way:

> Sungei Rual is divided into three settlement centres. *Puak* Pusu and *Puak* Meraju live together in nine houses; most of them still are of the traditional 'lean-to' dwellings, about one kilometre from the main settlement where the school, clinic and storehouse are located. *Puak* Mat Din, *Puak* Lanas and *Puak* Macang have their houses at the main settlement. They live in 14 houses built close to each other. About one kilometre north from the main settlement is the third hamlet occupied by *Puak* Teras.

To provide a graphic representation of how Rual settlement has changed over the past twenty years, Maps 4.3, 4.4 and 4.5 are of the settlement in 1978, 1988 and 1999 respectively. A comparison of the maps shows that, apart from the expansion of the built up areas with more houses and other structures, such as the community hall and the prayer houses, the settlement

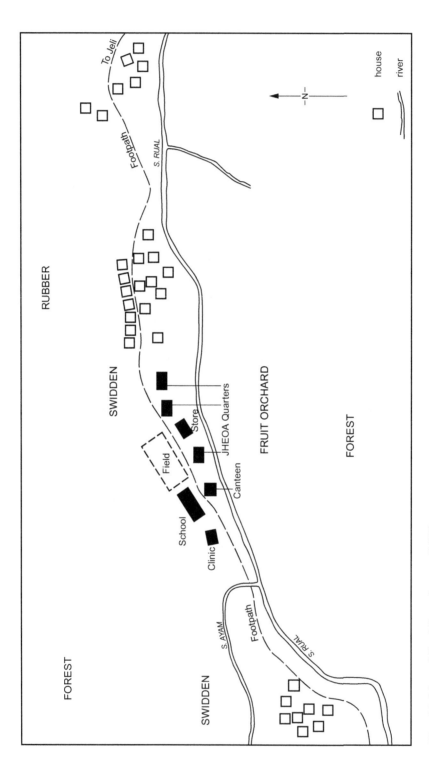

Map 4.3 Map of Rual Resettlement (1978)

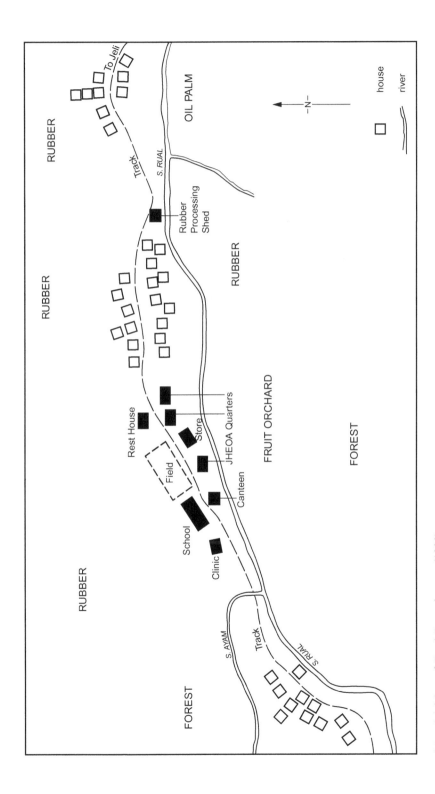

Map 4.4 Map of Rual Resettlement (1988)

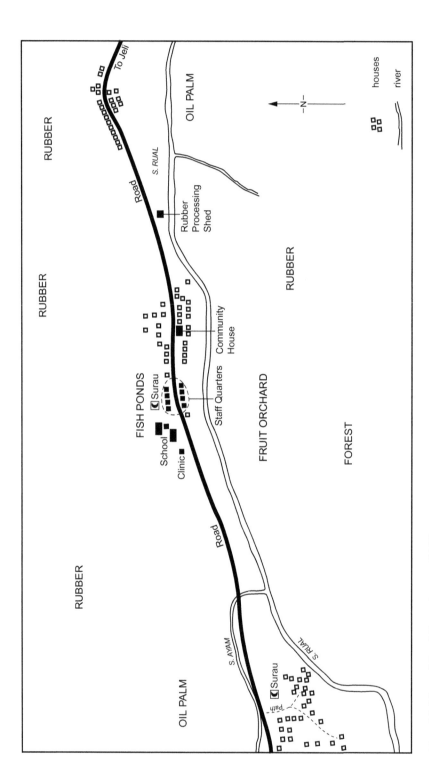

Map 4.5 Map of Rual Resettlement (1999)

pattern has not changed radically over the years. The dwellings have for the most part remained in the same location even though they have been rebuilt several times. The houses are located along what used to be a footpath in the 1970s and is now a road. The subsidiary hamlets of Manok and Kalok have retained a semblance of the traditional camp-like arrangement with dwellings arranged in a semi-circle. The expansion of the settlement is obviously to cater for the growth of the Rual population. Let us now look at the population composition and dynamics of the Rual settlement.

Rual demography

The first census I conducted for the Rual population in 1976 enumerated a total population of 184, comprising 90 males and 94 females. In the census I carried out in 1999, there were a total of 331 people at Rual. The population of Rual in 2006 had expanded to about 475, representing a population increase of 291 people in thirty years or about nine per year. Overall the Menraq population grew at an annual rate of about 4.8 per cent per annum through natural increase and in-migration.

Tables 4.1, 4.2, and 4.3 provide the age-sex composition of the Rual population in 1978, 1988, and 1998[9] respectively, based on demographic surveys conducted in 1978, 1988, and 1999.[10] Figures 4.1, 4.2, and 4.3 present this data graphically. The Rual population can be characterized as young. From the data presented in the tables and the population pyramids, it is evident that the proportion of the younger cohort, those below the age of 14, hovers above the 40 per cent mark, with 50.8 per cent below 14 years of age in 1978, 41.2 per cent in 1988 and 46.8 per cent in 1998. The mean ages were 20.1 years in 1978, 21.1 in 1988, and 20.7 in 1998.

Table 4.1 Age and sex composition of Rual Menraq population (1978)

Age (years)	Male	Female	Total	%
60 over	2	2	4	2.1
55–59	3	2	5	2.6
50–54	–	5	5	2.6
45–49	1	1	2	1.0
40–44	7	2	9	4.7
35–39	4	2	6	3.2
30–34	6	8	14	7.2
25–29	9	4	13	6.7
20–24	6	13	19	9.8
15–19	7	11	18	9.3
10–14	13	11	24	12.4
5–9	19	18	37	19.2
0–4	18	19	37	19.2
Total	95	98	193	100.0

Table 4.2 Age and sex composition of Rual Menraq population (1988)

Age (years)	Male	Female	Total	%
60 over	3	1	4	1.6
55–59	2	2	4	1.6
50–54	5	1	6	2.3
45–49	3	1	4	1.6
40–44	6	10	16	6.3
35–39	11	5	16	6.3
30–34	8	9	17	6.7
25–29	6	15	21	8.2
20–24	16	11	27	10.6
15–19	15	20	35	13.7
10–14	15	13	28	11.0
5–9	18	22	40	15.7
0–4	16	21	37	14.5
Total	124	131	255	100.0

Table 4.3 Age and sex composition of Rual Menraq population (1998)

Age (years)	Male	Female	Total	%
60 over	7	1	8	2.4
55–59	5	3	8	2.4
50–54	4	4	8	2.4
45–49	8	2	10	3.0
40–44	10	10	20	6.0
35–39	11	9	20	6.0
30–34	9	10	19	5.7
25–29	12	13	25	7.6
20–24	14	16	30	9.1
15–19	13	15	28	8.5
10–14	11	14	25	7.5
5–9	31	26	57	17.2
0–4	41	32	73	22.1
Total	176	155	331	100.0

Further analysis of age cohorts indicates that while more than a quarter of the Rual population was over the age of 40 in 1978, this proportion dropped to 13 per cent and 16 per cent in 1988 and 1998 respectively. This is due to an increase in the younger cohorts in 1988 and 1998 rather than a reduction in life expectancy. The proportion of women of reproductive age (15 to 44 years) has increased from 41 per cent in 1978 to 53 per cent in 1988. It dropped to 47 per cent in 1998. As far as sex ratios (male/female multiplied by a constant) are concerned, there is an interesting pattern of change.

The sex ratio dropped from 96.9 for the 1978 census to 94.7 for 1988, which indicates that the excess of females in the total population had increased in the span of ten years. However, there was a drastic shift in the sex ratio in 1998 measured at 114, a discrepancy most probably the consequence of chance.

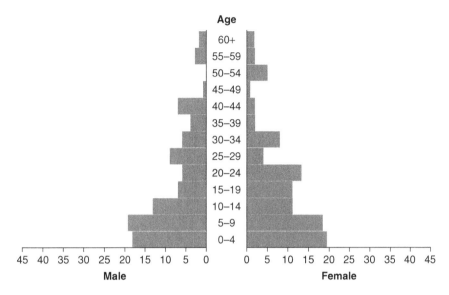

Figure 4.1 Rual Menraq population, 1978

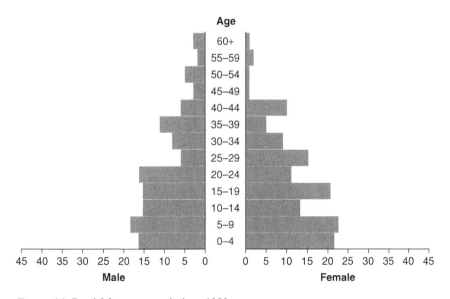

Figure 4.2 Rual Menraq population, 1988

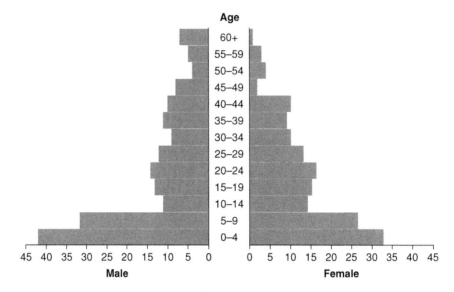

Figure 4.3 Rual Menraq population, 1998

Table 4.4 provides data on fertility levels for the Rual Menraq population in 1978, 1988, and 1998. To provide an indication of fertility levels, I have employed four different measures: child–woman ratio,[11] total maternity ratio,[12] maternity ratio,[13] and crude birth rate.[14] The child–woman ratio and crude birth rate tend to suggest that fertility levels have fluctuated in a see-saw manner over the three census periods while the total maternity ratio (TMR) and the maternity ratio (MR) indicate a constant increase from 1978 to 1998.[15] In twenty years, the TMR has increased by 24 per cent and the MR even higher at 41 per cent, signalling a substantial increase in the number of children born to Menraq women during the intervening period.

Table 4.5 shows the maternity ratios according to the age cohorts of the women in the three census periods. As one would expect, the maternity ratios increase quite consistently from the youngest cohort to the oldest in all the three census years. Table 4.6 presents data on the number of children of women above the age of 45 for the three census years. The range in the

Table 4.4 Rual Menraq fertility levels for 1978, 1988 and 1998

Fertility Measures	1978	1988	1998
Child–woman ratio	925	521	973
Total maternity ratio	4.5	5.2	5.6
Maternity ratio	2.9	3.3	4.1
Crude birth rate	71.10	50.98	69.49

Table 4.5 Number of children born to living ever-married women, 1978, 1988, and 1998

Age cohort	No. of women			No. of children			Maternity ratio		
	78	*88*	*98*	*78*	*88*	*98*	*78*	*88*	*98*
15–19	7	20	9	7	32	11	1.0	1.6	1.2
20–29	18	21	26	41	61	84	2.3	2.9	3.2
30–39	10	15	19	48	64	104	4.8	4.3	5.5
40–49	3	11	12	15	66	71	5.0	6.0	5.9
Total	38	67	66	111	223	270	2.9	3.3	4.1

Table 4.6 Number of live births to post-reproductive (> 45 years) Menraq women

Year	No. of women	No. of children														$\bar{x}$	SD
		0	*1*	*2*	*3*	*4*	*5*	*6*	*7*	*8*	*9*	*10*	*11*	*12*		
1978	12	–	–	1	5	1	2	–	1	2	–	–	–	–	4.5	2.1
1988	13	1	–	1	1	1	4	2	1	1	–	–	–	1	5.2	2.9
1998	16	–	–	1	1	4	3	–	2	4	–	1	–	–	5.6	2.3

numbers of children that these women have given birth to is staggering, from none to 12 children, with an average of 5 children per woman.

All in all, the figures clearly show that fertility levels in the Rual population have risen over twenty years. Why are Menraq women having more children? In an earlier publication (Gomes 1982), I attributed this increase in fertility to the changes in economic conditions resulting from resettlement. I argued that being sedentary and less involved in foraging had meant that the heavy burden of nursing more than one small child at a time was much reduced and hence women were prepared to have more children. My contention was inspired by what has been referred to as the 'backload model' (Pennington 2001) explaining the reasons for the common finding (for example, Lee 1979) that women in hunting and gathering populations tend to manage long birth intervals, usually four-year intervals. According to this model, women in foraging societies maintain 'wide birth intervals because they cannot care for more than one small child at a time due to the constraints of foraging activities and lack of weaning' (Pennington 2001: 186). This would explain the low fertility level when the people were actively engaged in foraging. To control births, Menraq have told me that they used several kinds of traditional contraceptives and abortifacients. However, the strict observance of their postpartum taboo of sexual abstinence for two years would also be a factor in fertility reduction.

The change in economic activity from foraging to sedentary agriculture would remove the 'backload' factor in family planning among the Menraq.

It would also potentially alter Menraq views regarding children. In my earlier study, I contended that the high demand for labour in the agricultural projects and the food rations that school children had brought back to share with their family members (see Chapter 6 for details of the rationing) would have accentuated the value of children to Menraq households. This, I argued, could have spurred Menraq families to have more children. This contention, which lends support to the view that resettlement has been successful as far as demographic factors are concerned, however, is partly flawed. In a subsequent study (Gomes 1990), it became clear to me that the high Rual Menraq fertility rate could actually be a conscious attempt by women to compensate for the very high child mortality they were experiencing. To appreciate why Menraq were having more children, it is therefore necessary to look at mortality at Rual.

Extrapolating from genealogical records, reproductive histories, and comparative analysis of the population censuses, I counted 178 deaths in the Menraq population from 1978 to 1998. This means that an average of nine people died each year and in a population ranging from 193 to 331, this is a rather high number of deaths in a year. The population grew by 138 individuals during this period. Hence, in absolute terms it is apparent that more people have died during this period of twenty years relative to the addition in the population. These deaths have certainly minimized the potential growth of population, as calculations will show that if each woman had 4 to 5 children (which is the average birth rate) this should result in a population size of anywhere between 392 to 490 in 1998. The population in 1998 totalled 331 and this includes about twenty or so in-migrants.

From a comparison of death records compiled in different survey periods, it appears that more people in Rual are dying annually than before. In my survey of the period between December 1974 and April 1978, I counted 23 deaths, which averages to seven deaths per year, two less than in 1998. Of course one could argue that the absolute number of deaths is bound to increase as the population size expands. There are, however, several statistical measures that can be used to provide a more accurate and precise estimation of the level of mortality. In the absence of a reliable system of vital information registration, one method of extrapolating the level of mortality is to examine comparatively the survival rates of the offspring of post-reproductive women. Table 4.7 lists the numbers of children that have survived for post-reproductive women according to the census year while Table 4.8 draws a comparison between numbers of liveborn children extracted from Table 4.6 and the numbers of surviving children of post-reproductive women. A comparison of the differences in the figures for surviving children and liveborn over the three census periods suggests a considerable increase in the level of mortality in the Rual population. The number of children dying before their mothers has gone up from 0.67 in 1978 to a staggering 1.69 in 1988, which means each post-reproductive woman living in 1988 had lost one child more than her counterpart living in 1978, to 2.13 in 1998.

Table 4.7 Surviving children of post-reproductive Menraq women

Year	No. of women	No. of Children										
		0	*1*	*2*	*3*	*4*	*5*	*6*	*7*	*8*	*x̄*	*SD*
1978	12	–	–	4	3	1	1	2	–	1	3.83	1.99
1988	13	1	–	3	2	4	1	1	1	–	3.54	1.85
1998	16	–	2	1	5	5	2	–	1	–	3.50	1.51

Table 4.8 Comparison of surviving children with total liveborn children per post-reproductive woman

Total no. of children	Year		
	1978	*1988*	*1998*
Liveborn	4.50	5.23	5.62
Surviving	3.83	3.54	3.50
Deceased	0.67	1.69	2.13

Crude death rates (CDR, the number of deaths per 1,000 people) for the Rual population add further support to the estimation of high mortality levels at the Rual Resettlement.[16] In 1979 I estimated the Rual Menraq annual CDR at 32.6 over the period 1956 to 1979 (Gomes 1982). For the period 1978 to 1988, the CDR had risen to 45.1 (Gomes 1990) but dropped to about 26.3 for the period 1988 to 1998. For the twenty-year period of 1978 to 1998, the annual CDR for Rual was about 34 per 1,000 population. For the Satak Semai, who, like the Rual people, have been resettled, Fix (1977) estimated the annual CDR for the period 1960 to 1969 to be 30. Compared to the national CDR of 4.5, these CDR figures are extraordinarily high. So why are the death rates so high? Why are more people dying each year at Rual than in the past? As I will elaborate in Chapter 7, the high mortality is related to the high incidence of disease, an outcome of the changing conditions resulting from resettlement.

Social and political re-organization

As one would expect, the amalgamation of several separate bands into three hamlets entailed some re-organization of the social and political arrangements. In the traditional system as outlined in Chapter 2, Menraq live in groups referred to by anthropologists as bands (*puak*). Each band has a recognized leader, usually an older male noted for his decision-making abilities as well as his talent for dealing with outsiders. In the past, Menraq referred to their leader by the kin term for grandfather, *Tok*. Nowadays *puak* leaders are addressed formally and to outsiders as *Penghulu*, a government-accorded title. They are paid a salary by the government and are expected to wield their influence and authority over their wards. Given strong egalitarian values among the Menraq, such expectations are never easily, if at all, fulfilled.

With eight bands coming together in Rual, there were eight leaders until recently when the JHEOA decided not to appoint replacements for two of the headmen who had died in the last two years. It is not entirely clear as to how the different bands came to be settled in their respective hamlets. Apparently, the divisions grew along lines of dialect group affiliations. The residents of Kampung Kalok are primarily Jahai, belonging to *Puak* Meraju and *Puak* Bernas with a smaller Mendriq band (headed by Langsat). Those residing in Kampung Rual are mixed Batek and Mendriq with a few Jahai (who have married into the bands) and one Temiar (non-Menraq) (*Penghulu* Lanas). Kampung Manok consists of *Puak* Teras who are mainly Jahai. Each hamlet or kampong tends to be autonomous with the people making decisions regarding 'village matters'. The *puak* leaders are expected to consult their members or pass on instructions from the government officers.

The JHEOA has established an administrative structure with the appointment of one headman, Mat Din, to be the main Headman (*penghulu kanan*) of Rual Resettlement. The *Penghulu Kanan* serves as the intermediary between the government and the other *puak* leaders who in turn act on behalf of their *puak*. This appointment and the fact mentioned above that the JHEOA has not replaced headmen for two bands seem to indicate the government's intention of consolidating a village-type administrative organization in place of the traditional Menraq band organization. This has established a hierarchical order in the resettlement, which is not altogether popular among the residents. On numerous occasions I have heard complaints by disgruntled people from the other hamlets, mostly to do with unfair distribution of handouts from visitors and the government by the main headman. The establishment of a hierarchical political system at Rual goes against Menraq traditional egalitarian values and sets in train intra-community social differentiation, an issue I will discuss at greater length in the chapters to follow.

Plans for the future

What plans do the government have in store for the Rual people? In 1998, the Kelantan State Development Planning Unit together with the Department of Urban and Rural Planning of the Ministry of Housing and Local Government conducted a study of the Rual Resettlement and produced a 'development plan' for Rual, which was referred to as *Kampung Baru* (New Village). The researchers identified several economic, infrastructural, and social 'developmental issues'. Among the economic issues noted were the lack of secure income sources, the continued dependence on fast-disappearing forest products, relatively unproductive rubber trees, and absence of village provision shops. As for the settlement, the researchers indicated that it was too close to rivers and hill slopes, opening it to risks of floods, landslips, and landslides, and the houses were arranged disorderly. It was also pointed out that the drainage system at Rual was poor, the road to the Malay kampung was unsatisfactory, and there was a lack of playing fields and social centres in the hamlets of Kampung Kalok and Kampung Manok. Interestingly, the planners also mentioned the negative impact of logging and encroachment by outsiders into the Rual settlement due to unclear boundaries as problems requiring attention.

The authors of the plan proposed several projects to be implemented in a period of ten years till 2010, with an estimated total cost of RM2.1 million (US$552, 630). The main principle of the plan is that Rual 'needs a process of change and modernity relative to the development that has been accepted by the surrounding Malay villages'. Apart from the expansion of the current rubber and oil palm holdings and infrastructure development such as roads and public halls, the Plan recommended the building of a mosque estimated to cost RM60,000 (US$15,790) by 2005 and building more prayer houses (*surau*), from the current two to three in 2005 and four by 2010. It also advocated as part of its *Bina Insan* ('Character Building') programme more teaching of the Koran and other Islamic religious classes. Another interesting proposal is to landscape the area surrounding Rual for 'recreational purposes', with a budget of RM63,250 (US$16,650), possibly for eco-tourism and/or cultural tourism. The other infrastructural plans to be completed by 2010 include road construction at an estimated cost of RM1 million (US$263,158), building four community halls, developing more sport playing fields (from one to four fields), and setting up four provision shops and a waste disposal centre. It is clear that the focus of the planners is on infrastructural development and the consolidation of Islam in Rual but they do not address several key developmental issues. While there is mention of the issue of encroachment by outsiders and logging companies and the recognition of the problem of unclear boundaries, there are no proposals or recommendations of how these problems might be best resolved. Neither is there a proposal for the allocation of legal rights to land to the Rual Menraq.

Summary

The main purpose of this chapter was to provide a historical, demographic, and geographical background to the growth of the Rual resettlement village. In order to appreciate the setting up of Rual better, it was also necessary to outline the political and economic aspects and discourses underlying the policy of resettlement. Over the years, a range of concerns has steered the policy of resettlement for the Orang Asli. In the early years, Orang Asli were relocated primarily for national security reasons. Subsequently, it was the expressed motive of economic advancement that prompted the government to set up resettlement or regroupment projects for the Orang Asli.

Underlying this motive is the notion that nomadism is inimical to modernity. However, there are other agendas too for resettlement. In many cases Orang Asli resettlement was simply a ploy to remove people from areas coveted by more powerful interests. Orang Asli have been moved to make way for commercial timber extraction, land development schemes for Malays, mining, plantations, and hydroelectric projects.

Since its establishment in 1972, Rual has experienced substantial social and economic change, primarily arising from the implementation of government-sponsored development projects. The environs at Rual have also been transformed. The lush rain-forest cover has almost completely disappeared, due mainly to commercial logging and clearing for oil palm and rubber plantations and Malay settlements. In the past thirty years, the Menraq population has almost doubled, largely due to natural increase but this is not as significant in terms of population pressure on resources as the growth of the Malay population in the areas around Rual, primarily as a result of land development schemes benefiting Malays. The following chapters will focus on the implications of these economic and ecological transformations as well as the social and cultural consequences of Menraq involvement with government and closer contact with the wider Malaysian society.

5 Menraq as foragers

The decisive change in economic focus among the Menraq since 1972 is perhaps the most immediate step we can see in their confrontation with modernity. Broadly speaking, this alteration is related to the wider transformations in the Malaysian economy in general and Kelantan State in particular, which are in turn responses to the changing global economic system. In specific terms, the economic shift in Rual is more directly an outcome of resettlement and changing ecological conditions. As noted earlier, the Menraq are not unaccustomed to the market economy, as they have been involved in the trading of forest products and the purchase of commodities from merchants and shops for a very long time. However, resettlement and the various accompanying development programmes implemented in the past three decades have pushed the people deeper into the market economy. Consequently, they now engage more and more in the production of goods to earn cash. This is because their need for money has grown immensely as they now have to buy most of the things they need, including food, from traders and shops. In the process, they have been entrapped in the commodity 'exchange' or circuit. They have to work to produce commodities to sell in order to buy other commodities, which they are increasingly dependent on. This focus on commodity production has engendered many changes in Menraq economy and society. In economic terms, it has, among other things, led to a decline in subsistence-oriented foraging as people devote more time and effort to growing cash crops and participating in other market-oriented activities.

Foraging is no longer a viable or rewarding economic option for the Rual people for another reason. The ecological and social changes in the region have had a negative impact on foraging. The forests where people used to forage have been either cleared or drastically depleted of resources, or they are under the control of new Malay settlers in the vicinity. Timber companies have clear-cut large tracts of forests surrounding Rual since the late 1970s and the area is now almost completely devoid of primary forest. Deforestation has led to a nearly total disappearance of an important subsistence option in the form of gathering and hunting for the Rual Menraq and in the process has reinforced their dependence on the market for most of their food needs. In order to provide a clearer view of the extent of this change, in this chapter I describe first the foraging economy which was the basis of Menraq livelihood until about 30 years ago.[1] In the following chapter I then proceed to a discussion of the new – and irreversible – economic configuration in the Rual community resulting from government-directed resettlement and development programmes.

Opportunistic foragers

In the *Cambridge Encyclopaedia of Hunters and Gatherers*, Lee and Daly (1999: 3) define foraging as 'subsistence based on hunting of wild animals, gathering of wild plant foods, and fishing, with no domesticated animals except the dog'. Like the Ju/'hoansi (!Kung) of the Kalahari Desert and the Mbuti of Congo's Ituri Forest, Menraq are often presented as a classic example of a hunting and gathering people (also referred to as foragers). In early anthropological writings, Menraq are often depicted as people living in pristine, Stone Age like, conditions. For example, in one widely used textbook, originally published in 1934, Forde (1971: 12) notes, 'the Semang, save where occasionally they have interbred with Malays and adopted their habits, raise no crops and have no domestic animals, but are dependent on the wild products of the forest'. By pointing out that the Menraq used stones rather than iron implements to fashion wooden and bamboo tools and weapons such as digging sticks and bows and arrows, Forde implied that their technology had not evolved much from the Stone Age era. Hence the impression one gains from most of these early writings and some of the anthropology textbooks is that the Menraq engage in a simple foraging economy to eke out a living from the tropical forest.

In reality, the economy of the Menraq is by no means as simple as these summaries suggest. In fact Menraq follow a rather complex mixed economy, combining a range of activities carried out for subsistence as well as for cash income. They hunt, gather, and fish for subsistence and collect a variety of forest products for trade. They also farm but not as intensively or extensively as their horticulturalist neighbours. Currently, they also engage in cash cropping as a result of development programmes. The true complexity and intricate pattern of living among the Menraq is neatly summarized in Benjamin's observation, first made in his introduction to the 1973 re-publication of Schebesta's *Among the Forest Dwarfs* and repeated more recently:

> The various populations who follow the Semang pattern are not simply hunter-gatherers, for they forage off *anything* that comes their way, including the Malay state. They have worked the fields for Malay farmers, served as porters for forest travellers, sold or bartered forest products with outsiders, and even desultorily cultivated their own swiddens. Of course, they will also forage by hunting and gathering if the opportunity arises – as it frequently does – but their foraging is not necessarily

definable in terms of hunting and gathering. On the other hand, what the Semang do *not* do is just as interesting. Even now, they avoid both trapping and long-term integral swidden farming, for these activities would require them to reside for long periods in the same place.

(Benjamin 2002: 34, emphasis in original)

This observation has prompted Benjamin (1973: viii) to refer to the Menraq as opportunistic foragers. Such a diversified economic behaviour is, however, not a recent adaptation to changing economic conditions or modernity. Kirk Endicott notes that there are late nineteenth- and early twentieth-century reports of instances of Menraq engaging in agriculture, trade, and wage labour (Morgan 1886, Skeat 1906, Evans 1937, Schebesta 1924 in Endicott 1974: 32–3). As Endicott (1974: 33) concludes, 'the evidence suggests that at least some agriculture has been practiced by some Negritos for at least a century, and there is no reason why this could not have gone on for many years before'. Menraq involvement in trading supports revisionist studies of foraging societies that challenge the view that hunting and gathering peoples have little or no links with the outside world.[2]

According to anthropologists, the foraging economy has a strong bearing on the group's lifestyle, social organization, and cultural perspectives and expressions. Such activities require mobility since the resources people extract or tap are scattered over vast areas of the forests and are dictated by seasonal changes. Nomadism is hence a social and cultural adaptation to hunting and gathering. People do not just wander aimlessly in search of food or products: they move and set up camp in particular areas within their territorial zone on the basis of their in-depth knowledge of the ecological conditions such as fruiting seasons and availability of edible food and valuable resources. Such economic practices also impose direct or indirect restrictions or limitations on certain social behaviours such as settlement or population size, long-term future orientation, and accumulation of property.

On the basis of economic orientation, Woodburn (1980) has classified foragers into two types: immediate-return and delayed-return. The Menraq fit into the immediate-return category which includes the Ju/'hoansi, Mbuti, and Hadza of Africa, and the Paliyan of India. According to Woodburn (1980: 99), immediate-return foragers share the following characteristics:

All these societies are nomadic and positively value movement. They do not accumulate property but consume it, give it away, gamble it away, or throw it away. Most of them have knowledge of techniques for storing food but use them only occasionally to prevent food from going rotten rather than to save it for some future occasion. They tend to use portable, utilitarian, easily acquired, replaceable artefacts – made with real skill but without hours of labour – and avoid those that are fixed in one place, heavy, elaborately decorated, require prolonged manufacture, regular maintenance, joint work by several people or any combination of these. The system is one in which people travel light, unencumbered, as they see it, by possessions and by commitments.

It should, however, be noted that Menraq nomadism is not just an adaptation to their foraging and forest trading. As Endicott (1974, 1997) and Lye (1997) have indicated, it is also conditioned by several social and cultural factors. Frequent mobility was, and continues to be but on a lesser scale, a survival strategy from slave-raiders in the past and intruders. It is a way of avoiding conflict, as several researchers studying the Orang Asli have found. People would typically choose flight over fight in any confrontation or altercation. Lye (1997: 255) indicates that nomadism is also a means by which Menraq 'retain tenure of forest' by demonstrating utilization, and by implication, ownership of forest tracts or *sakaq* (territory). Since Menraq have become known, for better or for worse, as nomadic peoples, their nomadism, as Lye (1997: 255) observes, has become an 'ethnic marker' of Menraq in the same way as the blowpipe has come to be regarded as a marker of Orang Asli identity.

Another aspect of an immediate-return system type is the adherence to a short-term orientation. As one of Kirk Endicott's informants indicated:

> the Batek want to look for food and eat it the same day and the next day look for food again and eat it; they want to be able to move around. Malays want to get food and put it away, get more and put it away; they want to be rich and give feasts.
>
> (Endicott 1974: 162)

It must be pointed out that two important aspects of an immediate-return system, namely the lack of future orientation and lack of desire (or ability) to accumulate, are inimical to a 'modern' economy based on the production of commodities. I will discuss this in the following chapter but now I turn to a description of the various activities in the Menraq foraging economy.

Gathering

Gathering wild foods and materials from the forests was a primary economic activity among the Menraq. These days they no longer depend on forest resources as much as previously. Many of the wild foods have been replaced with rice and vegetables bought with cash. In the past, Menraq foragers had to move regularly to avail themselves of wild foods and materials scattered widely in the forests. A Menraq band set up camp in a particular area within their *sakaq* (territorial zone) for a few days to several weeks to harvest food available in the surrounding locale. These camps were usually located close to streams, which form a natural break in the forest, allowing sunlight to reach the forest floor and stimulate the growth of diverse and lush vegetation.[3] Menraq gathered a variety of wild tubers, greens, and mushrooms for

9 Menraq woman returning from gathering firewood (1979) Photo: A. Gomes

10 Two Menraq women gathering vegetables (1979) Photo: A. Gomes

food, and rattan and bamboo as material for tools, shelter construction, and household implements. They also harvested fruit and honey. Small groups of mostly women ventured into the vicinity of the camp in search of edible wild tubers and vegetables. When they came across a plant, usually a creeper, they recognized as a plant with edible tubers, they cleared the ground around its stem and dug with a machete and a digging stick, usually a piece of sapling cut for the purpose. The tubers were dislodged, brushed cleaned of dirt, and put into rattan baskets or cloth bags fashioned out of old *sarongs*. They were then carried back to the camp where they were cooked, either roasted or boiled, and eaten with vegetables, meat, and fish.

In my first visit to Rual in 1975, I observed Menraq gathering several types of wild tubers, with the main ones being *takop* (*Dioscorea orbiculata*) and what people call *ubi garam* (possibly another *Dioscorea*).[4] A rather small plant with a thin stem, *takop* belies what it stores in the ground. One plant can produce about 20 to 50 potato-sized tubers spread deep into the ground. In the forests around Rual, I have come across large holes which are evidence of *takop* gathering. Endicott (1974: 40) notes that a woman can gather 200 tubers in a day. However, when I visited Rual in 1975, Menraq no longer ate as much *takop* as in the past, preferring tapioca and rice to this wild tuber. For Menraq, *takop* ceased to be an important foodstuff and, instead, became an icon of past lifestyle. I have often heard people say 'during the times when we ate *takop* things were easier' or 'we no longer wear *cawat* (loin-cloth) like the days when we used to look for *takop*'. This change of food preference could be a reflection of changing tastes among the Menraq. Having a desire for more highly flavoured carbohydrate foods, Menraq have commented that *takop* is 'rather tasteless and needs a lot of salt to make it tasty'. Similarly, Endicott's respondents (1974: 40) remarked that the tuber is 'not as delicious' as rice. There could, however, be an ecological reason for this dietary change: environmental transformations in the area, particularly deforestation, would have made it exceedingly difficult to find *takop*.

I have been told by Menraq that most of their vegetables and fruit were obtained through gathering in the past. During my field visits, I have observed people gathering several types of wild cabbages (referred to as *umbut*), ferns (*pucuk paku*), tapioca leaves, fungi, and mushrooms for their own consumption. They also harvested honey from bee's nests by driving the bees away with a smoking torch and then quickly grabbing the honeycomb and dropping it into a bamboo container. Menraq also cut pandanus leaves to make mats and other things, rattan for baskets, bamboo for house-building and cooking implements, and palm fronds (*bertam*, *Eugeissona tristis*) for thatching roofs. But such work is in rapid decline.

Hunting

Menraq wild game hunters use five types of weapons – blowpipes, shotguns, spears, catapults, and bush knives. In several pre-1900s reports, there is mention of the use of bow and arrow in Menraq hunting. By the early 1900s, however, the bow ceased to exist as one of Menraq weapons, as Schebesta ([1928] 1973: 77) observed:

> today the bow is an almost obsolete weapon among the Semang. The Jahai were the only tribe among whom I came across it, and yet two generations ago it was in general use, as the present generation still remember. The bow has been the only weapon of the Semang.

A Menraq elder told me in 1976 that he remembers people in Kelantan using bow and arrows when he was young in the 1920s. The question why the Menraq no longer use the bow and instead rely on the blowpipe has attracted the attention of several writers. Williams-Hunt (1952: 60) attributes the abandonment of the bow and the increased use of blowpipes to changes in the social and ecological situations among the Menraq:

> formerly the Negritos were living in much more open areas where the bow would be superior to the blowpipe. Malay and Chinese expansion has forced them into the hills and the foothill jungles are much more suited for the blowpipe than the bow and this I feel is the probable explanation of its disappearance.

As a hunting weapon, the blowpipe is only effective for small tree-dwelling game such as squirrels, monkeys, bats, and birds, and for this reason alone its use is restricted to the forest. In open areas air movement can easily deflect the more or less weightless darts. Furthermore, it is less time-consuming to make darts rather than iron-tipped arrows and consequently losing darts in the thick undergrowth is not costly. The proven effectiveness in forested conditions may explain the continued use of the blowpipe but it does not illuminate why people have abandoned the bow. Endicott (cited in Rambo 1978: 211) offers another plausible explanation:

> It is likely that big game hunting required not only a more powerful weapon than the blowpipe but also a large number of persons working together. Possibly, as the Negritos were pushed back into the jungle by immigrant agriculturalists, and scattered by the predations of slave hunters, it became impossible to organize the large hunting parties needed to kill large animals safely. The greater efficiency of the blowpipe for killing small game in the treetops would have favored it among hunters forced to seek only such prey.

Nonetheless, big game hunting is still pursued among the Rual Menraq. During our six-week stay in 1976, people told Rambo and me that they had killed four wild pigs and two barking deer although, as Rambo (1978: 212) observes, they used shotguns to do this. Menraq access to guns is by no means recent; there are several late 1800s and early 1900s records (see, for example, Rambo 1978) of Menraq use of guns. Rambo (1978) contends that Menraq ceased using the bow and arrow simply because they had access to a more effective weapon in the shotgun. The fact that Menraq had obtained their guns from the Europeans and Malays suggests that the change in hunting technology can be seen as a consequence of their external relations. Endicott (cited in Rambo 1978: 211) has even gone further to attribute the change of weaponry to slave raiding on the Menraq by immigrant Malays, which had caused people to flee from their open lowland homesteads into the forests in search of refuge.

While the blowpipe remains today the main hunting weapon of the Menraq and their Orang Asli counterparts, it is not, however, just a hunting weapon. It has become an important ethnic marker or symbol of Orang Asli identity. For example, it is displayed as an icon on the coat of arms of the JHEOA and the Orang Asli Association. Blowpipes are also made for sale to tourists and collectors as souvenirs and display objects. It will be recalled that two of the victims in the Jeli incident were reported to have died from the effect of blowpipe-propelled poisoned darts.

Blowpipes are made of specially chosen, but not easily found, bamboo (usually *Kinabaluchloa wrayi*) that has widely spaced (about 1.7 metres) internodes. The blowpipe consists of an inner and an outer tube; the inner is referred to as the *anak* (child) and the outer, the protective tube, is called the *sarong* (as in the cloth-wrap garment in Malay dress). At one end is the mouthpiece fashioned out of soft wood and glued on with resin. A typical blowpipe is about 1.8 metres long. The dart is about 20 cm in length and made out of palm-leaf rib, usually from the *bertam* palm (*Eugeissona tristis*); its tip is coated with the highly toxic processed sap of the ipoh tree (*Antiaris toxicaria*). During a hunt, the darts are stored in quivers made out of a length of large bamboo.

Blowpipe hunting is a male activity and is usually solitary, although hunters do occasionally set out in groups of two or three. In a hunting expedition, the hunter walks along the forest paths seeking out potential game in the trees. Upon spotting an animal, he sneaks up slowly and positions himself as close as possible to take the shot. The blowpipe is usually effective within a range of 30 to 40 metres, but it takes several minutes for the poison to take effect. Hunters occasionally have to track the quarry before it falls to the ground. The productivity from blowpipe hunting is variable. As Endicott (1974: 116) observed of Batek hunting:

> two or three monkeys brought in per week is considered good results. In a camp of 30 persons, the average number of men hunting each day is two (i.e., six adult males each hunting every third day), giving 14 man-days of hunting per week or 5–7 man-days per kill. Such results are not efficient in terms of calories expended for those gained, but the protein is important enough to warrant the necessary subsidizing of hunting by

collected vegetable food. Under certain special conditions, better results can be obtained, but such conditions are rare and short-lived.

The shotgun, as mentioned above, is certainly a more efficient weapon for obtaining larger game. But it is not readily available for hunters to use. At the time of my fieldwork in the 1970s, there were only two shotguns in the settlement. Although these were supplied to the settlement by the JHEOA for security purposes, the department did not prohibit the people from using these weapons in hunting. In fact, there were occasions when JHEOA officers requested Menraq to hunt deer with the government-issued shotguns, supplying the cartridges in exchange for a share of any quarry obtained. Only a few people were allowed to use shotguns and they were given a limited supply of shotgun cartridges. Cartridges were sold freely in Jeli town but Rual hunters could rarely afford to buy them. Since the supply of guns and cartridges was limited, the use of the shotgun was not extensive. Nevertheless, as mentioned earlier, hunters were able to kill four wild pigs and two barking deer during my one-month stay in 1976. This may imply that the Menraq are accomplished shotgun hunters. However, the following extract from my field journal written in 1976 would suggest otherwise:

> After it had rained, several Menraq men came out of their huts and appeared to be discussing something. Macang was carrying a shotgun on his shoulders. I joined them to find out what was going on. They said that they were getting set to go out hunting. I asked to join the party of five men. We walked along the path leading to Jeli. It was late afternoon and the path was wet and slippery. We chatted and shared jokes along the way. About twenty minutes later, one of the men who was walking ahead signalled to stop talking and when we approached him, he whispered that he had heard sounds coming from the bushes. Macang, who was holding the gun, then proceeded into the bushes and we followed him quietly. Just about ten metres or so ahead of us was a band of pigs. Macang took aim and fired but missed. The pigs darted off in all directions. The members of the hunting party then examined the area to see where the pellets landed. They spent some time at the scene deliberating on how the shot did not hit the pigs rather than how Macang missed his mark.

Menraq hunters also use spears or spikes to kill large animals such as wild pigs, deer, and bears. Many of the animals killed are obtained incidentally when people are out walking in the forest or engaging in some other activity. I have observed people digging out animals such as bamboo rats and porcupines from burrows they have chanced upon in the forest. They would at times set a fire and fan the smoke into the burrow to drive the animal out. People have also reported clubbing animals such as monitor lizards encountered by chance. In 1999, a Menraq man speared a female honey bear which he claimed was about to attack him. People later admitted that he killed the bear upon spotting it in the forest with its young cub, which he brought back to the settlement to be raised as a pet. The mother bear's meat was distributed among several families in the band.

Large kills, as we have just seen, are shared, but it was difficult to obtain accurate records of small game taken in hunting because, as Rambo (1985: 72) notes:

> Successful hunters are secretive about their catch to avoid having to share it with others so that it was impossible to obtain any record of the number of animals killed during the fieldwork.

Menraq do not engage in trapping as frequently as other Orang Asli people. Among Semai swiddeners, as I found, a large amount of meat is obtained through the use of several kinds of ingeniously made traps and snares. In one trapping operation for rats, involving four Semai men, I recorded that each trapper obtained between 6 to 7 kilograms of rats in three days of setting about 60 snares per person (Gomes 2004: 105). The reason why the Menraq do not imitate their more sedentary Orang Asli counterparts is unclear. Endicott (1974: 117) offers a possible explanation:

> the making, setting, and tending of traps seems to require more pre-paratory work than the Batek consider worthwhile and more diligence and regular habits than they have. It may well be that being tied to a series of traps, even for relatively short periods, would inhibit their ability to take advantage of unexpected opportunities which is the hall-mark of most of their subsistence techniques.

Fishing

Fishing is another important source of food protein for the Menraq. They use a range of techniques to catch fish from rivers and streams close to the Rual Resettlement. The water courses in the vicinity of Rual are no more than small streams, from which there is little hope of a good catch of fish. Fishing with hook and line is common at Rual. Menraq use worms, grubs, flesh of certain fruits, and insects as bait on a hook attached on a line tied to a *bertam* (*Eugeissona tristis*) palm-leaf rib. In such fishing, I observed that more time is spent on traversing the banks of the river or streams in search of suitable spots than in actual line casting. During the 1970s, spear-gun fishing was popular among men and young boys, a fishing technique apparently adopted from the Malays living nearby. Wearing store-purchased goggles, Menraq would dive in the river pools in search of fish hiding beneath rocks or debris. They would then shoot at the fish with home-made spear guns made of wood, with rubber bands serving as the propellant. The spears

11 Menraq man with fishing cast net (1979) Photo: A. Gomes

are bicycle spokes made into barbed metal spikes. My records show that on average spear fishing produces in an hour about 300 grams of small fish (approximately 3 or 4 cm each). On rare occasions spear fishermen took fish larger than 6 cm in size. Another fishing technique which Menraq have learned from the Malays is the use of cast nets, purchased from shops. In the 1970s, a few men owned such nets and would go out fishing regularly, especially after a rain. The catch from cast-net fishing is usually small because of the lack of good fishing spots along the rivers in the Rual area; the streams and rivers tend to be shallow at most times of the year except during the rainy seasons. Menraq also use fish traps and weirs but these are not as elaborately made as the ones other Orang Asli, particularly the Semai and Temiar, use. The most common fish trap is called *bubu* in Malay, and resembles a funnel-shaped basket made of rattan strips.

Occasionally, Menraq set out fishing in fairly large groups. People in such groups used hook and line, as mentioned above. Apparently these fishing excursions are undertaken more for leisure and sociality than to obtain food. Despite its social aspect, such fishing is still individualistic in the actual productive aspects as people will cast their own line and mostly keep the catch for their own (and family) consumption. In other words, there is minimal, if any, cooperation in the actual fishing activity in such group excursions. At times though, people do engage in cooperative group fishing, which usually involves the use of stupefacients. The following is a description of one such fishing expedition that I attended in 1979:

The fishing group was fairly large: 13 women, 7 men and 8 children. Seven of the women were carrying their infants on their back. They walked about 1500 metres upstream along the Rual River. They then barricaded a section of the river using rocks and debris. One of the men then poured a bottle of pesticide into the water upstream from the barricade and in no time, stunned fish of different species and sizes began to swim erratically on the surface and everybody present waded into the water scooping out the stupefied fish by hand. In just a total of two hours or so, including the walking to and fro from the settlement, of fishing, people obtained about 90 kilograms of fish. The fishing party distributed the catch equally among the families involved, irrespective of who actually picked up the fish. The fish caught included *tengas, keli, rong, baung, tilan, sembarau,* and *duan* [various species of carp and catfish].

Menraq in the past used derris root but, in the case described above, they used chemical pesticide, which has become common. Repetitive pesticide fishing can of course lead to irreparable destruction of rivers. It takes months or even years for the river fauna populations to recover from such chemical damage.

Menraq also hunt frogs, turtles, and tortoises along the rivers and streams. While these animals were formerly hunted for own consumption, these days they are taken to be sold to outsiders. Turtle hunting became for a time a significant commodity production activity. But turtles are now difficult to find near the settlement. The following from my field journal describes a turtle hunt in 1999:

Four Menraq men approached Kamal and me and asked us whether we could drive them to a riverbank close to Batu Melintang about 14 kilometres away to search for turtles. They told us that they were intending to catch and sell turtles to a Chinese middleman. We drove approximately 20 kilometres and then walked through a Malay homestead to reach the river. After several hours of hunting, the men caught one turtle with a shell about 40 centimetres in diameter. Instead of selling the turtle the men cut it up and distributed the meat among themselves for their own household consumption.

Some animals are trapped neither for consumption nor for sale but for domestic uses. As Rambo (1985: 72) observes:

Small wild animals such as monkeys and bamboo rats are occasionally captured as infants and are raised in captivity as pets. One bamboo rat was being raised in this fashion during the period of field work. Monkeys may be sold to the Malays for use in gathering coconuts.

Like most of the subsistence-oriented activities carried out by Rual people, hunting and fishing have declined in economic prominence primarily due to the drop in their productivity. The diminution of the forest has led to severe depletion of wild fauna, and therefore potential game. Extensive logging around Rual has also adversely affected the water quality of the rivers and streams and, in turn, the faunal populations. The wanton use of chemical pesticides has been noted. The faunal population has also been severely depleted as a result of intensification of hunting and fishing by a denser population, in both Menraq and Malay settlements, utilizing the remaining forests and the rivers in the area.

Forest collecting and trading

Hunting, fishing, and gathering once supplied the bulk of the Menraq's subsistence and material needs. However, as mentioned in Chapter 2, they also engaged in trading to obtain goods that they desired but did not produce themselves. Among these items were rice, tobacco, iron knives, salt, and certain condiments. To secure these goods from the outsiders, they collected tradeable forest products such as rattans, bamboos, *damar* (resins), and parts of wild animals. The collection of forest products for trade has a lengthy history among the natives of the Malay Peninsula and other parts of the Southeast Asian region. Dunn (1975) maintains that this trade has been going on for about two thousand years, involving the predecessors of the Menraq and their neighbouring Orang Asli forest communities. As Dunn (1975: 108) writes:

> The forest aboriginals were, until the 19th century, the only people available to exploit most of Malaya's forest land. As forest-adapted people
> . . . they were also the only people armed with the necessary experience
> and knowledge to seek out and wisely exploit the resources of their
> forest subsistence zones.

This trading intensified as people's dependence on externally produced goods increased.

At the time of my first visit to Rual in 1975, forest collecting was an important source of cash income to the Menraq. They actively collected and traded various species of rattan, and such edible fruit or vegetables as *kerdas* (*Pithecellobium bubalinum*), *petai* (*Parkia speciosa*), and *keranji* (*Dialium indicum*). They also occasionally sold honey, medicinal herbs and roots, and aphrodisiacs and love potions to Malay villagers. During my fieldwork in 1976, one old Menraq man regularly offered various dried plant materials such as roots and leaves to me in exchange for money and food. Among these were *tongkat ali* and *buah pamoh*, noted among Malays and Orang Asli alike as aphrodisiacs.

Orang Asli are renowned for rattan collecting. Rattan is used mainly in the cane furniture industry and as binding in a range of craft manufactures. The main rattans which Rual Menraq collect for sale are *rotan manao*

(*Calamus manau*), *rotan putih* (*Calamus javensis*), and *rotan udang* (*Karthalsia echinometra*). Collecting rattan, especially the larger ones, is arduous work. First the collector has to trek in usually difficult terrain in search of the vines. Then the vines must be dislodged from the host plant by cutting off the crown and this may involve climbing a tree next to the host plant to reach the crown. Sometimes the climb is 15 or 20 metres high, making it hazardous. Once the vine is cut from its crown, the collector needs a lot of strength to pull the vine off the host. The thorny skin of the vine has to be removed before the vine is cut into stalks of about 2 metres. The final tasks in the collection are the bundling of the stalks and transporting the heavy bundles on the shoulder, usually through rough terrain to the trading site. In 1976, Menraq told me that it was still easy to find such rattan in the vicinity of the Rual settlement. This is no longer the case. Logging and forest clearing for land development schemes have cut the supply of rattan drastically. Thus, people do not bother to spend much time and energy on collecting rattan, even if the price of this product is relatively high these days. Occasionally, a few Menraq nowadays travel by bus to forest areas about 20 to 30 kilometres away to collect rattan. Nagata (1997b) observed this same tactic among a group of Menraq in Kedah. Writing about the Kg. Lubuk Legong people, Nagata (1997b: 18) notes that 'it now being usual for them to ride buses and taxis to reach their principal hunting and collecting areas (their blowpipes occasionally can be seen sticking out of taxis' windows)'.

I came across Menraq collecting rattan to trade just a few times during the 1970s. In March 1976, several Menraq men collected 3,300 stalks of *rotan manao* and received a total of RM1,650.[5] However, during the following month they worked fewer days and produced only 660 stalks fetching them RM330. For a period of three weeks in 1979, 28 Rual men engaged intensively in collecting 2,129 stalks of *rotan manao* that they sold for RM2,554. The following from my fieldwork journal is my record of the trading event that took place at Abdullah Hassan's (JHEOA field officer) shop in April 1979:

> Between 6.30 and 8.00 in the morning, about 100 or so Menraq set out from Rual on their approximately two-hour walk to Jeli. Most of the rattan was transported earlier on the timber-laden trucks to the unloading depot near Jeli. My informants told me that Pah Lah [Abdullah] collected 10 cents per stalk as a fee for transportation purportedly charged by the logging company. The people suspected that Pah Lah instead of giving the money to the logging company had pocketed it for himself. At the shop we waited for the Chinese trader. It seemed like a rather convenient place for Pak Lah as I observed Menraq buying lots of drinks and cakes from his shop. The Chinese trader arrived at about 11am. Pah Lah and another Malay man escorted the trader to the two sites where the rattans were unloaded. The trader then counted the stalks. Each collector identified his pile of rattan and the trader recorded the

number of stalks in his book. The JHEOA evidently had set the price at RM1.81 per stalk of diameter 3.75 cm and above. With assistance from Pak Lah and the Malay man the Chinese trader negotiated a lower price. He asserted that the stalks varied in size and offered RM1.20 per stalk as a reasonable price. The Menraq expressed privately to me their disappointment at the price reduction but said that they were not prepared to argue for a better price, especially since Pak Lah had affirmed the trader's offer. The trader then calculated the amount each collector was to be paid. The Menraq approached the table where the trader was seated in turn to receive their share of the rattan income. The money was placed on the table and Pak Lah's son and another Malay shopkeeper took whatever money owing to them before handing it to the Menraq. In most cases, the money collectors received minus the debts amounted to just a few *ringgit*.

As is evident from this typical case of rattan trading, Menraq were regularly underpaid for their effort. Furthermore, the cash they earned dissipated quickly as people were on a spending frenzy at the shops after the rattan sale. The expenditure on drinks and food at the trading venue tended to make such events costly for them. In some cases, they even fell further into debt with the shopkeepers.

Another forest-related cash earning activity among the Rual people in pre-resettlement times and during the early years of resettlement was the collection of bean-pods from a number of different leguminous trees, mainly *petai* (*Parkia speciosa*), *kerdas* (*Pithecellobium bubalinum*), and *jering* (*Pithecellobium jiringa*). The beans were eaten either raw or cooked. They were often important ingredients in Malay cuisine such as in *sambal* and curries. The seasonal fruiting of these trees worked well in spreading the collecting effort and income throughout the year. *Petai* was harvested in the months of August to November. To pluck the pods, the collector climbed the 20–30 metre tall *petai* trees to reach the ripening pods. This made *petai* collecting a hazardous activity. The collector normally used a pole to dislodge the pods from the tree. Males did the actual plucking and women and children or older males unable to climb the trees assisted in gathering the pods on the ground. The seeds were then removed from the pods and sold to traders or to neighbouring Malay villagers. The going price for *petai* seeds in 1976 was RM1 per *cupak*, which is the volume of a 'bowl' fashioned out of a coconut shell. Sometimes, the pods were tied in bundles and traded in that form. Alias (1977: 96) reported that the Rual people earned about RM4,000 from the sale of *petai* beans during the 1975 fruiting season.

During my fieldwork in 1976, many men and women collected *kerdas* for sale. The *kerdas* season is from February to May. Unlike *petai*, *kerdas* pods were allowed to fall and were collected off the ground. The seeds were removed from the pods and transported in cloth bags or rattan baskets to waiting traders. The *kerdas* were sold at 50 cents per *cupak* in 1976. Each collector earned about RM5 to RM8 per day from the sale of *kerdas*. *Keranji* was collected in a similar way as *kerdas*. However, since the fruiting season from October to February coincided with the rainy period, hampering effective collecting, Menraq did not earn as much from *keranji* as from *petai* and *kerdas*. Rual Menraq also occasionally sold *durian*. Unlike other Orang Asli groups such as the Semai, for whom the sale of *durian* was a major source of village income, Menraq had only small holdings of *durian* trees. Consequently, they did not produce enough quantities of fruit to make trading worthwhile for *durian* buyers. Furthermore, Menraq were reluctant to carry the heavy loads of *durian* to the trading centres, located about 8 kilometres away. In my research among the Semai in the early 1980s, households earned an average of RM2,300 per year from the sale of *durian*, making this a fairly lucrative enterprise (see Gomes 2004: 93).[6]

Some Menraq claimed that they used to make thatch roofing (*attap*) out of *bertam* palm leaves for sale to Malay villagers. This activity seemed to have ceased by the time I made my first field visit. Apparently, the demand for such roofing had dropped as a result of the increased availability of corrugated iron roofing. Endicott found that the Batek he studied in the early 1970s still partook in this activity. As he observes:

> Attap roofing is also made in special jungle camps which are, in effect, small factories located near the source of the raw materials used . . . The roofing consists of a series (twenty-five to thirty pieces) of palm leaves, which look something like the fronds of sword ferns, with all the leaflets folded to the same side and tied in parallel rows of three rattans which run perpendicular to the leaves. The panel formed is about five feet wide (the length of the fronds) and seven feet long . . . All the members of a camp participate in making attap roofing. Usually the men and older boys bring in the palm fronds, though women may help with this when there are still some thatch palms near the camp. The time-consuming process of folding . . . is done mainly by women, including the very old ones, with some help from children and old men.
>
> (Endicott 1974: 153–4)

He reports that the roofing was sold for RM2 to 3 per roll, and an average Malay house would need about six to ten rolls. While it may not seem like a lucrative enterprise in terms of cash earned, Endicott (1974: 154) notes that the demand for such roofing is steady as they need to be replaced once every two or three years.

As the *attap* case illustrates, the demand for a particular type of forest product tended to vary according to changes in tastes, preferences, and fashion. Another example is rattan. Menraq would set out to cut rattan if there was a firm request from a trader. The demand for rattan had been erratic, fluctuating according to the popularity of rattan furniture. Rual Menraq also collected *gaharu*, aromatic wood used mostly in the Middle

East for making perfumes and incense. The collector would need to chip away tediously to dislodge the resinous wood of tree trunks. This is hard work but the rewards can be good. *Gaharu* collecting was popular among young Menraq males in the late 1980s and 1990s.

In the late 1990s, Rual people were still collecting rattan sporadically at RM3.50 per length of *rotan manao* and on a more regular but on a smaller scale *petai* (sold at about RM15 to RM25 per bundle of 100 pods), *kerdas* (fetching RM2 to RM3 per kilogram), and herbal remedies and aphrodisiacs. To these, two new items were added: soft back turtles selling at RM8 to RM16 per kilogram, and frogs, fetching about RM16 per kilogram. I was not able to record sales of such lucrative items but some turtle and frog collectors claim that they can earn about RM100 or so per outing.

Wage labour

Wage labour is not a new activity among the Menraq. As noted in Chapter 2, observers in the 1920s and 1930s (see, for example, Schebesta [1928] 1973: 32–3, Evans 1937: 33–9) have reported Menraq working as farm labourers for their Malay neighbours in exchange for part of the harvests or for goods such as machetes, clothes, and salt. Some Rual Menraq, mostly men, still occasionally work for money in nearby Malay villages on casual terms. Nowadays they are mostly employed as agricultural labourers in Malay-owned rubber and oil palm plantations, taking up tasks such as weeding, applying fertilizers and pesticides, and harvesting. The wage varies but is usually about RM10 per day. As I discuss later, Rual Menraq also earned cash by working in the government-sponsored development projects. A few Rual villagers, all males, held salaried positions in government departments, primarily the JHEOA, and in the military and police forces, mainly with the *Senoi Praag*, an Orang Asli auxiliary police force originally formed in the 1950s during the Emergency.

While Rual Menraq are willing to work for money when such opportunities are available, they tend to approach paid work with caution. I have heard complaints from many Rual villagers of being cheated by employers, some of them officers with the JHEOA and other government agencies. In one case in the late 1990s, two Malay men, identified to me as JHEOA staff, hired several Menraq to work in a 2.4-hectare watermelon and pumpkin plantation, believed to be a joint concern between the Malay men and a Chinese entrepreneur. With a promise of a wage and a share of the harvest, about 20 Menraq carried out every aspect of the cultivation, from clearing the area, planting and maintaining the fields to harvesting the crops. After the harvest, the Malay men refused to pay their Menraq workers the wages owing and instead gave each of them '3 bowls of rice and salt fish'. My Menraq informants estimated that the watermelon and pumpkin they harvested would have fetched the plantation operators about RM40,000 (US$10,525 at 1997 exchange rate). This experience left the workers annoyed and disillusioned and all those I talked to about it thought it unlikely they would ever work for outsiders again.

In general, I found that Menraq, in keeping with their foraging outlook, prefer to work on a casual and flexible basis. They tend to choose jobs they can do when they feel like it and work that does not compromise their personal autonomy. Such jobs, as Endicott (1974: 159) noted for the Batek, 'are thought to provide a good return on one's effort without unduly restricting his overall freedom, since the jobs can be dropped or turned over to another Batek at will'. Furthermore, the returns in casual employment are usually immediate. As Endicott (1974: 159) observed, cash wage employment is attractive to the Batek because 'the money comes in regularly so they do not have to organize themselves and plan ahead as they do in full-time agriculture'.

Swidden farming

Although Menraq were foragers, they were not totally opposed to farming whenever there was an opportunity. Imitating their Orang Asli neighbours the Temiar, renowned for planting large swiddens, Menraq have occasionally cleared small areas of forest and cultivated hill rice and other crops. Unlike the Temiar, however, the Menraq did not give their agricultural pursuits the sort of seriousness, consistent attention, and dedication, particularly in weeding, required for making this economic activity worthwhile. Endicott (1974: 147) offers a plausible reason for the Menraq tendency to avoid swidden farming:

> The high value placed by the Batek on freedom of movement and variety of daily activities promotes the efficient exploitation of widespread and transient resources, partly by increasing knowledge of what resources are available at a given time. By varying the daily tasks, a person is able to survey a wide range of different localities, and by visiting widely among different camps, a great deal of indirect information is obtained. Such irregular habits, although much favored in hunting and gathering, are inimical to sound farming in which success is cumulative and depends on the faithful carrying out of each phase of a chain of interdependent activities.

Apart from the rice swiddens the JHEOA directed them to plant in the initial years of resettlement, I have not come across Rual Menraq planting rice on their own since that time. As I discuss in the next section, these plots yielded very little rice in any case. They were cultivated in a way similar to the planting of swiddens by the Semai I studied in the early 1980s (Gomes 2004). Using bush knives and axes, Menraq cleared a forested hill slope and waited for the felled vegetation to dry before setting it alight. Burning the plot clears the dead brush and releases nutrients into the soil. Once the soil cooled, Menraq planted a variety of crops, such as hill rice, corn, tapioca, and leafy vegetables, by dropping seeds into holes in the ground made by dibble sticks. Unlike the other Orang Asli peoples known for swiddening, Menraq did not weed or carry out other swidden maintenance tasks unless instructed by the JHEOA officers to do so. Due to this lack of attention to the swiddens, it is not surprising that the yields were poor. For the Batek, Endicott contends that agriculture as practised by the people in 1971 was 'incapable of satisfying the people's full subsistence needs'. He found that:

> The total amount of food produced would in most cases be insufficient even without bad luck, and most of the food grown becomes available at one time, leaving long stretches of time without any fresh source of cultivated food. The immediate causes of these problems are plain. The small amount of food is due to small areas planted, inadequate weeding and protection of the growing crops, and the absence of any means of preventing Batek who did not help with the growing from taking a share of the crop.
>
> (Endicott 1974: 143–4)

For Menraq, swiddening was apparently carried out not simply to produce food crops but for the wild animals such as pigs, deer, rodents, monkeys, and birds that such crops attract. These animals are preyed upon by Menraq hunters. More recently, tapioca cultivation seems to have become popular among the Menraq. During my visit in 2001, I was given some cooked tapioca harvested from swiddens planted by *puak* Teras. However, it would be reasonable to say that most of the more successful farming at Rual in the past thirty years is related to the various government-sponsored agricultural projects such as rubber and oil palm plantations and fruit tree cultivation as part of the *Bumi Hijau* ('Green Earth') development programmes. To that extent the Malaysian government had begun to convert foragers into farmers, an issue we will look at in the next chapter. For now, attention will focus on generalized reciprocity, a cultural practice and norm closely associated with a foraging lifestyle.

Generalized reciprocity

For the traditional hunter-gatherer Batek people, Endicott declares that food sharing is 'an absolute obligation to the Batek, not something that the giver has much discretion over'. He observes that:

> A person with excess food is expected to share it and if this is not done others do not hesitate to ask for some. And it would be virtually imposs-ible for someone to hoard food in the open shelters of a Batek camp without everyone knowing about it. Recipients treat the food they are given as a right; no expression of thanks is expected or forthcoming,

presumably because that would imply that the donor had the right to withhold it.

(Endicott 1988: 117)

Why do foraging people accord such importance to sharing? A standard anthropological explanation (see, for example, Sahlins 1972) is that sharing is a way of redistributing resources which are naturally spread widely and unequally among people in a group in order that everyone benefits and nobody is disadvantaged from the vagaries of the food quest. According to this view, people give food to others at times of plenty with an expectation of being reciprocated at times of need. Governed by the principle of generalized reciprocity, a donor does not expect to receive a return gift from his or her recipient. Instead the donor's generosity is likely to be reciprocated by someone else in the group of people involved in reciprocal exchanges. In generalized reciprocity, sharing occurs within a group of people and the obligations to make a return gift are shared by the members of the group.

Several anthropologists (for example, Woodburn 1980) associate sharing with egalitarianism, a salient feature of immediate-return foraging societies. The variation in productivity as a result of differences in skill, fortune, and labour capacity and efficiency, as one would expect, can impose some pressure on an egalitarian ethos. It is contended that increased productivity and the provision of greater quantities of food and other products may accord higher status or privilege to the producer. To minimize this or to remove this possibility, individuals are socially obliged through a set of rules, beliefs, and norms which function to encourage, stimulate, or subtly coerce people to share. Sharing is hence perceived to be a form of levelling mechanism, which serves to militate against accumulation and in the process, operating to thwart or retard the development of inequalities of wealth, power, and prestige.

When asked why they gave their food to their fellow camp members, Menraq offered reasons such as 'we must help each other', 'it's *adat menraq*' (our custom), 'we've always done this, it's a custom from our ancestors', and 'it's *punan* (tabooed) not to do so'. These reasons touch on the sociality created by sharing in the functionalist sense that it establishes and maintains social relations among members of the band. As Endicott (1988: 112) contends, '[t]he unity of a camp is based not on political organization . . . but on a moral obligation incumbent on each family to share food with all other families in the camp'. The concept of *punan*, which appears to derive from the Malay *kempunan*, meaning yearning or desire, seems to be central in justifying as well as motivating sharing and gift-giving in general among Menraq and in most, if not all, other Orang Asli communities. Endicott (1988: 117) describes *punan*, which he spells as *pohnen*, among the Batek as 'a belief that to refuse a reasonable request for something can cause harm to the person refused'. My understanding of this concept differs from Endicott's. Rual people's explanation of *punan* appears to be similar to the Semai concept of *pehunan* which Robarchek (1977: 105) explains as the 'state of being unfulfilled, unsatisfied, or frustrated in regard to some specific and strongly felt want'. Similarly, as in the case of the Semai, someone who has incurred *punan* among the Menraq is believed to be at risk of attack by super-natural forces and/or wild animals and/or susceptible to accidental injury, illness, and even death. Aptly, Van der Sluys (2000: 445) defines the concept (which she spells as *pehunen*) as 'accident proneness'. *Punan* refers to the experience of unfulfilled desire as well as the sanctions or punishment result-ing from it. Since people in a camp are likely to be kin-related and generally socially close to one another, a state of *punan* in one of its members is going to have implications for the whole group. As Van der Sluys (1999: 310) observes, 'Affliction falls on the victim, thus reinforcing the ethic of caring for one another'. In order to avoid *punan*, a person may drop hints of his or her desire by making statements such as 'I haven't eaten rice for a while' or 'you have lots of tapioca in your rattan basket'. Among the Menraq, people may demand a share of food or tobacco. This is a form of sharing that has been appropriately referred to as 'demand sharing' and appears to be a common practice among foragers. As Peterson (1993: 860) points out, 'observation and ethnographic evidence suggest that much giving and sharing [in forager groups] is in response to direct verbal and/or nonverbal demands'. Hence, sharing in this way occurs 'by taking rather than giving' (Peterson 1993: 861) and is not governed by unsolicited generosity.

During my field research I have observed people giving food to one another on a regular basis. People do not just share wild foods that they obtain from hunting and gathering but also habitually distribute purchased food such as rice, dried fish, sugar, salt, and biscuits as well as other consumables such as tobacco and cigarettes. In such distribution, the donor follows an order of priority according to social distance; as Endicott (1988: 116) observes, 'they must give shares first to their own children and spouse, then to any parents-in-law or parents present, and finally to all other families in camp'. Occasionally, this food giving practice appears to be economically irrational, as people would give each other the same sort of food. I have come across people giving rice they have bought in the market or a shop to their neigh-bours who would make a return in kind. There is no obvious benefit in levelling or redistribution in such food exchange. Endicott (1988: 116) says that '[t]his apparently unnecessary distribution confirms that sharing of food is a dominant value in Batek culture'. There is, however, an element of levelling in the case of the distribution of large animals obtained in hunting. Such distribution is procedural. The following is an extract from my field journal relating to the distribution of a wild pig I witnessed in 1976:

> The pig was laid on a mat of leaves at the back of the house of the headman. Several people were present, some squatting, some standing and a few sitting on the ground. One of the men then started cutting up the pig with a machete. He seemed to be butchering the carcass according

to a prescribed technique. The meat is separated into heaps made out of similar cuts or from the same part of the animal. The butcher then picks up portions of the meat from each heap and places them in a set of separate smaller heaps arranged around the large heaps of meat. He ensures that each small heap has almost equal portion of meat from all the different parts of the animal. A member of each family then collects a heap of meat to take home.

Summary

This chapter has outlined the various foraging activities of the Menraq. These forest-dependent activities which fulfilled the subsistence and material needs of the people for a very long time, and which served as a source of identity for the Menraq, are now no longer economically important, both in terms of effort that people devote to them and the amount of food and material that these activities contribute. Part of the reason for this has to do with the obliteration of the forests in the vicinity of Rual, and another factor is the increasing acceptance of cash crop cultivation and other government-mandated development projects. There are a number of cultural practices and norms, such as the generalized reciprocity, discussed in this chapter, and band social organization and egalitarianism covered in Chapter 2, associated with a foraging lifestyle that are also under threat. One could say that Menraq have had to give up foraging, rather involuntarily, to take up commodity production on their trek towards modernity. In the next chapter, we will look at the economic transformation of the Menraq from foragers to commodity producers.

6 From foragers to commodity producers

In Chapter 4, I outlined the physical transformation of the Rual settlement resulting from various development projects – construction of houses, schools, the community hall, medical clinic, sporting facilities, and prayer houses. All these built spaces seem to follow a plan to re-shape the settlement to one resembling a Malay *kampung*. Such a design clearly adheres to the government's primary objective for the Orang Asli which is to integrate them into 'mainstream society', and that, as noted earlier, means turning them into Malays. Simply altering the way the settlement looks represents only part of the overall programme of change.

As mentioned in Chapter 3, an important aspect of Malaysian government policy towards the Orang Asli is economic modernization. In the case of Rual this policy took the form of projects designed to transform the Menraq economy from subsistence foraging to primary commodity production. Among these projects were the cultivation of Hevea rubber and oil palm, animal husbandry, and fish farming, and they have all served to vitalize the process of commoditization of the Rual economy. What are the effects of commoditization on the Menraq? How has it changed the Menraq socially and culturally? These are the questions addressed in this chapter. It will show that the Rual Menraq have now become increasingly dependent on the government and the market to satisfy their daily needs, and that they are also more exposed to exploitation by outsiders and external agencies. Commoditization has also had an adverse impact on the Rual natural environment, and it has also had transformative effects on Menraq social and cultural life, particularly in the realm of intra-community sharing and interpersonal relations. In particular, it has spurred incipient social differentiation in a society noted for its egalitarianism. According to the government plans, changing the Menraq into primary producers and wage labourers has made them more like rural Malays economically. As will be shown in the following chapter, the government has one further objective in its plan to bring the Menraq into the modern Malaysian 'mainstream', and this is Islamization, the conversion of the Menraq to the religion of the Malays. The remainder of this chapter sets out the economic framework of this visionary modernization programme.

Resettlement economy: a tool of development

In 1975, the Rual Menraq, as mentioned previously, were still heavily dependent on foraging, but there was evidence of what I would refer to as the 'resettlement economy'. While the new settlers were still engaged in hunting, gathering, and fishing, their ability to gain from these activities was beginning to be restricted by several factors related to changes in economy and ecology. In the month I spent in the resettlement in 1976, as mentioned earlier, hunters killed two barking deer and four wild pigs using shotguns, and killed several smaller animals, squirrels, and monkeys using blowpipes. They also procured small fish, turtles, and frogs using homemade spear guns, by trapping with hands, and the use of poisons. Rual Menraq collected for sale forest products such as rattan, *gaharu*, *petai*, *kerdas*, *jering*, and some *durian*. From this commerce they received cash with which they bought a range of goods from shops in the nearby Malay villages and in towns. While some foods were culled directly from the gardens, fields, and forests, the shops and itinerant peddlers offered foods and supplements such as rice, dried fish, canned food, packaged noodles, sweetened biscuits, salt, spices, tea, coffee, sugar, bottled soft drinks, and cooking oil. Everyday household goods included kerosene, matches, soaps and detergents, flashlights, batteries, cooking pots and utensils, clothing, toothbrushes, and hairbrushes. Menraq also bought beauty products like lipstick and shampoos and occasionally luxury items such as television sets and video recorders, and house furnishings like cupboards, dressing tables, and lounge sets. They also spent on cigarettes and tobacco regularly, and on alcoholic drinks occasionally.

They had to buy rice from the shops even though they planted swiddens with rice and tapioca, among other cultigens, on about 25 hectares of forestland. The swiddens were intended to produce food to supplement the rations provided by the government as inducements to secure the participation of the Menraq in the various agricultural projects and as a reward for sending their children to school. But, as mentioned previously, very little rice was harvested due to neglect of the fields. Hence, the dependence on rations was immense. Rations included tinned food, rice, salt, sugar, tea, and dried fish and were airdropped regularly, once or twice a month from 1972 to 1979. One could say that in the early years the resettlement economy was a domestically unproductive, dole-driven economy. Many of the subsistence requirements of the settlers were fulfilled by external inputs rather than through local effort. This should not be interpreted to say that the people had developed a dole mentality or that they were indolent. On the contrary, the ration system was very much in keeping with their foraging mindset, where to the Menraq government handouts had become just another source of food open to them to 'forage'. Waiting for rations rather than working on some other activity makes perfect economic sense for opportunistic foragers like the Menraq, who would seize any chance that presented itself in order to eke out a living. It may seem immoral, as some of the JHEOA officers have hinted, but it is certainly economically rational even if viewed from a non-foraging perspective. From the JHEOA's point of view the rations were at most temporary to see the people through the transitional period until their cash crops reached production.

Rubber and oil palm cultivation

In 1974, the JHEOA with assistance from RISDA (Rubber Industry Small-holders' Development Authority) started a rubber plantation at the resettlement. The model for this project was the FELDA (land development) schemes, where beneficiaries were expected to repay the cost of the agricultural projects once their plantations were income generating. In other words, the rubber project was a 'loan' to the Menraq which had to be repaid. However, it was subsequently converted into a grant or, as one JHEOA officer put it, a 'gift' to the people.

In the first year of the project (1974), an area of approximately 16.2 hectares was cleared and planted with rubber seedlings. Menraq were paid at a rate of 50 cents per seedling planted. Several JHEOA officers, including Abdullah Hassan, the field officer based at Jeli, supervised the planting, which was carried out in stages till 1981. By that time a total of 64 hectares had been planted with rubber trees. The Menraq carried out all the work involved, from planting the seedlings to maintenance work like applying fertilizers and weeding. For every task they undertook they were given money or rations. Once the trees were ready for tapping, the JHEOA divided the plantation among about twenty families for tapping, with each receiving about 2 hectares. The rubber trees were first tapped in 1983 but since only the trees planted first were mature enough to produce latex, the income from rubber in the initial years was necessarily small.[1]

In the early years of production, the rubber tappers processed the latex into sun-dried sheets and sold them to shops in the nearby Malay villages. In 1986, RISDA began buying the rubber directly in an effort to shield the tappers from exploitation at the hands of the shopkeepers. RISDA officers visited Rual twice a month to buy rubber. During a 11-month period in 1986 and 1987, Rual rubber tappers sold a total of about 6,600 kilograms of sun-dried rubber sheets amounting to roughly 800 kilograms per month (excluding the rainy months of November to January when rubber trees are not tapped) (Rokeman 1988: 68). In the 1980s, with the price averaging RM1.45 per kilogram, each family earned an estimated RM60 per month from rubber tapping. In the month of April 1987, six Rual Menraq sold a total of 284 kilograms of rubber sheets, ranging from 28 kilograms to 68 kilograms (Rokeman 1988: 70), receiving an average cash income from rubber tapping of RM65 for that month. The RISDA truck also served as a mobile shop. It was stocked with a range of foodstuffs and household goods. Rokeman (1988) observed that people spent most of their rubber income on food and other goods supplied on the truck. RISDA officers claim that they

12 Menraq selling rubber sheets to RISDA officer (1987) Photo: A. Gomes

offer this service not just for people's convenience but also to protect Rual
Menraq from being cheated by shopkeepers. Currently, RISDA and FELCRA
handle all the trading of Menraq products, such as rubber and oil palm.

Rubber tapping is now the main economic activity at Rual. Rubber occupies about 202 hectares, including areas recently replanted to rejuvenate
tracts first planted in the 1970s. Following the national trend of diversifying
primary production, in the late 1990s the government introduced oil palm
cultivation at Rual. In 1997, RISDA started the project with a plan for 150
hectares of oil palm. Three sites already cleared by logging operations were
selected. Several Menraq residents, mostly men, were then hired to prepare
the land and plant seedlings supplied by RISDA. The total area under oil
palm in Rual today is about 100 hectares. As part of the privatization policy
(discussed in Chapter 3), a subsidiary company of RISDA, referred to by its
acronym RSPSP (RISDA Smallholder Plantation Limited Company) undertook the further development of the oil palm plantation and marketing.
Being a privatized business enterprise, it is more likely to be driven by such
commercial predilections as profit maximization and business viability than
by the potential benefits to the Menraq.

It is not entirely clear whether the Menraq will gain title to the oil palm
plantations in the future or, if so, how the FELCRA plantation is going to
be subdivided among the various households in Rual. At the time of my
field visit in 1999, several Menraq, mostly male, were paid to work on the

planting and maintenance of the oil palm holdings. Promised a wage of RM14 per day (8am to 1pm), they received RM10 per day. The Menraq were naturally displeased and complained that they had been underpaid. The JHEOA officer explained the lower wage as a reasonable payment for the actual amount of work that the Menraq did in a day. He indicated that his employees started work late and took far too many breaks in between and therefore did not put in the expected number of hours. Another source of grievance was the disbursement for tree planting. A Menraq worker was supposed to be paid RM1.20 for each oil palm seedling planted but according to several of my informants, they received only RM1 for every seedling they planted. They accused the FELCRA officer of short changing them and pocketing the difference in wages. Apart from the dispute regarding wages, another thorny issue was the hiring of several foreign workers to carry out work meant for the Menraq in the Rual oil palm plantation. The Rual villagers openly expressed their displeasure to the authorities at being replaced by foreign workers (believed to be Indonesians or Thai Malays) who quit working after immigration officers caught them for not having valid work permits.

The Menraq have shown little enthusiasm for the oil palm project and the grievances in relation to wage discrepancies have further dampened this to the extent that they did not carry out their work efficiently. To meet the necessary labour requirements, the project implementers hired labourers from outside and this only compounded the problem. The Menraq began to wonder who the real beneficiaries of the project were: themselves, FELCRA officers, or foreign workers? Some of the government officers have interpreted the Menraqs' poor enthusiasm and inefficiency as 'laziness', 'inability to value economic opportunities', and 'dole mentality'. But this case illustrates the importance of considering the concerns of people regarding any grievances, whether perceived or real, in order to secure full participation in the project. A half-hearted devotion to the project will not bring success to the development effort.

Animal husbandry and fish farming

While attempts to introduce cash cropping to the Rual economy have been moderately successful, the efforts to establish animal husbandry through what were referred to as a 'cattle project' (*projek lembu*) and a 'chicken project' (*projek ayam*), and through aquaculture have been almost complete failures. In the 'cattle project', the JHEOA supplied Rual with 39 cattle over two years in 1978 and 1980. The Menraq were instructed to clear about 20 hectares to be used as grazing land and to build fences and cowsheds. The project was short-lived, as within a couple of years Rual had no cattle left. Some cattle were lost in the forest, but many were discreetly sold to Malay villagers. Rual people complained about the many demands of cattle raising, such as having constantly to keep track of the grazing cows, rounding up the herd in the evening to lead them into the makeshift cowsheds, maintaining fences (to stop the cattle from getting into the home gardens), and cleaning up after the animals, which tend to dirty the village land. Perhaps the only benefit the Menraq saw in the cattle project was the surreptitious sale of the herd to outsiders. The 'chicken project' did not fair so badly. In 1986, the JHEOA supplied Rual settlement with 350 chickens, and when I visited the settlement in 1988, there were about 80 chickens left. Many of the chickens succumbed to disease and many more were given or sold to outsiders. In my visit in 2001, there were about the same number of chickens in the village as in 1988 but in 2006, I did not find as many chickens grazing the village grounds.

In 1994, the Kelantan state development agency (KESEDAR), as part of its poverty alleviation programme, implemented a fish-farming project. It funded the construction of nine freshwater ponds and the supply of fish fry. As in most development projects in Rual, the aquaculture project failed. Hardly any of the fish supplied survived, due to poor water quality, the result of neglect of pond maintenance and cleaning. This project was revived in 1999 with the supply of about 8,600 fish fry. Two of the original ponds were cleaned and refilled with water; *tilapia*, *liku*, and *jelawat* species were released in one of the ponds and the other was used for raising *keli* (catfish). While this project was intended to operate commercially on the expectation that the fish would be sold through a government marketing scheme, it was also aimed at providing much needed protein in Rual people's diet.

'Greening' the village

Since the 1970s, the JHEOA has carried out its *Bumi Hijau* ('Green Earth') programme in Rual, directed towards the production of food as well as a means of beautifying the village with fruit trees and home gardens. Ostensibly, the *Bumi Hijau* programme is yet another design to transform the resettlement into a settlement resembling a Malay *kampung*, just as in the case of the dwelling houses and village infrastructure. Fruit trees, especially coconut trees, and home gardens with vegetables and spice plants are visible features of a Malay *kampung*.

The *Bumi Hijau* project in Rual was started in 1975, and since then a large variety of fruit trees have been grown. In the first year of the project, about 10 hectares were planted with rambutan, *durian*, *petai*, bananas, jackfruit, *rambai*, *langsat*, and coconut. The Menraq were also given seeds – beans, corn, chilies, watermelon, and tobacco – to plant in their kitchen gardens. From 1975 to 1984, a total of 43 hectares of fruit trees was planted, mainly on the bank of Rual River. The JHEOA provided the seedlings and directed the planting. As in the other projects described above, the people were given food rations as inducements. The fruit plantation project, however, was not very successful. A large number of seedlings did not survive, partly due to neglect but also because of severe microclimatic and poor soil conditions, as well as destruction by both wild animals (such as pigs) and cattle. When I visited Rual in 1988, there were only 20 hectares of fruit trees left. Of all the trees planted, coconut palms appear to have had the highest survival rates. Coconuts are plucked regularly, mainly for domestic use. On hot days, Menraq pluck young coconuts and drink the sweet and refreshing water contained in the shell. The flesh from the matured coconuts is shredded and used in cooking, while the shells make useful containers and the husks are used as cooking fuel. Apart from their economic function, the coconut trees have an aesthetic role. A village dotted with swaying coconut trees is how a typical Malay *kampung* is portrayed, and Rual with its coconut trees, as noted earlier, has come to resemble a *kampung*. The 'greening programme' is also an attempt to minimize the drastic ecological repercussions resulting from resettlement and forest clearing.

Ecological changes

Endicott (1974: 29) has observed that

> the Batek feel at home in the jungle, especially the primary jungle, but feel out of place in clearings and in villages outside the jungle. This attitude is expressed in their belief that the jungle is healthy because it is cool and clearings unhealthy because they are hot.

Rual Menraq have often expressed to me their preference for the forest, particularly during hot days. They complain about having to endure the very hot conditions at the settlement. The cutting of forests from logging and agriculture has affected the microclimate of the area. In his study of the climatic conditions prevailing at Rual in 1976, Rambo (1985: 54) found that

> Daytime air temperature was always higher in the settlement than in the forest, averaging 29.4 °C in the settlement clearing compared to 27.2 °C in the forest. There was a daily range of 11.3 degrees between the lowest and highest temperatures (22 ° to 33.3 °C) in the settlement compared to 8.5 degrees (22 ° to 30.5 °C) in the forest.

Rambo's study was conducted in 1976 when there was still substantial forest cover. With the almost complete deforestation at Rual, the current situation would certainly be worse. It is a common finding in studies of Orang Asli resettlements or regroupment schemes that the land chosen for settlement is not of good quality for agricultural development. Mohd. Tap (1990: 69) refers to the land provided to Orang Asli as 'second class land', that is plots rejected by other people because they have poor soils, are located in remote areas, 'devoid of any commercially viable resources like timber and minerals', and are mostly unsuitable for agriculture, unless they are 'well rehabilitated'. The soil at Rual is mostly sandy at the settlement and lateritic (subject to leaching) in other parts. It is generally of poor quality.[2] Hence, land around Rual needs to be 'well rehabilitated' and this involves the heavy use of fertilizers. In the oil palm cultivation at Rual about 10 per cent of the initial cost was for the supply and application of fertilizers. In traditional slash and burn or swidden agriculture in forestlands, the nutrients in the vegetation are released into the soil through burning, which effectively enhances soil quality and enables productive farming (albeit with regular rotation) without the use of artificial fertilizers. The use of chemical fertilizers and pesticides in the various agricultural projects at Rual is bound to have ecological implications for the quality of the land and water in the area, but I do not have data to support this.

Another consequence of resettlement with ecological implications is the depletion of resources due to overexploitation. Higher population density in the area and the accumulative tendencies in commodity production have led the Menraq (and their Malay neighbours) to increase harvests in order to redress reduced output from subsistence-oriented production and to meet demands for imported commodities. I have mentioned earlier the ecological travesty of fishing by poison. To this we can add the overexploitation of certain new commodities, such as frogs and turtles, which has led to an almost total disappearance of these animal species in the Rual vicinity. The Rual case resembles the predicament of the Miskito of Nicaragua. In his research on the Miskito, Nietschmann (1973) observed that the market demand for turtles had pushed hunters to over-harvest the species, leading to a vicious cycle ultimately destroying the turtle population. Much of the impact on the environment is, however, exogenously imposed.

As I have already indicated several times, commercial logging has greatly affected the Rual environment. Intensive logging began in April 1976, when a logging company was given a concession to extract timber near Rual and in parts of the resettlement area. By 1979, there were six logging companies operating in the Rual area. The environmental impact of logging in tropical forest is well documented. Dentan *et al.* (1997: 98) provide a summary of the ecological changes resulting from logging:

> The absence of shade raises the temperature of the soil to desert conditions, so that it no longer holds water well and easily blows away . . . Since there are no roots to hold the thin, dusty topsoil in place, heavy rains then flush the topsoil into the rivers. Mud bars choke the rivers, making them unavailable for transportation and killing the more sensitive fish on which rural people depend for food . . . Logging roads, even more than loss of trees, cause erosion. Exposed to torrential rains, the soft laterite soil washes away as soon as the loggers move on. Logging roads also interrupt drainage, creating stagnant pools, ideal breeding places for the mosquitoes that carry malaria. Often the land is left too eroded to allow the forest to regenerate. Eventually, the succession is to grassland, typically of useless *lalang* grass.

13 Timber trucks passing through Rual Resettlement (1979) Photo: A. Gomes

During the height of logging in the late 1970s and early 1980s,[3] more than ten timber trucks daily would ply up and down through the Rual settlement to transport logs to the depot at Jeli. Each time a truck went past it left behind a cloud of dust and sand, which was blown into the dwellings. Logging has also transformed the Rual landscape and waterways. In 1975, the hills surrounding the Rual settlement were covered with lush green vegetation, making it seem very much like a settlement in the deep forest. The Rual River had clear running water. A few years later, during my 1979 visit, I noticed that the hills were almost barren and that the settlement appeared more like a homestead in an abandoned tin mining area, with obviously dirty streams and pools. But it is not just the aesthetic implication of deforestation that is of concern; it has also had an adverse impact on people's ability to meet their subsistence requirements from foraging in the immediate environment.

Dependent economy

A major consequence of the resettlement economy has been the increasing dependence of the Menraq on the government for their day-to-day survival. The provision of food rations to secure people's involvement in the projects has spurred such dependence. Menraq expectations of rations or gratuities reached such a level that they would refuse to participate in state-sponsored activities that did not come with handouts. In 1978, when their requests to the JHEOA field officer for food rations appeared to be falling on deaf ears, they threatened to uproot the rubber seedlings they had just planted. Their requests were quickly met. This dependence seems to have conditioned the people to behave differently with outsiders. People frequently asked for food and other things from Kamal, my research assistant, during our stay in Rual in 1999 and 2001 rather than from me, pointing out that I am an 'old friend' of theirs.

Writing about a similar situation among the Semai at the Betau Regroupment Scheme, Nicholas (1990: 78) contends that:

> With much of their traditional structure being eroded and their ability to be self-sufficient and self-reliant being drastically impaired, the Semai have been forced to seek government aid in almost every sphere of development. Consequently, in place of traditional self-confidence, the Semai were reduced to a state of 'imitative dependence'. This is a highly degraded state associated not only with an inability to provide themselves adequately with the material means of sustenance but also with the loss of cultural and psychological integrity.

This state of economic dependence is, however, not only limited to Orang Asli in resettlement projects. As Mohd. Tap (1990: 486), a former high-ranking JHEOA officer, candidly noted, 'Orang Asli have been transformed to a community that is totally dependent on the Department and the government for even the most trivial of things, like buying pencils for their school-going children.' Apart from being dependent on the State, with the process of growing commoditization of their economy, the Menraq have become increasingly reliant on the market for most of their needs.

Commodity production, commoditization, and market dependence

While the government's development programmes have had mixed success in terms of productivity and people's participation, they have, however, intensified Menraq links with the market economy. Both before and during the initial period of resettlement, the Menraq continued to engage in the trading of forest products, linking them to the cash-oriented market economy. However, the resettlement economy has pushed the Menraq into a greater dependence on commodity production and stimulated the increasing commoditization of their village-based economy. Commoditization is a 'process of becoming involved in producing things for exchange and by extension the obtaining of things offered for exchange by others' (Peterson 1991: 2). How have the Menraq come to terms with growing commoditization? What is the impact of commoditization on the Menraq subsistence ethic?

On one of my field visits in 1978, I witnessed an amusing encounter between a group of Menraq and an agricultural extension officer that illuminates the contradiction between commodity production and the subsistence ethic.

With a brief to show people how to plant rubber seedlings, the officer visited Rual after the delivery of rubber seedlings to the resettlement. He organized with the Rual headman to demonstrate planting techniques at the rubber plantation site. About twenty Menraq men were present. At the start of the demonstration, the officer instructed a youth to dig a hole in the ground. The officer then placed a rubber seedling in the hole and pushed the soil around the seedling with his feet to secure the plant and declared, 'This is how you plant these seedlings the government has given you'. One of the onlookers, an older Menraq man, retorted, 'You know we are stupid (*bodoh*). Can you show us again how to do this?' Holding a seedling upright, the elder continued, 'Do you put it in this way or the other way round?' Throwing his arms up in the air, the officer exclaimed to me in English, 'These people are so stupid!' The officer packed up his things and left the settlement. In my attempt to seek explanations for their behaviour, a Menraq man, apparently speaking for the others, told me that they were not keen to plant rubber trees. The man who annoyed the officer then spoke, 'We know it takes many years before we can tap rubber. Then we have to sell it to traders. They give us low prices for it. And the prices, the Malays tell us, change all the time. They are not definite. What if we slip and fall and spill all the latex we collected. We'd lose everything. And if we are hungry, we can't eat rubber!'

From this anecdote, it is abundantly clear that the Menraq do have some understanding of the vicissitudes of rubber growing. What they staged for the extension worker was feigned ignorance, one of the several strategies in what the political scientist Scott (1985) refers to as 'passive forms of resistance'. Dallos (2003: 82) provides another example of such resistance among the Lanoh (another officially classified 'Negrito' group). In response to interrogation by state forestry officers about cutting down trees planted by the Forestry Department, a Lanoh leader responded:

> We are Orang Asli and we are ignorant. The Forest Department people are clever people. But we know that if we want to take the fruits of our neighbors, we have to ask them. This is our land. Nobody told us whose trees these were and who planted them. If somebody had told us that these were Forest Department trees, then we would have asked why they were planted here on in (sic) our land. So if we did anything wrong, then we can be arrested. But we did not do anything wrong. If the Forest Department plants trees on Chinese land, on Malay land, they have to pay rent. So had we known, we would have asked for rent as well.

> (Dallos 2003: 82)

This is a cogent argument; it exemplifies not only the use of feigned ignorance as a strategy of resistance but also the ability of the Menraq to detract from their 'wrong doing' by counter-accusations made in a polite and diplomatic yet forceful manner.

To return to the Rual example, the Menraq complaint 'if we are hungry, we can't eat rubber' is poignant, for it encapsulates the inherent contradiction in participation in commodity production while still being rooted in an independent subsistence ethic. Commodity production and commoditization have become entrenched in the Menraq economy. It is evident that the Menraq are devoting more time and effort to working for cash than in sustaining their former self-sufficiency.[4] This preference is not only the result of the dictates of the resettlement economy with its growing dependence on the market for fulfilling subsistence needs and earning money, but also because the opportunities for their traditional subsistence-oriented activities of hunting, gathering, and fishing have dwindled drastically in the past twenty years or so due to deforestation and the loss of their traditional territories to outsiders.

Commodity production and subsistent-oriented foraging differ in several significant ways. First, as mentioned above, commodity production entails greater dependence on exchange relations with outsiders, such as shopkeepers, traders, and marketing agencies, to earn money to buy food and other needs. Producers must have access to a reliable market for their products in order to ensure continuity of their commodity production activity. In contrast, the exchange relations in a foraging economy, mostly in the form of gift-giving and reciprocal sharing, are predominantly among fellow band members. Second, in commodity production people are driven to produce more so that they can purchase more. People are caught in a treadmill of consumption with a strong and unrelenting desire for commodities and cash associated with capitalist-oriented development. In the process, things that were once considered luxuries have become necessities of life. Among the Menraq, things like jewellery, cosmetics, and television sets, which people did not see the need for in the past, are presently goods they strive to own. There is a desire to accumulate material things. As foragers, it did not make sense to accumulate things, as it would simply hinder their movement; and besides they generally did not have the means of storing things, especially food (see, for example, Leacock and Lee 1982). Hence, they would give away their surplus or extra things. In terms of food and resources, foragers would only gather and collect what they and their families needed. In commodity production, people can accumulate because their products can be converted almost readily into cash or wealth objects, which in turn can be saved and amassed. Third, in commodity production, unlike in foraging, there is a tendency for producers to compete with one another in the quest to produce more. Commodity production is usually driven by a sense of individualism, particularly in terms of keeping the income and profits of one's labour or capital to fulfil individual needs. While foragers do frequently work alone, they tend to share extensively the products of their labour with other members of their community. There is therefore a strong sense of reciprocal mutualism among foragers which engenders cooperation, not specifically at the stage of production but at the time of consumption. Fourth, as mentioned previously, Menraq foraging is predicated on immediate-return of their labour. They forage to satisfy their immediate needs and there is little, if any, consideration for future requirements or plans. This is in stark contrast with commodity production, which requires future-orientation and planning. In the various commodity productive activities, the Menraq have had to devote effort and energy to tasks which will reap benefits several years later. As discussed in Chapter 2, the Menraq foraging lifestyle, especially the mobility imperative and immediate-return attitude, is intimately connected with their social and cultural organization. Commoditization therefore is likely to have a disintegrating effect on intra-community relations. But what is certain is that it has crystallized changes in the Menraq social and cultural milieu.

Anthropologists have long been concerned with the impact of commoditization in foraging societies. Using a Marxist framework, Leacock (1954) examined the impact of fur trading on the social and territorial organization of the Algonguian Indians of Canada. She asserted:

> My hypothesis is, first, that such private ownership of specific resources as exists has developed in response to the introduction of sale and exchange into Indian economy which accompanied the fur trade and, second, that it was these private rights – specifically to fur-bearing animals – which laid the basis for individually inherited rights to land.
>
> (Leacock 1954: 2)

Murphy and Steward (1956) developed Leacock's contentions in a classic comparative study of the impact of mercantile exchange among Algonkian and Athabaskan fur trappers in Canada and Mundurucú rubber tappers in the Brazilian Amazon. The ideas presented in these studies were examined in the context of several foraging societies in an edited collection, *Cash, Commoditisation, and Changing Foragers*, by Peterson and Matsuyama (1991). Several conclusions about social changes resulting from commoditization can be gleaned from these studies: (1) the likelihood of the formation of nuclear families in place of extended families; (2) the emergence of intra-community competition rather than cooperation among producers; (3) decline in sharing and distribution; (4) changing property tenurial systems from communal access to resources to exclusive access. In other words, there is an increasing trend towards the privatization of property within the community. It will be interesting to examine these findings in the context of the Rual case.

Commoditization and the practice of sharing

The question is what happens to the ethos and practice of sharing when people become increasingly involved with cash and the market. Many anthropologists argue that capitalism and its attendant process monetization have an adverse effect on sharing in small-scale societies. For the Semai, Dentan (1979: 50) contends:

> The introduction of money has a devastating effect on this aboriginal Semai economy. As a standard of value, money necessarily introduces the forbidden element of calculation into economic exchanges. Moreover, money unlike food does not spoil so that sharing does not increase the amount of wealth available. Finally, it is much easier to hide money than food so that identifying 'selfish' people becomes harder.

It is, however, not the introduction of money which has a stifling effect on sharing systems. As I have noted earlier, it is the contradiction between sharing and the accumulative tendencies associated with commodity production that affects intra-community sharing and reciprocity. The question is how is sharing affected by increased commoditization. Has the extent of sharing declined? And/or, has the nature of sharing been transformed? In his study of the Agta Negritos of the Philippines, Griffin (1991: 219) observed sharing to be 'decreasingly important as nuclear families work hard to collect their own rattan, receive payment in cash and kind, and retain use of most of what is acquired'.

With the lack of precise data on intra-community exchange transactions, it is difficult to say whether the custom of sharing has declined in Rual. Some of the people I interviewed assert that their fellow villagers do not share their food as much as formerly, but there is no definite consensus on this. There are, however, several changes in the village economy that could work against the widespread practice of sharing. In the main Menraq production activities of hunting, fishing, and gathering, the allocation of labour will produce perishable food which, in the absence of storage facilities, will need to be consumed quickly. Furthermore, it was not possible to conceal food in the camp or hamlet given the openness of daily life in houses and hamlets. Hence, people will share surplus food with other families. The money earned from the sale of forest products is used to buy mostly food, which is shared in a similar way as domestically produced food. In the early days of resettlement, there was little cash available to producers or opportunities to buy consumer items such as manufactured goods, clothes, household goods, or cosmetics and ornaments. Neither did they earn enough to have money left over to hoard or save. Nowadays, with the greater range and quantities of consumer goods available to the Rual people from visiting traders and well-stocked shops in Jeli, people are presented with more than just foodstuffs to spend their money on. Furthermore, there are no obligations for the Menraq to share cash which, unlike food, can be hidden from others and hoarded.

As I have outlined in Chapter 5, hunters are expected to share their game with other members of their band. The question is: what happens if the wild meat can be sold for cash? In my study of the Semai, I found that, in contrast with the past, when hunting primarily served subsistence purposes, people now hunt for commercial reasons. They sell game such as wild pigs mostly to outsiders. With commoditization of hunting, a type of sharing of wild meat has emerged since the 1970s. I have referred to such sharing as commodified sharing, where the hunter would offer the game to his fellow villagers with an expectation of money in return. Hunters typically sold their game to other villages at the time of my research in the 1980s, as it was then, as before, regarded improper to receive money from fellow villagers for wild meat (Gomes 2004: 161–2). The meat is distributed as in the traditional way, with two major differences: the cost of the meat is shared equally with each portion priced accordingly and recipients may request more than the one share that they are traditionally entitled to. I have not so far come across such a practice in Rual, but there seems to me no reason why it could not develop in the future. While the Menraq hunter may be tempted to take his game animal to the local market, social pressure is still strong enough that the animal is usually cooked or shared in the community. Hunting as such continues to be a collective benefit. However, the fact that people sell some game like turtles and frogs rather than consume them domestically would mean that they are no longer considered as food to be shared. Since such food can be readily converted into cash, it may end up being removed from the sphere of generalized reciprocity, indirectly reducing the number of things shared within the community. However, Endicott (personal communication) points out that Batek still share food from the forest, such as saleable *petai* and honey, but it is the person who gathers it that decides how much to sell and how much to keep and share.

While it would be safe to assume, and in accordance with Rual people's claims, that sharing is in decline, there are instances of modifications and adaptations of traditional sharing practices to suit 'modern habits'. In 1976, on one of my trips to the shops in Jeli with Menraq from Rual, I witnessed an interesting sequence. On our way back to the resettlement, laden with provisions bought at the shops, Salim accidentally dropped a large watermelon he had bought. The melon broke into several pieces. Our party stopped, some picked up the pieces of watermelon from the ground and began eating the fruit. A short while later I observed each person giving some money to Salim. When I later asked two of the people who gave money to Salim why they had done so, I got several intriguing responses: 'we help one another', 'we have to share our losses', 'it's not fair to Salim if we don't give him money as we ate something he paid for'. The reasons given fit the Menraq sharing ethic squarely, but what is particularly interesting and revealing about this case is the encroachment of money into the traditional system of sharing. The fact that the watermelon was purchased and as such was a commodity removes it from the sphere of generalized reciprocity, where traditionally the food would be shared without an expectation of immediate return.

How has commoditization affected labour cooperation? Traditionally, while Menraq may go out gathering or collecting forest products together, there is little labour cooperation in these activities in the strict sense of the term. Married couples may work cooperatively in certain activities like collecting rattan or fishing. Occasionally, people may cooperate in certain activities, such as fishing with poisons or hunting, as described in Chapter 5. Contrary to expectations, I have not observed a growing trend of individuation of production as a result of commoditization. In fact, in many of the government-directed projects, people have been grouped into 'work gangs' to carry out certain tasks like clearing, planting, and weeding jointly. Hence, in such situations, people have been compelled to work cooperatively with one another. But what has emerged in these labour arrangements is recognition of leaders who are expected to pass on directives from the government officials to the other workers and to ensure that co-workers carry out the tasks. Invariably, these leaders are male, which brings us to the question of gender inequality, an issue I will take up below. But, first, I discuss the impact of commoditization on property ownership.

Privatization of ownership

Traditionally, land is communally owned in Menraq society. Furthermore, as Endicott (1988: 113) writes:

> The idea of exclusive ownership of land is an absurdity to the Batek. They say: 'Only the Batek *hala'* [superhuman beings] can own [Malay: *punya*] the land'. They believe the land was created for all people to use, both Batek and non-Batek, and no one has the right to exclude anyone else from living or working anywhere they wish.

However, as discussed in Chapter 2, people do recognize a traditional connection with a territory which they refer to as *sakaq*, but the rights to this land and its resources are communally held by members of the *puak* (band) recognized as the 'owners' or custodians of the *sakaq*. I have mentioned that some fruit trees and the ipoh tree may be individually owned. In the traditional system of land and property ownership, every member of the band has equal access and rights to the land and its resources.

There is, however, an interesting aspect of property ownership and the rules related to distribution of yield that appears to share a similarity with the capitalist system. Among the Menraq, the owner of an object used to produce something has the right to the product regardless of whether he or she has participated in the production activity. For instance, in the case of blowpipe hunting, as Endicott (1988: 115) notes, 'it is technically the owner of the blowpipe, not the hunter, who is the owner of the animal killed'. I have also observed this to be the case in the use of cast nets and spear guns in fishing. While the owner has a right to the products of someone else's labour on the basis of his or her ownership of the 'capital', this right is not always exercised. Furthermore, unlike in a capitalist system, this right does not imply a right to regulate or direct the production process.

The question is whether communal property ownership and equal access to resources can continue in a regime of commoditization where privatization of property is said to be more compatible. Privatization of property ownership complements individuation of production, where people work on their own primarily to avoid having to share products or income with others. As I mentioned above, this goes in tandem with a growing desire to accumulate surpluses. In the case of the Menraq, much of the individuation of ownership that I have come across appears to be an unintended result of government intervention. The groves of rubber and fruit trees cultivated as part of the government-sponsored development projects were parcelled out to the various individuals who participated in the projects. While the oil palm plantation has yet to be subdivided, I predict that the agency responsible for the project will devise a similar sort of system of division of property. However, it should be stressed here that for the Menraq, ownership does not imply exclusive use. I found that that even though these trees are considered to belong to particular individuals, the rights to them are not strictly exercised or observed. For example, some people occasionally tap rubber trees belonging to others, mainly from the same band. It must be said, however, that they do so upon obtaining the permission of the tree owners. While the system of property ownership is still flexible, this is likely to change with the intensification of cash cropping, particularly once the lucrative oil palm ventures mature.

Social differentiation

As discussed in Chapter 2, Menraq, like many other contemporary foragers, are noted for their social egalitarianism. Woodburn (1982: 431) observes:

> Equality is achieved through direct individual access to resources; through direct individual access to means of coercion and means of mobility which limit the imposition of control; through mechanisms which allow goods to circulate without making people dependent upon one another. People are systematically disengaged from property and therefore from the potentiality in property for creating dependency.

Endicott (1988: 122) contends that among the Batek an egalitarian ideology is related to ownership and rights to resources combined with their practice of sharing and reciprocal obligations which tend to hinder 'any individual or group from establishing a monopoly over some necessity of life and using that monopoly to gain control over other Batek'. Do economic changes that promote unequal access to cash incomes and employment opportunities threaten egalitarianism in such societies? In her study of southern African Kalahari foragers, Kent (1995: 531) concludes:

Massive economic transformation has resulted in changes throughout Ju/'hoansi and Nharo culture: sharing patterns have broken down, politics are more male-oriented, division of labour is increasingly rigid, and architecture and camp layout now promote privacy and the accumulation of possessions. All these factors contribute to an erosion of formerly egalitarian values and attitudes.

In my first visit to Rual in 1975, I found little disparity in terms of ownership of dwellings and possessions among the Menraq. With the exception of several of the headmen who were allocated comparably more elaborate houses by the authorities, most people resided in small bamboo houses and a few, particularly the families in the bands that occupied the subsidiary hamlets, still lived in lean-tos. People had few possessions – as noted earlier, an adaptation to a nomadic lifestyle. Now, thirty years later, Rual settlers own substantially more things. Endicott (n.d.: 12) observed a similar trend among the Batek in 1990, following his previous visit in 1975–76:

> Trade had also brought people unprecedented amounts of material goods, such as plastic sheets for roofing, cotton blankets, mosquito nets, fishing nets, mats, flashlights, radios, cassette recorders, and plastic toys. Whereas most people once had only a few articles of clothing, now most families had one or more suitcases full of bedding and clothing: shirts and trousers and thong sandals or plastic shoes for the men; sarongs and blouses for the women; shirts and shorts for the children.

What is abundantly clear in Rual is the substantial variation in ownership of houses, household goods, and other possessions. People who are less actively involved in the cash economy or in the various government-sponsored development projects tend to live in decrepit houses with hardly any material possessions. Conversely, Menraq who have access to a more secure and regular source of cash income, particularly the salaried employees of the JHEOA and commercial plantations or members of the armed forces, live in modern-style well-furnished homes with television and hi-fi sets, video players, and sewing machines. Many of these relatively affluent villagers also own motorcycles. In my recent visit in September 2006, I noted that three Menraq owned cars and about 21 people possessed motorcycles. This is similar to what has occurred among the Agta, as Griffin (1991: 219) observes:

> Inequality within groups is evidenced by the entrepreneurship of especially capable Agta men and women, who are able to produce more by their skill and industry. They buy more non-essential items, be it coffee and sweetened milk, or be it radio-phonographs or tape cassette players.

It would be easy to jump to conclusions at this point, but I would argue that this visible affluence is not social differentiation in the strict sense of the

14 Menraq family 'on the move' (2002) Photo: Kamal Solhaimi

15 A government-built concrete house next to a traditional bamboo-walled house
at Rual (2006) Photo: A. Gomes

term. In order for social differentiation to emerge, people would need to have access to investment opportunities where surplus product and savings can be converted into capital and used in profit-making ventures. In the case of the Menraq, people currently do not have access to adequate funds to invest in capitalist-oriented, profit-earning enterprises.

Several ethnographic studies have documented the emergence of a class of rich entrepreneurs among poor villagers through the success of intra-village capitalist ventures. In a study of Buhid swidden farmers in the Philippines, Lopez-Gonzaga (1983: 182) found:

> With the differential Buhid responses to the new opportunities for the investment of their surplus, an incipient form of economic differentiation is emerging. Within the past two decades of direct participation in the lowland market economy, small-scale entrepreneurship among these people had led to the creation of a segment of producers with larger landholding, surplus to hire seasoned wage labor, and capital for investment in new tools of production such as the plough and carabao. The institution of private landholding and the concomitant demarcation of land among the emergent local elites may be seen in such instances as Buhid entrepreneurs buying out land from fellow Buhid debtors unable to pay their debts.

In my study of Semai swidden farmers I came across similar kinds of entrepreneurial activities, but these were not entirely successful. With too little capital and confronted with the difficulties of running a business with co-villagers as clients who called upon customary obligations to share and so on, these commercial ventures earned profits too small to make them viable in the long-term. Endicott (2002) has also reported attempts by a few Batek who began the buying and selling of products from their fellow villagers for a profit. These entrepreneurs, according to Endicott, had succumbed to countervailing pressures, such as the Batek obligation to share and the high value on personal autonomy and independence, and these ventures failed. I have not yet observed intra-village commerce at Rual and, judging from the poor rate of success of such enterprises in other Orang Asli villages, it will take quite a lot of effort and time before this becomes a factor in intra-community social differentiation.

A more potent source of inequality in the short run is the reorganization of Menraq social structure promoted by government policies and in the activities of outsiders. As discussed in Chapter 2, the granting of power and authority to the headmen is one such example. Apart from a government salary, headmen receive gratuities from logging companies and traders wishing to operate or trade in Rual. While there is a tacit expectation for the headmen to share this revenue with their fellow band members, not all of them do so. There is also a new class of educated young Menraq who seem to be more assertive and confident than the older villagers. With their more extensive knowledge of the outside world and particularly being conversant in the national language, Malay, these young Menraq have been able to gain considerable influence in village politics. One youth who married into a band appears to have used his formal education and erudition in Malay to good effect by becoming the 'acting headman'. He would have been an unlikely choice in the traditional system of leadership where age and seniority are important criteria. It can be said that new forms of social order are slightly ahead of the economic transformations in accounting for social differentiation in Rual, at least in the short run.

Gender inequality

Several anthropologists have commented on the prevalence of gender equality in many foraging societies. Turnbull (cited in Karen Endicott 1981: 1), for example, states that among the Mbuti of Congo, 'A woman is in no way the social inferior of a man, and there is little absolute division of labour along sex lines.' In the case of the Ju/'hoansi, Draper considered them to 'the least sexist of any [group] we have experienced' (Karen Endicott 1981: 1). Traditionally, what little division of labour that prevails among the Menraq is predominantly, but not rigidly, based on gender. There is minimal sex typing of tasks. The rationale underlying sex typing is related to the two spheres of social interaction and work: domestic and public. Women's work and women's interactive space generally are domestic. Menraq women are responsible for the setting up and maintenance of the campsite, such as making the lean-to shelters, collecting firewood, fetching water, craftwork (like weaving mats and baskets), cooking, and childcare (see, for example, Endicott 1974: 159). Men's work is focused on activities performed away from the camp or with people from outside the group, such as traders or state officials or security personnel. Nonetheless, Menraq accord equal importance to male work and female work. Furthermore, women are not prohibited from performing male work. For instance, women may on occasions join their husbands on hunting excursions and may even kill game they encounter by chance. Males are clearly not averse to carrying out domestic tasks, as I have observed men on numerous occasions cooking or taking care of their children while their spouses are out gathering food or firewood or doing the laundry.

Will this relatively equal status of women prevail after sedentarization? In a study of the Ju/'hoansi hunters in Botswana, Draper found that sedentarization had led to a 'decrease in women's autonomy and influence' through new notions and behaviours such as:

> increasing rigidity in sex-typing of adult work; more permanent attachment of the individual to a particular place and group of people; dissimilar childhood socialization for boys and girls; decrease in the mobility of women contrasted with men; changing nature of women's subsistence

contribution; richer material inventory with implications for women's work; tendency for men to have greater access to and control over such important resources as domestic animals, knowledge of Bantu language and culture, wage work; male entrance into extra-village politics; settlement pattern; and increasing household privacy.

(Draper 1975: 78)

However, Kent (1995: 531–2) emphasizes the point that the change comes not from sedentarization itself, but rather from the 'inegalitarian cultural attitudes of groups from whom subsistence tasks are borrowed'; this borrowing, possibly accompanying development projects, brings about the inegalitarianism in gender roles and relations in the Kalahari.

Inspired by Marxist writings, particularly those of Engels, some researchers (for example Leacock 1987, Sacks 1974) have contended that involvement with a capitalist economy tends to erode women's autonomy and status, and concomitantly leads to an emergence of gender inequality. As Sacks (1974: 221) asserts:

since industrialization women have been heavily involved in public or wage labor. Meeting the heavy labor burden that capitalism places on the family remains socially women's responsibility. Responsibility for domestic work is one of the material bases for present barriers to women working for money and for placing them in a more exploitable position than men in the public labor force.

Howell (1983: 79) in her study of the Chewong, another Orang Asli foraging group, found 'indications that Chewong society is becoming stratified along sexual lines, and that individual men are beginning to emerge as leaders'. She attributes this incipient 'social imbalance' to the emergence of the 'malacca cane' (rattan) trade and the increasing frequency of interaction between Chewong people and members of other ethnic groups. In contrast to the collection of other rattan species where men and women worked together, the collection of malacca cane excludes women, as the work involved is relatively more strenuous and hence is carried out solely by men. The trading of malacca cane proved to be a lucrative venture for the Chewong and as a consequence, as Howell notes, men devoted many hours to this activity and earned large amounts of money from the sale of the cane. They bought household and personal items such as radios and clothes from the proceeds of these sales and began to establish exclusive ownership rights to these new goods. Conversely, the women no longer had opportunities to earn cash and became increasingly dependent on their husbands for money. Howell implied that this dependence, combined with alien notions of gender inequality that Chewong adopted from their dealings with non-Chewong, had induced a nascent gender imbalance in the traditionally egalitarian Chewong society.

Let us return to the Rual Menraq. To what extent has the resettlement of Menraq foraging people, with the attendant process of commoditization, led to a general loss of autonomy and status among women and promoted gender inequality? With the decline of such female-dominant economic activities as gathering and hook and line fishing, the contribution of women in the resettlement economy has dropped substantially. Women formerly contributed the bulk of the subsistence needs of the camp. These days they are more homebound, rarely venturing into the forests or along the rivers to gather and fish. Their work time is allocated primarily to domestic chores, such as cooking, laundry and house cleaning, and childcare. In contrast, men's contribution to the economy has increased substantially, as most of the new cash earning activities tend to favour males. Men have greater access to money and knowledge of the outside world. The development projects implemented in Rual favour men, as these are sponsored and directed by Malay-dominated agencies imbued with androcentric values and attitudes. Almost all the government officials – extension workers, JHEOA officers, and health and education personnel – who visit or work in Rual are male. They generally hold the assumption that males are the decision-makers in Menraq society and consequently only consult with the males at the resettlement about development plans and projects. Men are also regularly invited to visit towns, and attend seminars and workshops sponsored by the JHEOA

16 Menraq women and children (2006) Photo: A. Gomes

and other government agencies. In November 1999, seven men attended a meeting in Kota Bharu under the auspices of the JHEOA. Women very rarely interact with outsiders and are mostly excluded from the various development activities. Occasionally, women are asked to do chores like weeding and rubber tapping, but generally almost all the development projects implemented are strongly male-biased. This is also the case with employment in the logging operations, which offer jobs to males only. Such economic changes could inadvertently promote inequality as males, like their Chewong counterparts, now have greater access to cash and opportunities to acquire more possessions while females have become more dependent as a consequence of the decline of gathering and fishing. This should not be overstated however, as Endicott (n.d.: 19) observed of recent times in Batek society:

> The women were still bold and self-confident as they went about their activities, whatever their activities were. The nuclear family continued to be the most significant autonomous social unit, and husbands and wives shared equally in decision-making. Although the increased importance of trade meant that most of the family's income came from the husband's efforts, spouses decided together how to spend the money. It was not uncommon to see men receive money from traders and immediately hand it to their wives; the partnership of spouses was very much in evidence.

This certainly suggests that people place such a high value on gender equality that the women's autonomy and status appear to be minimally affected by the economic changes that favour men and the imposition of patriarchal attitudes. Gender symmetry is also maintained by the Menraq system of bilateral inheritance that allows women to acquire ownership and control of property and affords them equal rights and access to land and resources. However, while greater gender differentiation and inequality are likely to develop with the intensification of the process of male-focus commoditization, I would contend that the main threat to gender egalitarianism among the Menraq will occur when people fully adopt contemporary Islamic (and Malay) values and culture. I discuss the implications of Islamization in the next chapter.

Summary

This chapter has focused on the economic and ecological changes affecting Menraq society. Resettlement and the various development projects implemented in conjunction with it were ostensibly carried out to draw the Rual people into Malaysian modernity. In the state's vision, economic modernization can only occur through the imposition of capitalism and this involves the replacement, as much as possible, of a subsistence-oriented economy with one that is cash-oriented and linked to (and effectively controlled by) the wider national and international economy. In the Rual case this change involves a shift from a subsistence-oriented foraging economy to one that is primarily oriented to the production of commodities, such as rubber and oil palm, associated with a sedentary way of life. This shift has set in train several processes such as commoditization and monetization and has begun to increase Menraq dependency on outsiders and their loss of personal autonomy. The social fabric traditionally kept intact by the binding forces of sharing and generalized reciprocity has been undermined by the individualistic tendencies and self-aggrandizement associated with petty commodity and capitalist-oriented production and consumption. There is evidence of incipient social differentiation. Social inequality will make for radical change in Menraq communities, given that egalitarianism is a salient feature of their traditional way of life. Commoditization has also contributed to environmental problems. The causes of these environmental problems are, however, not simply or exclusively due to the internal dynamics of the Rual economy. Commercial logging and land development schemes for Malays have led to a significant growth of population in the vicinity of Rual and have compounded environmental problems. The dire state of affairs at Rual is not solely the outcome of economic and demographic changes. It is also the product of the social and cultural transformations accompanying commoditization and state sponsored development programmes. This socio-cultural dimension in the Menraq experience of modernization is the subject of the next chapter.

7 Social and cultural change

Among the Meratus Dayak in the south of Indonesian Borneo, Tsing (1993: 92) found that 'the goal of state policy [of resettlement] is not just military control, but new forms of order in daily life'. The Rual resettlement programme, as we have seen, has also introduced new forms of social order into the everyday lives of the Menraq, through the more visible projects such as formal education, health, and Islamization, but also through more subtle attempts at cultural modification. One example is the arrangement of houses and its effect on social relations among the Rual people. There are also attempts to impose Malay values and customs on the Menraq to 'civilize' them. These include Malay culinary practices and social etiquette, or what is called 'proper behaviour' (*sopan santun*) – manner of speaking, greeting, demeanour, and giving of presents. The social and cultural impact of the various 'civilizing projects' has been nothing short of remarkable. The culture of the Menraq has been overwhelmed by a host of exogenous concepts and living habits through schools, Islamic teachers, medical personnel, and increased contact with the outside world. This chapter focuses on the transformative effects of these 'civilizing projects' on Menraq social organization and culture, beginning with formal education.

Education

The introduction of schooling in Orang Asli communities has been one of the key modernization projects implemented by the Malaysian government. This is a common government strategy which is said to affect tribal peoples adversely. For example, Bodley (1990: 103) asserts:

> In many countries schooling has been the prime coercive instrument of cultural modification and has proved to be a highly effective means of destroying self-esteem, fostering new needs, creating dissatisfactions, and generally disrupting traditional cultures.

Before 1995, the JHEOA carried out the Malaysian government's educational programmes for the Orang Asli. These programmes were designed to prepare Orang Asli children to enter the national education system after three years of schooling. The JHEOA set up about eighty schools specifically for Orang Asli communities in remote areas (Endicott and Dentan 2004: 36). These schools were generally poorly equipped and children were taught by JHEOA Malay and Orang Asli field officers rather than by professional teachers. After completing the initial three years, the children were sent to one of several primary schools set up in larger Orang Asli communities. These schools offered education till standard six. Students passing the Standard Six Exams were then eligible to attend government secondary schools, mainly located in towns or close to large Malay kampungs. Orang Asli secondary students mostly stayed in JHEOA hostel accommodation at several urban areas.

The JHEOA educational programme has been declared a 'dismal failure' by government officials and Orang Asli advocates alike. A key problem was the dropout rate, as Endicott and Dentan (2004: 37) indicate:

> According to JHEOA statistics, the dropout rate in the 1980s was extremely high, especially in the lower grades . . . On average 25 per cent of the children who started primary schools, mostly in JHEOA schools, dropped out after only one year, and about 70 per cent of all students dropped out by the end of grade five.

A 1994 survey revealed that about two-thirds of Orang Asli children (47,141 out of 70,845) between 5 and 18 years old were not going to school at all (Endicott and Dentan 2004: 37). Why is the dropout rate among Orang Asli school children high? Government administrators regularly blame Orang Asli attitudes for the high dropout rate. The media statement by Jimin, a former director-general of JHEOA, quoted in Endicott and Dentan (2004: 37) exemplifies this view:

> Firstly, it must be realised that there is no formal education in Orang Asli society. None of the Orang Asli tribes have their own alphabet or writing. Moreover, the introduction of a formal education process was met with general apathy. Orang Asli children go to school because there is a hot-meal programme. They will stay away from school if they are scolded by their teachers. Then there is the problem of parents taking their children away for weeks – to look for wild fruits during the season.

Several anthropologists (see Dentan *et al.* 1997, Endicott and Dentan 2004, Nagata 1995, Nicholas 2000) attribute the high dropout rate to problems with the education programme. One problem raised is the relevance of the curriculum to Orang Asli needs. It has been argued that Orang Asli parents generally felt that their children stood to gain little from subjects such as Malaysian (Malay-centric) history and mathematics. Another, perhaps more significant, issue is the quality of education provided at Orang Asli schools.

In particular, a thorny issue is the appointment of 'inferior teachers' in Orang Asli schools, as Endicott and Dentan (2004: 38) explain:

> Teachers in the three-year primary schools were JHEOA field staff with no training as educators (Jimin *et al.* 1983: 72; Mohd Tap 1990: 269, 295 n. 24). Teachers in six-year central schools came from the Ministry of Education, but were generally those who had failed their Lower Certificate of Education exams. Many resented being assigned to JHEOA schools (Mohd Tap 1990: 269), and they often took out their resentment and frustration on their students.

Recognizing the lack of success of the JHEOA education programme, the government shifted the responsibility for Orang Asli education to the Malaysian Ministry of Education in 1995. Since then, there has been some improvement in terms of the quality of infrastructure and teachers in Orang Asli schools, which in effect means that the strategy of imprinting social and cultural values and beliefs through schooling has been enhanced. As Knauft (2002b: 175) indicates, schooling influences 'children's configuration of social relations, their sense of themselves as contemporary subjects, their relation to persons and images of authority, and the production of status or class relations within the community'. It is in the course of education that the values and sentiments of the nation are articulated and imparted to the Orang Asli children. At issue now is how schooling has affected the Rual Menraq community.

17 Menraq school children with food rations (1976) Photo: A. Gomes

18 Rual School (1979) Photo: A. Gomes

19 Rual School (2006) Photo: A. Gomes

One of the initial government-sponsored projects at Rual was the introduction of formal education. The first school built at Rual was a rectangular shed about 8 by 15 metres in size. It was built on the ground with no proper flooring. The school building was rather rudimentary, with a corrugated iron roof and bamboo walls. It had just one large classroom furnished with about twenty tables and chairs, and a writing board. It had an attached room with cooking facilities where food was prepared and cooked for the students. The school accommodated about 20 students. Over the years, the school expanded both as a building with furnishings and in the number of students. Today, the school building is made out of concrete walls and flooring, iron corrugated roof, with four classrooms fully equipped with desks and chairs. It is now almost indistinguishable from schools in rural Malay villages. Along with the improvement in its fabric has been the enhancement of professionalism of the teaching and the curriculum offered. The following is an edited extract from my field diary during my visit in 1976:

> It was early in the morning and rather misty. In the yard in front of the school, several boys and girls appear to be getting ready for their classes. They were in school uniforms, some shabbily dressed and many in faded and tattered clothes. Just about 7.30 am, the teacher emerged from her lodging and summoned the children to line up. What seemed like a well-rehearsed daily ritual the children started singing the *Negara Ku* (National Anthem). The children sang with tremendous enthusiasm but not altogether in tune. Once the national ritual was observed, the teacher waved the children into the classroom. The children sat in their respective places and the teacher proceeded to the front of the class and began writing a list of numbers on the board. This appeared to be the mathematics class. Without explaining the additions and subtractions she wrote on the board she asked the students to copy what she had written into their exercise books. She then left the students in the classroom and returned to her lodging. I then noticed that the teacher had walked down to the river to do her laundry. In her absence the children were playing and chattering in the classroom but they stopped as soon as the teacher reappeared about half an hour later. It was now time for the next class: Bahasa Malaysia (National language). The didactic method was the same as in the math class. Soon it was time for the cooking. With the assistance of several students, the teacher cooked large quantities of rice and dried fish and then each student returned home from a day at 'school' with a plateful of food to share with their household. Food was offered as a form of enticement for the children to attend classes. It was also the reason that appears to be why their parents were keen for their children to go to school. This explained why the children turned up to school with plates and pots rather than textbooks.

It is evident that schooling involved recognition, copying and rote memory of words and mathematical problems and solutions, neglecting lessons on how to develop creative thinking or skills. There is pronounced regimentation in the way the school day is sequenced into time periods, beginning with the assembly, during which Menraq students are commanded to stand in line in a disciplined manner. Such regimentation goes against Menraq predisposition towards lackadaisical behaviour. Schooling also deviates from the traditional Menraq socialization process. Menraq children learn by imitating their parents and other adults. When they are very young, they start participating in domestic and foraging tasks. This type of education is based on example rather than words. Furthermore, the schoolteacher, unlike a Menraq adult, is likely to be a disciplinarian.

In the early years of resettlement, the government had to continually persuade parents to send their children to school. Handing out food to the children was a key strategy, but JHEOA officers also had to convince the Menraq that schooling was going to benefit their children in the future. This was, however, not a straightforward task, as Endicott (1974: 78) indicates: 'the Batek understand the value of having their children fed better than they understand the abstract value of education, and it is certain that these rations have helped school attendance'. Their initial experiences of the government schooling system and the stories they have heard about schools in other Orang Asli settlements have not helped to create a good impression of government-sponsored education. Endicott's reasons for why government schooling was not popular among the Batek in the 1970s would apply as well to the Rual Menraq:[1]

> Although the official policy of the J.O.A is that no pressure should be put on the Orang Asli to change their religion or customs, this has not prevented some teachers, who so far have all been Malays, from showing lack of respect for the Batek and for their customs, especially when they contravene the teachings of Islam. The students have been told, for example, that it is evil for them to eat pork. Sometimes, they have been called 'stupid savages' when slow at their lessons and at least one teacher gave students Arabic-style names and forbade them to use their Batek names in school.
>
> (Endicott 1979b: 180)

It appears that the Menraq are more receptive to formal education now. Students seem quite enthusiastic about attending school which has provided them with a new avenue and form of socialization. Over the years the educational facilities have improved, particularly since 1995 after the Rual School was incorporated into the national schooling system under the jurisdiction of the Ministry of Education rather than the JHEOA, which, as mentioned previously, lacks expertise in the delivery of formal education. The Ministry posted four fully qualified teachers at Rual School in 1995 and now the school has six teachers. In 2004, the school had 100 Menraq students distributed into six primary standards. Twenty-four students had passed the Standard Six national examination and were admitted into the secondary school in Jeli. They have been provided with hostel accommodation in town and appear to be doing reasonably well in their studies. Apart from an academic curriculum, schoolchildren have been introduced to different sports, from soccer to volley ball to *sepak takraw*. Of these it appears that *sepak takraw* has picked up in popularity, and young Menraq males play it almost daily. They have formed teams and have entered Kelantan state-wide competitions.

Compared to other Orang Asli communities, the success rate in schooling among the Rual Menraq has been less impressive in spite of the provision of over thirty years of formal education in the village. The only person to make it to college is a young boy who has been admitted to an Islamic religious school. This low success rate is primarily due to the poor standard of education provided in the initial years of the Rual School with poorly qualified and unprofessional teachers and the racial discrimination that Menraq face when attending national-type schools. Nevertheless, schooling has created a new educated class among the Rual Menraq. Members of this class maintain a confident sense of themselves when dealing with outsiders or when visiting towns or other villages. They display an assured and assertive disposition in meetings and modern discourse, speaking the national language, and travelling to other parts of the state and the country. They have the capacity to 'talk big' in a manner 'just like a town Malay' (*Melayu Bandar*) and engage in 'playing politics' (*main politik*). One could say that they have attained a modern sense of self and personhood. While schooling has had an impact on Menraq youth, it is the practice of informal 'schooling' or 'disciplining' that appears to have a greater impact on the cultural lives of the Menraq in general. This is the imposition of Malay values.

Cultural modification

There is no doubt that Menraq have adopted aspects of what are usually described as Malay 'culture' or 'customs' (*adat*, which is a Malay word that people use in reference to customary behaviour and ideology) as a result of the longstanding contacts they have maintained with their Malay neighbours. However, such cultural borrowing is by no means extensive, as Menraq still display their distinct culture. Furthermore, Menraq are keen to maintain an identity that is distinct from Malays. This self-conscious pattern of limited cultural borrowing is, however, changing. There are several salient features of quintessentially and recognizably Malay *adat* which appear to have been advocated and promoted as part of the resettlement package to 'modernize' the Menraq. The most significant of these is the adoption of the Islamic religion, which I discuss in the following section. With the aim of 'civilizing' the Menraq, providing them with *kebudayaan* (Malay word for culture) and inculcating them with civic consciousness, Malay visitors (including government officers) have introduced certain Malay practices, and the Menraq have picked these up in a seemingly willing way. Examples of these include culinary styles, home decoration, planting of home gardens, village grounds maintenance, and the village hall (*balai*) as a centre of social interaction.

On the premise that Menraq have 'no tradition of village cleanliness', people have been taught cleanliness. Women have been urged to sweep and tidy up the house and houseyard regularly. I have heard Abdullah Hassan on many occasions lecturing Menraq on how they should always keep their homes 'clean' and 'tidy' and not 'live like chickens'. Menraq have also been taught various crafts, mainly the making of Malay cultural artifacts and dress. Malay teachers and officers have also frequently given informal cooking lessons on how to prepare and cook Malay food. In a recent visit, one of the Menraq who invited me to share a meal with his family commented on how his wife, unlike in the past, can now cook 'tasty' food 'just like the Malays'. He pointed out that their cooking used to be simple. They either roasted their meat over a fire or stewed it in a bamboo container with few seasonings from the forest. These days Menraq will often add curry powder, prawn paste (*belacan*), and soy sauce to their dishes.

Menraq are also encouraged to 'dress like the Malays'. Women have been asked to cover their breasts. Nicholas (2000: 134) cites a high ranking 'Culture, Arts and Tourism' Department official as saying about the Batek

20 Menraq walking along road at Rual Resettlement (2002) Photo: Kamal Solhaimi

that 'Although it is natural for women of the tribe to live half naked in the village, their photographs may give a wrong impression that Malays here are dressed in that manner.' While this promotion of Malay culture has been going on for some time at Rual, the most incisive reordering of the lives of the Rual people has occurred through their conversion to Islam. Today, we can find young girls wearing Islamic styles of dress like the *tudung* (head dress) to cover their hair and the *baju kurung* (Malay loose long dresses) just like their Malay neighbours. It is also not uncommon to find Menraq men wearing the *kopiah* (white skullcap) and *songkok* (Malay dark velvet hat).

Another aspect of cultural modification is the imposition of time management in the everyday lives of the Menraq. Traditionally, Menraq followed a cyclical system of time reckoning focusing on the rhythms of nature, such as climatic seasons and plant flowering and fruiting cycles. They did not have set meal times; they ate when food was available and when they were hungry. They hunted, fished, and gathered in the context of how long it would take to meet their needs and not on the basis of time. When I first visited Rual, older Menraq could not tell me how old they were, as age in terms of years did not matter to them. Menraq lives were not regulated by the clock or calendar. Most Menraq did not have clocks or wristwatches and did not know how to read the time. Consequently, it was difficult, if not impossible, to organize a time for a meeting with them or for an event. Over the years the consciousness of linear and abstract time gradually permeated Menraq lives to the extent that almost every aspect of life has become increasingly governed by the clock. Social and economic activities nowadays are largely organized around time or on the basis of time. The Menraq are expected to start work in the plantations at 7.30 am and finish at 2 pm. The work tasks are divided and measured according to the amount of time required for their completion, and workers are paid according to how much time they have worked. Menraq workers have to 'clock in and clock out', and they are watched carefully to ensure that they do not 'waste time'. Many Menraq now wear wrist watches, own clocks, and are aware of time, in terms of both hours and minutes as well as calendar dates and years. Their everyday lives are filled by numerous time-fixed events: school time, Muslim prayer times, Friday prayers, national TV news time, time for *Drama Minggu Ini* ('This Week's Drama') on national television and *Ramadan* (Muslim fasting month). The ordering of their lives on the basis of time occasions a form of discipline by which Menraq are no longer able to work or live flexibly according to their own desires or aspirations.

Islamization

For a long time now missionaries from the major religions – Christianity, Islam, and Bahai – have sought to convert Orang Asli. Christian missionaries were active during the colonial period, but are now restrained in their efforts in the face of government prohibitions on their proselytizing in Orang Asli communities. Islamic missionary work, known as *dakwah*, is, however, carried out zealously and with considerable encouragement and support from the government. Efforts to make Orang Asli into Muslims are by no means recent. As the Italian writer, G. B. Cerruti (1908: 109 cited in Dentan *et al.* 1997: 142) at the turn of the previous century reveals:

> In an era of fanaticism, invasions were made upon them [Orang Asli] with the object of converting them to Mohammedism but the only result was fire and bloodshed and after each conflict the surviving Sakais fled further into the forest (into those parts which had never been before explored) or to the natural strongholds of the far off mountains.

Since the 1980s the Malaysian government has stepped up its Islamization programmes in Orang Asli villages under the guise of what it calls 'spiritual development' and on the premise that Orang Asli, with the exception of the few who are Muslims (like the Orang Kuala) and Christians, 'have no religion'. Orang Asli traditional religions are commonly referred to as mere *kepercayaan* (beliefs) by Malay Muslims and not as *agama* (the Malay word for religion), a word reserved for the major religions such as Islam, Christianity, Judaism, Buddhism, and Hinduism. This is not just an issue of semantics. Underlying this doctrine is the assumption of the centrality of Islam in Malaysian politics and any set of beliefs and practices that shares some resemblance to Islam, like the worship of a supreme deity, is regarded as religion. For Muslims, however, Islam is not just a religion but also a way of life. Hence, conversion to Islam for the Orang Asli would entail much more than simply the adherence to a set of religious beliefs and practices. Since Islam is a central defining criterion in Malay ethnicity in Malaysia, conversion to Islam is also viewed as changing one's ethnicity to Malay. In fact, the colloquial term for Islamic conversion was (and is) *masuk Melayu* (lit. 'entering Malaydom', 'becoming Malay', in practice 'converting to Islam' or *jadi gob*, as the Menraq put it, where *jadi* is the Malay word for 'becoming' and *gob* is the Menraq label for Malay people and more generally for outsiders).

Despite several concerted efforts on the part of Malay *dakwah* enthusiasts to convert Orang Asli to Islam, the success rate has been rather poor. Only about 10 per cent of Orang Asli have become Muslims. Many of them are only nominally Muslims but are still counted as Muslims in the official statistics. There are a number of possible factors for this general lack of success in conversion. First, the association of Islam with Malay identity has made Islam unappealing to the majority of Orang Asli, who are generally resentful of Malays for treating Orang Asli harshly in the past. In the eyes of Orang Asli, Islam is the religion of their oppressors. Second, Orang Asli generally view the religious practices of Islam as incongruous with their lifestyles and food habits. For example, Orang Asli point out that the food tabooed (*haram*) in Islam, like pork and the meat of several wild animals, are in fact the food they prefer. They also say that it would be difficult for them to pray five times a day or fast during *Ramadan*, given their irregular work patterns. Third, as Dentan *et al.* (1997: 148) indicate, 'One major sticking point is the requirement that Muslims be circumcised . . . The idea of chopping off flesh is repugnant to most Orang Asli.' Finally, once again as Dentan *et al.* (1997: 148) argue:

> On a theological plane, Islam seems alien and incomprehensible to many Orang Asli. Although Muslim missionaries ignore this fact, most Orang Asli groups have full-blown religions of their own, which make sense of their world and give meaning to their lives. Their beliefs, prohibitions, and rituals are intricately woven into their everyday lives.

The government's, and particularly the Islamic missionaries', zeal to convert the Orang Asli is inspired by several agendas, some explicit and others hidden. In a 1983 JHEOA document, it was made explicit that the government aims to achieve 'the Islamisation of the whole Orang Asli community and the integration/assimilation of the Orang Asli with the Malays' (Nicholas 2000: 98). While previous efforts to draw the Orang Asli into the 'mainstream of society' focused on economic development projects, it now appears that the government has extended its focus to include Islamization. Critics see such an assimilationist strategy as a form of ethnocide, a means of eradicating the Orang Asli and in the process removing a sore point in Malay claims to indigenous status. The Orang Asli are considered, albeit privately, as the true indigenous peoples by many non-Malays in Malaysia on the basis of being descendents of populations that inhabited the country long before the arrival of Malays. Eliminating the Orang Asli category would then certainly strengthen the Malay *bumiputera* ('princes or sons of the soil') assertion. As an Orang Asli man shrewdly declared, 'when all Orang Asli have become Malays, then Malays will become Orang Asli' (Dentan *et al.* 1997: 82).

It is apparent that the Islamic missionary fervour of the late 1980s and early 1990s coincided with the global Islamic revivalism during that period. In the Malaysian context, the two Malay-based political parties, the United Malays National Organization (UMNO), the main political party in government, and the Islamic Party (PAS) engaged in competition for Malay favour by outdoing each other in their implementation of Islamic-oriented policies. The increased interest of the government in converting the Orang Asli must be viewed in this context. Stepping up its *dakwah* (religious proselytizing) programmes was not simply a battle for the 'souls' of the Orang Asli to gain divine favour. It also had an earthly dimension in the form of political ascendancy.[2]

While the adoption of Islam was claimed to be to the benefit of the Orang Asli, a sort of civilizing mission, the process of conversion was carried out through persuasion and the use of material inducements, referred to as 'positive discrimination' (Dentan *et al.* 1997: 144). As mentioned above in the context of the Batek, some of these attempts at conversion have been carried out through the village school (Endicott 1979b: 180). In the 1990s the persuasion became more subtle and insidious. At the end of 1991, 250 officers, who were initially called 'welfare officers' and later 'community development officers', were deployed in several Orang Asli communities to implement Islamic programmes. They were jointly trained by the JHEOA and the Religious Department (Nicholas 2000: 98–9). During this period the government also built double-storey community halls (*balai*), incorporating a prayer hall (*surau*) on the upper level, in several Orang Asli villages. By 1993, the government had built 265 of these halls, costing in total RM20 million (US$5 million) (Dentan *et al.* 1997: 146). Converts were rewarded with better facilities such as housing, electricity, water supply and roads, job opportunities, schooling, and health services. They were also given cash and material goods, in some cases, even motorcycles.

After several years of persuasion, the Menraq at Rual finally agreed to become Muslims in 1994. The circumstances of their conversion remain somewhat unclear, as people were reluctant to speak to me about the details of how and why they converted. When asked about their conversion, my respondents would simply say 'they asked us to become Muslims and we said yes'. Some would repeat the religious propaganda: 'It's a good religion. It will help us to be better humans. That's why we have embraced Islam.' Dallos (2003: 110–11) relates the way her Lanoh respondents were converted to Islam:

21 Surau (Prayer House) at Rual (2006) Photo: A. Gomes

One day, [two Lanoh men] were walking down to the store to get tobacco. They ran into the *ustad* [Islamic clergy] . . . [who] asked them 'Don't you want to join the religion?' They replied, 'what kind of religion?' The *ustad* said, 'The Malay religion.' At first they were not very enthusiastic, but then the *ustad* said 'It's so easy to enter this religion. Just put your fingerprints on this paper and you get 25 ringgit.' The people didn't have money, so when they heard they were going to get 25 ringgit, they quickly put their fingerprints down and converted right on the spot, at the roadside.

As for Rual, since so many people converted to Islam, I suspect that the Religious Department staged a large-scale, concerted conversion process.

Not all of the Rual Menraq converted. Of those who did, in many cases they merely followed their *puak* leaders, who received cash rewards and promises of future government handouts. Soon afterwards an Islamic teacher (*Ustaz*) was posted at the settlement with the tasks of conducting Islamic classes and holding prayers. By 1998, eight prayer halls (*surau*) had been built and the *Ustaz* took charge of their maintenance. He controlled the use of the halls; people had to seek his permission to use the prayer halls. I witnessed one incident in 1999 which illustrates this. Several people asked the *Ustaz* whether they could use one of the prayer halls to rehearse a traditional dance that they had been asked to perform at a formal Kelantan State function. The *Ustaz* refused permission to the dancing troupe on the grounds that they were performing a religious dance (*siwang*) and it would be offensive to Muslims if it were performed in a *surau*. The people decided to rehearse outside the hall albeit having to remain under the watchful eye of the *Ustaz*.

Apart from the rewards provided through positive discrimination, the religious authorities offer several other forms of inducement. In Rual, Menraq are given a packet of instant noodles each time they attend a prayer session at the *surau*. In some other communities, people are given rice. As Dentan (1997: 122) observes:

> Especially among the Temiar, government agents have created some 'rice-Muslims', analogous to the 'rice-Christians' of China. When payment of conversion money ceases, whether by plan or by corruption, people return to their ordinary lifestyles, although they remain on the government books as converts.

To what extent have the Rual converts actually accepted Islam? Endicott's (n.d.: 6–7) observation of Batek conversion is strikingly similar to the Rual Menraq case:

> Most of the Batek Teh and Batek Te' who lived permanently at Post Lebir [southeast Kelantan] had declared themselves to be Muslims,

although the degree to which they actually followed the prescribed practices varied. All of them had adopted Malay-style names and had been issued identity cards indicating their religion as Islam. Four men were known to have been circumcized, a few prayed from time to time, but almost no one followed the dietary laws unless Malays were present. Several of the Batek De' men who had houses at Kampung Macang had studied the religion and identified themselves as Muslims while in the presence of Malays, although they generally reverted to their Batek patterns of behavior when camped in the forest. A small number of other Batek De' men had adopted Islam at one time, but later had given it up. Because schoolteachers routinely bestowed Malay names on all schoolchildren and Department of Aboriginal Affairs census-takers recorded everyone's religion as Islam unless they strenuously objected – which many were too shy or too intimidated to do – the bulk of the people who maintained a presence at Kampung Macang were regarded by the government as Muslims, although their actual commitment to the religion varied from weak to non-existent.

I have witnessed several incidents at Rual that also go against the assumption that the people have 'accepted Islam fully'. Because of its sensitive nature and the possibility of retribution by the Islamic authorities I have to refrain from narrating these incidents here.

Displacement and spatial re-ordering

Evrard and Goudineau (2004: 938), in the context of Laos, indicate:

> The word 'resettlement' thus refers to a double process: *deterritorialization*, which not only means leaving a territory, but for many villagers also entails changing their whole traditional way of life (ecological, cultural, technical); and *reterritorialization*, which implies not only settling in a new environment but also accepting and integrating into the cultural references that are bound up with it.

Resettlement has removed Menraq from their *sakaq*, resulting in people losing control and ownership of the land that was once theirs. Land allocated to Orang Asli settlers is invariably less than and different from the land they occupied traditionally. As Nicholas (1990: 71–3) observes, the size of the resettlement areas ranges from 1.1 to 15 per cent of the size of their former territories. In one Semai community in the Betau Regroupment Scheme, he notes that the 95.1 hectares of land allocated to the village amounts to a mere 1.4 per cent of the approximately 7,000 hectares of their communal land. Every time I have visited Rual, people have complained about their localization into much smaller areas than they are accustomed to, about the Malay encroachment onto Menraq hereditary territory, and about its destruction by logging. Displacement from their homelands, loss of access to its resources and loss of other rights, as they see it, to their traditional land have been a source of much discontent among the Rual people.

On one of my visits to Rual in the late 1970s, I had an interesting experience that revealed the implications of deterritorialization. Early one hazy morning I heard voices outside my window and I got out of bed to see what was happening. I peered through the window and saw several Menraq speaking to two Malay men who looked like officials from a Kelantan State department. I enquired what was going on. One of the Menraq men replied that they were rounding up guides to help the Malay men to survey the area. He explained that the visitors were from the Forestry Department and they were going out into the forests to 'survey the trees'. I asked how long they would be away and whether I could join them. They said that the trek would not take long and that they would be back at the settlement by midday, and they invited me to join them. Without having eaten my breakfast, I started walking with the party of six Menraq men and the forestry officers. We walked for several hours up to the crest of the hill and then the guides suggested that we take a rest. While resting, I noticed that the guides were engrossed in an animated discussion. I then learnt that they were unsure which of the paths that radiated from the resting spot they should take. One guide explained to me and the Forestry officers that the paths led to different locations far from each other, one to Jeli, another to Rual and yet another to Batu Melintang, and they were not sure which of these paths would take us back to Rual. In other words, they were lost. I was baffled as I pondered: how is it that the guides, renowned as 'forest peoples', have become lost in a forest that they should know well? Don't they have mental maps that they have formed through all those years of moving and travelling in the forests or through instructions from their elders? It then occurred to me, after identifying the band affiliations of the guides, that they were all new to the area. They belonged to a band from a different *sakaq* (territorial subsistence zone), one which was resettled in Rual only a few years ago. Their knowledge of the territory was therefore limited by the little time they had spent in the place. Their willingness to be recruited as guides is perhaps an indirect expression of their 'rights' to their present *sakaq*. Or it could simply be an opportunity to earn some money from the Forestry Department for their services. Whatever the reasons were, this is clearly another ethnographic instance, as in the case of the Meratus Dayaks of Borneo, where Tsing (1993: 153) found that resettlement was turning people into 'strangers in their own lands'. As 'strangers', what are their rights to land? Do they have legal ownership of the land they claim as their own? The Jeli incident discussed earlier would suggest that claims of ownership and control are shaky. Furthermore, the boundaries of the 'territory' belonging to the Menraq are at best fuzzy. How then could the Malay farmers who tried to evict the Menraq band claim that they had 'bought' the land the people were residing on? I discuss the issue of land rights after exploring the implications of displacement and spatial re-ordering for Menraq social interaction and identity constructions.

Land – or more exactly indigenous conceptions of territory (*sakaq*) – is an important source of history and identity for the Menraq. As mentioned in Chapter 2, Menraq tell stories of past events in connection to the place where these events occurred. In other words, for Menraq, their past is inscribed in their land. In what I earlier referred to as a spatialized historical consciousness, spaces are transformed into places as they are incorporated into people's social and cultural maps. Place is also an important symbolic source and substance for Menraq social identity. Who they are depends largely on where they are from. Displacing them from their *sakaq* then has major implications for their identity and their history.

Resettlement also engenders the considerable spatial re-ordering that Evrard and Goudineau (2004: 938) have referred to as reterritorialization. It is possible to see some of the social implications of such re-ordering in a comparative analysis of the traditional camp and the current settlement. In a camp, the shelters are erected close to one another in a semi-circle with the main hearth in the centre of the camp. They are also open, with almost no privacy. There is an air of intimacy and closeness, and this, along with the open nature of spatial arrangement, facilitates social interaction and communication, sharing of food (as it is impossible to hoard food), and the exchange of knowledge. It also eases the decision-making process. In contrast to the intimacy of the camp, the settlement is structured in a grid form, where the houses are arranged in a row or clusters and the hearths are located inside the dwellings. In the new settlements there is less village intimacy and greater privacy, with the houses having doors that are usually closed and even locked when the residents are away. The closed and private nature of the houses makes possible hoarding or concealment of wealth and possessions. People can avoid sharing by hiding things they do not want to share. If, as discussed earlier, sharing is an adhesive in Menraq social grouping, then the spatial arrangement in the new settlements goes against the grain of the traditional culture of the Menraq. The temporary nature of the shelters in a traditional camp makes the camp more flexible than the new settlement where the houses are permanent with concrete floors and power connections. The flexible and temporary nature of the camp allows people to erect their shelters in accordance to their sharing network and social alliances. They can easily change the location of their shelters according to changing relations or shifting alliances. They can also avoid tension and possible confrontation if problems with other families emerge. People in the settlement do not have the option of moving houses whenever they like. Moving away is no longer an easy strategy for escaping confrontations or altercations with neighbours (see, for example, Endicott 1979b: 185). Fixity in settlement and housing not only has implications for social relations among Menraq but, as the Jeli incident reveals, it has also forced people to 'stand their ground' in the face of encroachment from outsiders.

To ensure a secure future for their economy, it is of critical importance for the Menraq to have unambiguous ownership and control of the cash-crop plantations which have emerged as the key sources of their income in the past decade. As Endicott (1979b: 190) pointed out quite sometime ago in respect of the Orang Asli in general, 'the amount of land acquired and the kind of rights to it that are obtained will have a crucial effect on the future of those groups'. Secure tenure to their land is certainly an issue of consider-able concern as, while the Menraq think of themselves as owners of the land they utilize, they have yet to obtain clear legal recognition of their claim. As Nicholas (2000: 38) contends:

> The dismal record of securing Orang Asli land tenure – coupled with increased intrusion into, and appropriation of, Orang Asli traditional lands by a variety of interests representing individuals, corporations and the state itself – remains the single element that is of grave concern to the Orang Asli today.

In the 1970s I was told that the JHEOA had applied to the Kelantan State government for the Rual Resettlement area to be gazetted as Orang Asli reserve. In Malaysia, all land that has not been registered as belonging to individuals or corporations is deemed to be state land.[3] While the conver-sion of the land to Orang Asli reserve would afford the people some security, the land would still be legally under state control. As Hooker (1976: 180) has indicated:

> The area of state land occupied by the Orang Asli is public domain and the greatest title which the Orang Asli can get, either as an individual or as a group, is tenant at will. There is no power in any Orang Asli to lease, charge, assign or mortgage such land although some dealings are possible with the consent of the Protector . . . Land as such cannot be owned and no one group can claim rights over it as against another group. All that may be owned is the produce of the land both cultivated and (in some cases) wild.

The area of 1,630 hectares designated as part of the Rual Resettlement has not been declared an Orang Asli reserve. It is unclear whether an applica-tion for reserve status was made at the time of the establishment of the resettlement or whether the application, if made, had been rejected. Cur-rently, the Rual people hold a 'temporary occupation licence' (or TOL) over the 1,630 hectares. They do not have secure rights to the land they occupy. Even if the resettlement land were declared as Orang Asli reserve they would be 'tenant-at-will', totally dependent on the State, which has the right to revoke wholly or partly its declaration of reserve status. Similarly, the State can withdraw its grant of TOL. With the numerous instances of Orang Asli being displaced to make way for development projects for others, particularly the politically dominant Malays, mining, plantations, road and dam constructions, and parks, Menraq rights to land are insecure. A lack of security of tenure of land means a lack of secure future for simple commodity production in the Menraq economy. Furthermore, the misconception held by the government and its agencies that Menraq do not have clear notions of land rights or links to territory continues to influence state policy in regard to land issues among the Menraq and other Orang Asli.

Orang Asli are commonly perceived as people without a clear system of land tenure and rights. Nicholas (2000: 103–4) provides quotations made by several ministers and high-ranking officials illustrating this prevailing perception. For example, the Chief Minister of the State of Perak stated: 'Perak will issue land titles to the Orang Asli on condition that they give up their nomadic ways and live in a certain area for a continuous period of time' (Nicholas 2000: 104). In my Semai research I recorded the following statement made in 1983 by a high-ranking state official:[4]

> It is difficult to give land to the Orang Asli. They just don't stay put in one area. They move all the time. I think it is because they are shifting cultivators. Anyway by allocating them some land we hope they will stay in one area.
>
> (quoted in Gomes 2004: 179)

Why should such a view prevail? It is interesting that H. D. Noone (1936: 4) noted that 'If you are a Malay who has his eye on a choice "dusun" [fruit orchard] planted up by these people you tell the District Officer how the "Sakai" [derogatory term for Orang Asli] are "here today and gone tomorrow".' Taking cue from this observation, it can be said that the prevalence of such a view tends to serve as a justification and legitimation for displacing and resettling Orang Asli. Government ministers and officials often state that they intend to *give* the Orang Asli land rather than declaring that the government seeks to *recognize* Orang Asli rights to land. In the process, the government is seen as 'settling the forest nomads' by giving them land. But the land 'given' will still be under the control of the state, and the people who have been resettled will be wards of the state, their destiny totally dependent on the state.

Health, nutrition and disease

Development policies for indigenous communities often include health and medical programmes designed to improve perceived health problems or to relieve or minimize the health consequences of economic development projects. Health programmes are also seen as an aspect in the enhancement of the quality of life. In the case of Malaysia, the initial medical care efforts in the 1950s were also steered by an instrumental aim to secure the loyalty of the Orang Asli. Civilizing them through the provision of Western medicines and health education was considered to be an important strategy in winning the people over from communist influence. The JHEOA was given the intrinsic role of implementing the health and medical programme in the late 1950s and it has run this programme ever since, with some assistance from the Malaysian Ministry of Health.[5] Endicott and Dentan (2004: 36) hold the view that the programme has been a 'qualified success, although the quality of care has not improved appreciably since the 1960s'. The central aspect of this programme is the 450-bed Orang Asli Hospital at Hulu Gombak on the outskirts of Kuala Lumpur. The JHEOA also provides health and medical care through clinics established at resettlement and regroupment schemes and through flying doctor services. The clinic at Rual was set up in 1972. Like the other clinics in Orang Asli communities, it is managed by a JHEOA medical assistant trained to treat minor medical problems. The clinic has an examination area, a few patient beds and a storage room for medicines. The first Rual clinic was a small hut made out of attap roof and bamboo walls. In the 1980s, the clinic was rebuilt out of timber. It was replaced in the late 1990s by a concrete building with more space and modern medical paraphernalia. Occasionally, medical teams visit Rual to carry out vaccination programmes against polio and tuberculosis and to conduct general health checks and health education classes. How effective has this medical programme been in catering for Orang Asli health care needs? Chee (1995: 63) indicates:

> There are still many problems and inadequacies [in the Orang Asli Medical Service]: it is, for instance, not based on the primary health care philosophy of community participation; largely oriented toward a curative approach with a vertical programme of disease eradication; and lacks trained staff, resources, and proper supervision, organisation, and management.

One major problem that has undermined the government medical programme is the high level of non-compliance by the Orang Asli. Generally, Orang Asli are unwilling to seek medical treatment from the government medical personnel because they are often discriminated against by the mostly non-Orang Asli medical staff. Menraq have told me that they are often treated in a condescending manner at the government clinics. They claim to have been ridiculed, laughed at, and scolded by medical staff. Menraq reticence in their communication with medical practitioners has on occasions led to misdiagnosis.

Assessing the effects of the JHEOA medical programme in disease control among the Orang Asli, Endicott and Dentan (2004: 36) note:

> Certainly many diseases, like ringworm and yaws, have declined dramatically since the 1950s. The infant mortality rate appears to be down, and the total population is increasing. Yet malaria and tuberculosis are still

serious problems, respiratory diseases are common, pollution-caused diseases have increased, and malnutrition is widespread.

Baer (1999b) reports that Orang Asli account for about 50 per cent of all reported malaria infections in Peninsular Malaysia. This amounts to roughly 450 to 600 reported cases of malaria per year, but the rates of infection are likely to be even higher since many cases of infection among Orang Asli are undetected by the authorities (Baer 1999b).[6] The incidence of tuberculosis among the Orang Asli is alarming; for the state of Perak, Devaraj (2000)[7] reports a rate of 240 per hundred thousand cases of tuberculosis among the Orang Asli which is 5.5 times higher than the overall rate for the state.

Most of the deaths, about 96 per cent, in Rual are brought about by disease. From the death records kept at the Rual administrative centre that I obtained in 1988, it was reported that twelve or 40 per cent of the thirty deceased whose deaths were registered with known causes suffered from chronic diarrhoea and blood in the stool, which are symptoms associated with such diseases as acute amoebic dysentery and cholera.[8] Another nine (30 per cent) people died of respiratory related diseases, such as acute bronchitis and tuberculosis. In 1993, there was a cholera outbreak with eighteen detected cases, which in fact led to the temporary relocation of many of the Rual people. This outbreak killed eight people in Rual. Pertinent questions that need to be addressed include, has there been an increase in the incidence of disease in the Rual community over the years? If so, is this increase due to the changing conditions emanating from resettlement and development? In the absence of data on disease occurrence before resettlement, it is not possible to answer the first question with any certainty. Several Menraq have commented that unlike in the past when living traditionally they and their family members fall sick more frequently these days. They also felt that more people in Rual seem to die from sickness these days than before. This view is clearly reflected in the mortality statistics discussed in Chapter 4, which show a rise in the mortality rate over the past thirty years. There is also supporting evidence from research on Orang Asli published before 1960. For the general Orang Asli population, several researchers (Noone 1936, Polunin 1953, and Williams-Hunt 1952) have reported that the health status of less acculturated Orang Asli communities was generally higher than that of their counterparts with greater external contact.[9]

In respect of the relationship between economic changes and morbidity, several researchers have maintained that economic development can lead to higher incidence of disease. According to Bodley (1990: 139–40), development induces a higher rate of disease in affected populations in at least three ways:

> First, to the extent that development is successful, it makes developed populations suddenly become vulnerable to all the diseases suffered almost exclusively by 'advanced' peoples. Among these are diabetes,

obesity, hypertension, and a variety of circulatory problems. Second, development disturbs traditional environmental balances and may dramatically increase certain bacterial and parasite diseases. Finally, when development goals prove unattainable, an assortment of poverty diseases may appear in association with the crowded conditions of urban slums and the general breakdown in traditional socioeconomic systems.

Often, different consequences of development combine to produce a deadly effect on health status or contribute to the increased occurrence of communicable diseases. An example of this is the rise of malaria transmission linked to land disruption as Baer (1999b: 302) notes:

> For the malaria vector in the interior, this land destruction [resulting from forest clearing] has produced a bonanza of seepages and trickling watercourses, ideal sites for larvae to develop. For the Orang Asli in the interior, the destruction has produced the opposite of a bonanza: a shrinkage of usable space for foraging, fishing, hunting and swiddening. Less food can now be procured from the environment, leading to lower nutrition and associated health problems. As a result, Orang Asli now may have less ability to cope with malarial attacks, both in terms of behavioural defences and in terms of physiological defences against the disease.

As for the health consequences of resettlement, Chee (1995: 50), among others, contends that 'Resettled communities which are at higher population densities . . . can sustain parasitical infections which could not previously be sustained; and crowding provides ideal conditions for the spread of infectious diseases.' As noted earlier, resettlement has brought about the concentration of Menraq into an area much smaller than they are accustomed to, resulting in deplorable sanitary conditions in the Rual Resettlement. The rubbish disposal system and toilet facilities in Rual have been poor ever since its establishment in 1972 and this will no doubt increase the susceptibility of people to such communicable diseases as dysentery and cholera. Another factor is the settlement layout which turns out to be conducive to the proliferation of certain diseases like malaria. As Baer (1999b: 303) indicates, the low-built and closely spaced houses, unlike the traditional living arrangements, prevent people from 'penning domesticated or wild-caught animals (alternative blood-meal sources for mosquitoes)' or making 'smudge fires' under their houses to drive off mosquitoes from the area. Having more people living close to one another, as Baer (1999b) also notes, facilitates the transmission of malaria from an infected person to others.

As Baer (1999a), among others, has indicated, there is a correlation between medical problems and nutrition. Good nutritional status undoubtedly ensures a balanced immunochemical system and therefore good health and better protection against disease. Traditional foraging societies are noted to maintain a reasonably good diet, as they typically have access to an adequate supply of animal protein, carbohydrates in the form of wild tubers, fruit, and vegetables from hunting, fishing, and gathering (see, for example, Dunn 1968). What happens to their diet when foragers are forced to settle down and/or become increasingly dependent on purchased foods? In a longitudinal study of several Ariaal and Rendille pastoral communities in East Africa, Fratkin *et al.* (1999) reported a drop in nutritional status as nomads settled due to a change in diet from high protein foods to cheaper and less nutritious staples. Consequently, 'childhood morbidity' had not improved despite 'sedentary populations' easier access to health care interventions and higher levels of immunization against polio, diphtheria-tetanus-pertussis, and measles' (Fratkin *et al.* 1999: 733).

Several studies report a decline in the nutritional status in Orang Asli communities that have been resettled. On the basis of nutritional surveys carried out in several such populations, Khor (1994:123) concludes:

Some 15 years after relocation, the nutritional status of Orang Asli children in regroupment schemes can be described as poor with a moderate to high prevalence of underweight, acute, and chronic malnutrition. Their dietary intakes are deficient in calories and several major nutrients.

Similarly, from anthropometric measurements taken at a Semai resettlement, Betau in southeast Pahang, Mohd Sham Kassim (1986, in Chee 1995: 61) found that out of the 499 children below the age of 10 examined, '54% was underweight, 21% severely underweight, 70% stunted, and 47% had poor mid-arm circumference (indicating poor protein and calorie reserves'. In another study in Kuala Betis, in Kelantan, Zulkifli *et al.* (1999) discovered considerable evidence of malnutrition such as underweight, stunting, and wasting among the 451 Temiar children they examined. The researchers attributed the malnutrition to 'the diminishing food source from hunting and gathering due to logging activities in the resettled area' and 'the impoverished state of the resettled Orang Asli communities' (Zulkifli *et al.* 1999: 125–6). These findings can equally apply to the Rual population. Factors such as the decline in hunting and fishing and the comparatively higher cost of market-supplied meat and fish have meant a reduction in the proportion of protein food in the typical Rual diet.[10] The following is an ethnographic snippet that reveals symbolically or metaphorically how the environmental and economic changes have impacted on nutrition and diet:

On one fine day in 1979 I saw a Menraq man checking his cast net. I asked him whether he was getting ready to go fishing. He looked surprised that I had asked a seemingly ridiculous question. He explained that there were no fish to be caught in the rivers. Seeing that I was holding my camera he offered to test his casting for me to capture the act on film. We proceeded to the track and he then pointed to an empty sardine can that was on the ground as his target. He spun the net over the can and then drew it towards him. Picking up the can, he exclaimed, 'Even the can is empty!'

Electronic media invasion

Not all the social and cultural changes in Rual are the outcome of direct governmental intervention. Some are the by-products of relative economic affluence and increased consumerism, associated with the culture of capitalism. The advent of media technology such as radio, television, and video in the village is a case in point. In the 1970s there were no television sets in the village. Several Menraq had battery-operated transistor radios and people listened to radio programmes when they could afford to buy batteries. They appeared to be keeping up with the latest national news broadcast on radio, although much of the information was considered by the Menraq to be of little significance to their everyday lives. Rarely did people discuss or debate issues related to the news items. They did, however, seem to enjoy listening to popular Malay and Hindi songs on the radio and I have on numerous occasions heard Menraq singing these songs. The most popular radio programme was the daily Orang Asli programme featuring news of events in other Orang Asli communities and traditional, mostly Temiar and Semai, ritual music. This instilled a sense of Orang Asli collective identity.

In the mid-1980s, a Menraq man with savings from his government salary bought a small television set. Since electricity was not available in the settlement, the television was powered by a car battery that required regular charging. Whenever the television was turned on, scores of Menraq men, women, and children would congregate outside the man's house to watch their favourite television programmes. Since the audience was usually too large for the house, the set was placed at the doorway so that the people seated or standing in the front yard could view the programmes. The programmes popular among Menraq were Malay melodramas and Indian Bollywood movies. However, the impact of television on the Menraq in the late 1980s was not strong, mainly because there was only one television set in Rual and it was not in operation regularly because of the inconvenience and cost of having to recharge the battery frequently. Today there are about ten television sets powered by electricity in Rual. Video recorders have also appeared since the late 1990s and so far there are five or more operational sets. Several homes have cable television. Electronic media are now more attractive and accessible to the Menraq. Villagers watch television and movies on a more regular basis and electronic media have become an important part of Menraq everyday life. Predictably, television and movies have introduced new values and ideas to the Menraq. Television and video watching in groups is an interpretative social event among the villagers, who engage in commentary on the films using Menraq understandings. People also now

22 Menraq house at Manok Hamlet. Note the satellite dish on the roof-top (2006)
   Photo: A. Gomes

talk about the films they have watched, and on occasion I have heard Menraq discuss issues derived from the films. One example is when I heard people musing over Indian marriage practices after they had watched a particular Hindi movie. It was interesting to hear their culturally mediated interpretations of caste and marriage among the Hindus. Electronic media have also promoted consumerism through commercials on television that create new desires and aspirations among the Menraq. In the process, Menraq have become increasingly aware of the variety of products in the market, many of which are unavailable to them, reinforcing a sense of relative deprivation among them. They have also developed an interest in national politics and now are more aware of wider political issues. Watching national news on TV has occasioned political debate among Menraq on an increasing basis. A positive outcome of this is that the Menraq are evidently no longer naïve about national politics and political parties can no longer deceive them as easily as in the past.

Summary

This chapter completes the picture of the implications of the Menraq experience of modernity begun in Chapter 5 by focusing on the social and cultural implications of development and resettlement. Combined with the adverse environmental effects of development, Menraq diet has deteriorated and, as this chapter has shown, this has led to poor health and a higher mortality rate. The social re-ordering through formal and informal education and religious conversion has been a major source of cultural turmoil for the Menraq. They have been pressured, albeit subtly at times but mostly in blatant form (for example, bribery), to cast away their traditional beliefs and ways of thinking and adopt 'modern' ways. The Malaysian forms of modernity offered to Menraq are economically capitalist and socially Malay-Islamic. In the process, people have lost control of their own destiny. They are often seen smiling when outsiders visit them but their smiles mask a deep sense of discontentment, disillusionment, and desperation.

8 Conclusion

By the late 1990s Rual seemed endowed with all the trappings of modernity. Cash-oriented agriculture, national-type education, bureaucratic administration, and new religious ideas now dominated. The Rual case study contributes to the burgeoning scholarship on the anthropology of modernity, much of which centres on theoretical and conceptual discussion, a key question being 'What does it mean to be or to resist being modern in world areas and locales that have different cultural histories?' (Knauft 2002a: 1). In this concluding chapter, I outline the main ethnographic findings of this study and return to the question posed at the beginning of the book: why did Menraq respond violently to a group of alleged Malay encroachers into their 'territory' in the so-called 'Jeli incident' of 1993?

The Menraq

Known as Semang or Negritos in official ethnological classification and in many anthropological studies, the Menraq belong to a category of tribal people called Orang Asli (Original Peoples). On the basis of their language, linguists surmise the Menraq to be descendants of an ancient people who inhabited the Malay Peninsula. There is no question of their indigenousness to the area but, as discussed in Chapter 3, the concept of indigeneity in the Malaysian context is fraught with logical inconsistencies and ambiguities, making it highly problematic. The politically dominant Malays claim to be the indigenous people of Malaysia and, together with the natives of Sabah and Sarawak and the Orang Asli, they form a group referred to as Bumiputera ('sons or princes of the soil'). The existence of a group of people like the Menraq linked to a population that settled on the Malay Peninsula before the Malays is a phenomenological glitch in the Malay claim to indigeneity. Therefore, it would not be absurd to say that the state's attempts at integrating and assimilating the Menraq and other Orang Asli into the Malay community constitute a strategy of resolving this conceptual issue. It is not only in the politics of indigeneity that Menraq are a thorn in the side of the nation; it is also in their 'primitive' existence as nomadic hunters and gatherers, a sore point in Malaysia's vision of becoming a fully industrialized nation.

Until the 1970s, the Rual Menraq fitted well the mould of a hunting and gathering or foraging society. In their survey of foraging societies, Lee and Daly (1999: 1) note:

> Hunter-gatherers are generally peoples who have lived until recently without the overarching discipline imposed by the state. They have lived in relatively small groups, without centralized authority, standing armies, or bureaucratic systems. Yet the evidence indicates that they have lived together surprisingly well, solving their problems among themselves largely without recourse to authority figures and without a particular propensity for violence . . . Most strikingly, the hunter-gatherers have demonstrated the remarkable ability to survive and thrive for long periods – in some cases thousand of years – without destroying their environment.

As Chapter 2 has outlined, Menraq have lived in small groups and their social organization was minimalist until they were resettled into government-mandated settlements. Their kinship structure and egalitarian predisposition were well suited to a life of nomadic foraging in the tropical forests of the Malay Peninsula. They survived this way for a very long time, but they also maintained trade relations with the outside world, supplying forest products in exchange for items such as rice, tobacco, salt, metal implements, and clothes. Menraq were gradually drawn into mercantile capitalism. In the late 1950s during the communist insurgency, external interventions in their lives expanded rapidly, and by the 1970s they finally bore the full brunt of modernization in the form of government-mandated resettlement.

As documented in this book, the changes in Menraq economy and society have been sweeping and far-reaching. The Menraq are, however, by no means alone in this respect; foragers, like them, all over the world have shared such experiences. Lee and Daly (1999: 1–2) surmise:

> In recent centuries hunters have retreated precipitously in the face of the steamroller of modernity . . . The twentieth century has seen particularly dramatic changes in their life circumstances. The century began with dozens of hunting and gathering peoples still pursuing ancient (though not isolated) lifeways in small communities, as foragers with systems of local meaning centered on kin, plants, animals, and the spirit world. As the century proceeded, a wave of self-appointed civilizers washed over the world's foragers, bringing schools, clinics, and administrative structures, and, not incidentally, taking their land and resources.

This is a statement of the general pattern of how the 'steamroller of modernity' has affected foragers. It summarizes in just a few sentences the findings of the many finely textured anthropological studies on the impact of development and modernity on small-scale societies in general and foragers in particular.[1] Summaries tend to lose the essence of specific experiences of people that ethnographies provide and the case study of the Menraq presented here underscores this tendency. While the Menraq share similar experiences of modernity with their fellow contemporary foragers in other parts of the world, their experiences are also special in some aspects. Many anthropologists have recently acknowledged that 'modernity is importantly regional, multiple, vernacular, or "other" in character' (Knauft 2002a: 1).

Modernity

This study provides ethnographic support to recent anthropological under-standings of the concept of modernity. For quite some time modernity has been viewed as an essentially Western project of transformation of societies. Embodied in this project is the imposition of ideas or actions of progress or advancement, rationality, and control or mastery of nature and other humans. It is a progress from old to new, traditional to modern, backward to civilized. Rationality is achieved through science and modern technology, through impersonalized and efficient bureaucracy and through capitalist economics. Control over nature and other humans in modernity takes the form of colonialism, capitalism, and the modern nation-state. Progress, rationality, and control are subjective ideas and actions; they are relative to local histories and cultures. What is progress in one culture, for example, may be considered as regression in another. In light of the observed divers-ity of modern forms, anthropologists have relativized and pluralized the concept of modernity (see, for example, Appadurai 1996, Kahn 2001, Knauft 2002a). As Knauft (2002a: 1), among others, has expressed it, 'standards of social advancement and progress are seen to differ depending on cultural and historical conditions'.

This book has revealed that the Menraq have had to encounter not just any modernity but a kind of modernity that I have labelled 'Malaysian (or Malay) modernity'. Islamic conversion, *Bina Insan* ('Character Building'), and Malay notions of civility and etiquette combined with the common features and effects of the culture of global capitalism, commoditization, consumerism, and bureaucratic rationalism produce a concoction of social, economic, and cultural conditions that characterize a Malaysian modernity. The portrayal of alternative modernities or the celebration of the differ-ences in modernities is only part of the story. There is a need to address the political economic impact of modernity, as Knauft (2002a: 3) contends, 'an emphasis on the plural modern sheds insufficient light on the deeper and longer impact of political economy – the historical forces of capitalism that shape contemporary globalization and undergird the sense of being or desiring to become modern'. Taking this significant point into considera-tion, attention was given in this study to how capitalism imposed through economic modernization programmes has shaped Menraq experiences of modernity.

Modernization

As Knauft (2002a: 41) indicates:

> Economic development projects, the green revolution, regimes of polit-
> ical intervention, and financial loans from wealthy nations were all
> designed to modernize social life and institutions in so-called develop-
> ing countries. It is now widely agreed, of course, that many if not most
> of these plans went greatly awry, had unanticipated and unfortunate
> consequences, and often intensified the problems they were ostensibly
> designed to resolve.

As this book has illustrated, the process of modernization, which effectively establishes the conditions of modernity, in the case of the Menraq, and for that matter for most of the other Orang Asli, has had 'unanticipated and unfortunate consequences' for the beneficiaries and in fact has created more problems for the Menraq. The process of modernization has taken differ-ent forms at different moments of Menraq history. In the government-sponsored effort at 'settling the forest nomads' and in the process, settling the problem of nomadism seen as inimical to modernity, modernization has taken the form of resettlement or 'regroupment'. This has resulted in dis-placement and dispossession for the Menraq. Modernization, as commonly perceived, was also carried out through the implementation of a range of development projects designed to transform the Menraq from 'traditional' subsistence-oriented foragers to cash-oriented commodity producers. Instead of improving the welfare of the people, this form of modernization has led to loss of autonomy and increased dependence on the government and external agencies, ecological woes, incipient social differentiation, an insecure and unstable economic future, and increased impoverishment.

Finally, modernization has also taken the shape of assimilation and integra-tion. In efforts to draw the Menraq and their Orang Asli counterparts into 'the mainstream of society', the Malaysian government has carried out a range of 'civilizing projects' including the establishment of national-type schools and Islamic conversion. In effect, these policies have had a more insidious agenda of transforming the Menraq and other Orang Asli into Muslim Malays, the dominant population in Malaysia.

Marginality

For the Menraq, one could say that modernization has resulted in increased marginalization, specifically because it has intensified the asymmetry be-tween the Menraq and the centre.[2] Menraq dependence on others, especially on the government, for the fulfilment of most of their needs has induced a loss of control of their means of production and survival. The Rual villagers, like many of their Orang Asli counterparts, do not have control over their land and resources. The legal and bureaucratic systems currently disadvantage the Menraq, as Nicholas (2000: 138) notes in respect of the whole Orang Asli population:

> In fact, the fundamental principle influencing current development policies and programmes for the Orang Asli is not one that treats the Orang Asli as self-identifying, autonomous communities; rather, it assumes the Orang Asli to be homogenous, discrete aggregates that can be moved about, or rearranged, to meet economically-determined or politically-designed objectives. With such a perception of the Orang Asli, it is inconceivable that these policies, for example, will recognise the need for Orang Asli communities to maintain organic links with their specific ecological niches or traditional territories in exchange for the benefits of modernisation – to be achieved by their incorporation into the national economy and their assimilation into the dominant culture.

Thus far, as Talalla (1984: 29) indicated, the Malaysian 'policy places an independent, subsistence oriented, non-capitalistic and non-competitive, culturally distinct group of people into a milieu of market dependency, competition, consumerism and alien values'. In examining the state's role in the affairs of the Menraq, it must be borne in mind that the state is caught in a web of conflicting interests – pandering to Malay demands, business concerns, Islamic interests, forest conservation, Orang Asli development – and its concerns for the Menraq tend to be sidelined by more influential interests.

Mobilization

The Menraq, together with their Orang Asli counterparts, are a minority in every sense of the term but they are increasingly speaking out about their plight and improving their political presence through such organizations as the Persatuan Orang Asli Semananjung Malaysia (Association of Orang Asli of Peninsular Malaysia, POASM). They are receiving growing support from other Malaysians and international organizations as awareness of their plight increases and spreads. Political activism by indigenous minorities is a growing global trend with the emergence and efflorescence of an International Movement of Indigenous Peoples.[3]

In Malaysia, one NGO, the Centre for Orang Asli Concerns (COAC) has been at the forefront in raising public consciousness about Orang Asli problems and has organized important campaigns to defend the rights of the people (see Nicholas 2000). COAC has been particularly active in organizing legal support in several court cases involving Orang Asli. An example of this is the court trial of the Menraq arrested in the Jeli case. COAC arranged a legal defence team comprising some of the most highly reputed lawyers in the country. It was also involved in a supporting role in a court case in 2001 where seven Temuan Orang Asli sued the Federal and State governments and two corporations for their displacement from their traditional land to make way for the building of a highway as part of the KL International Airport development. The Court ruled in favour of the Orang Asli, indicating that they possess 'proprietary interest in customary and traditional lands occupied by them and that they have the right to use and derive profit from the land' (COAC 2002). In his written decision submitted in 2002, the Judge stated:

> to be in keeping with the worldwide recognition now being given to aboriginal rights, I conclude that the proprietary interest of the Orang Asli in the customary and ancestral lands is an interest in and to the land. My view is that, although I am inclined to wear blinkers in considering the issues involved in this case by confining only to our existing laws and social conditions, I am compelled not to be blinkered by the decisions of the court of other jurisdictions which deserve as much respect, in particular on the rights of the aboriginal people which are of universal interest, especially when there is no clear and plain indication to the contrary in our laws.
>
> (COAC 2002)

The lifting of 'blinkers' covering Orang Asli rights and plight certainly provides a glimmer of hope for a brighter future for the Menraq and other Orang Asli. But there is still much more that needs to be accomplished. In particular, there is a need for a new land law that would recognize Orang Asli rights and this is something that POASM, COAC, and several other organizations are clamouring for at the moment. In short, there must be empowerment for the Orang Asli to carve out their own destiny.

The Jeli incident revisited

If we return to the question why the Menraq reacted so uncharacteristically in the Jeli incident, the reasons ought to be clear now. All in all, in their entanglement with Malaysian modernity, Menraq lives have been deeply and drastically affected, so much so that they no longer adhere to the fundamental principles of being non-violent and communally-minded foraging peoples. Here we have a group of people who have been displaced and consequently detached from their 'spatialized history', with an insecure economic future and frequently having to mourn the loss of their children to diseases associated with living in crowded and unhealthy conditions and being hungry, and having to retain their identity under attack from

Islamization and assimilation. They have been pushed into a small pocket of state-owned land, mainly devoid of the forests that they once depended upon for their livelihood. In general, there is a high level of discontentment, disillusionment, and despair in the Menraq resettlement. An attempt to evict them from this little plot that they think they own led to the sad event in their lives, the Jeli incident.

Glossary

adat	customary law, custom (Malay/Menraq)
agama	religion (Malay)
anak	child (Malay)
attap	thatched roofing (Malay)
bahasa	language (Malay)
baju kurung	loose-fitting Malay female dress
balai	community hall (Malay)
bangsa	ethnic group or race (Malay)
belacan	prawn paste (Malay)
bertam	a type of wild palm (Malay/Mcnraq)
bina insan	'character building' (Malay)
buah pamoh	an aphrodisiac (Malay)
bubu	fish trap (Malay/Menraq)
bumi hijau	'green earth' (Malay) used in reference to fruit and vegetable cultivation projects
Bumiputera	'princes or sons of the soil' (Malay), used as an ethnic label for Muslim indigenous peoples in Malaysia
cawat	loin cloth (Menraq)
cenoi	elf-like spiritual beings (Menraq)
cupak	a form of quantity measurement (Malay)
dakwah	religious proselytizing (Arabic/Malay)
damar	wild resin (Malay)
durian	a type of tropical fruit (Malay)
dusun	fruit orchard or plantation (Malay)
gaharu	fragrant wood (Malay)
gutta pecha	a type of wild resin (Malay)
halaq/hala'	shaman (Menraq/Batek Semang)
haram	taboo (Malay)
ipoh tree	tree that produces poison used in blowpipe hunting
jadi gob	'becoming Malays' (Menraq)
jering	a type of legume (Malay)
kampung	village (Malay)
kapal layar	sailboat (Malay)

Karey	thunder god (Menraq)
kebudayaan	culture (Malay)
kelamin	married couple (Malay), conjugal family (Menraq)
kempunan	food taboo or unfulfilled desire (Malay)
kepercayaan	beliefs (Malay)
keranji	a type of legume (Malay)
kerdas	a type of legume (Malay)
kopiah	skullcap (Malay)
langsat	a type of fruit (Malay)
lauk	'solid food' meat, fish but not vegetables (Malay/Menraq)
masuk Melayu	'entering Malaydom', a phrase referring to conversion to Islam (Malay)
masyarakat adat	adat/traditional communities (Indonesian)
menraq	human or people (Menraq)
menyusun	re-organize (Malay)
merdeka	independence (Malay)
nenek moyang	ancestors (Malay)
orang luar	outsiders or foreigners (Malay)
pehunen/pehunan	food taboo or unfulfilled desire (Jahai Semang/Semai)
penghulu kanan	village senior or main head (Malay)
penghulu	village or band head (Malay/Menraq)
petai	a type of legume (Malay)
puak	band (Menraq), clan or kin or family group (Malay)
pucuk paku	edible ferns (Malay/Menraq)
punan	food taboo or unfulfilled desire (Menraq)
pusaka	inheritance or heritage (Malay)
Ramadan	fasting month (Malay/Islamic)
rambai	a type of fruit (Malay)
rotan	rattan or cane (Malay)
Rukunnegara	national motto (Malay)
rumah kerajaan	'standard issue' houses supplied by contractors to government-sponsored schemes (Malay)
ruway	soul (Menraq)
sakaq	territory or traditional land (Menraq)
sambal	'toppings' to a curry, chosen from a tray of bowls and dishes (Malay)
sarong	Malay lower garment
saudara	siblingship and comradeship (Malay)
sepak takraw	Malay game played on a court with a rattan ball
siwang	ritual ceremony or seance, usually with shamanic singing, trancing and dancing (Semang/Temiar)
songkok	hat worn by Malay men
suku suku terasing	isolated communities (Indonesian)
sungai/sungei	river (Malay)

surau	prayer house (Malay)
Ta Pedn	creator god (Menraq)
takop	a type of edible wild tuber (Menraq)
Tohan	creator god (Batek Semang)
tolong menolong	mutual help (Malay)
tongkat ali	an aphrodisiac (Malay)
tudung	female head dress (Malay)
ubi garam	a type of edible wild tuber (Menraq)
umbut	edible wild cabbage (Menraq)
ustaz	religious teacher (Malay)

Notes

1 Introduction

1 For example, people commonly say 'we, Menraq eat meat from the forest'. To avoid confusion, it should be pointed out that the three terms – Semang, Negritos, Menraq – appearing in this book refer to the same people. The first two are ethnonyms other authors have used in reference to the people concerned and these terms will be met with in quotations in this book. Menraq are identified by the Malaysian government as 'Negritos'. Given the problems with using the ethnic labels Semang and Negritos, which I will discuss in the following chapter, I have decided to adopt the more appropriate autonym 'Menraq'.

2 I have used the term 'tribal' instead of the commonly used label 'indigenous' because the latter term includes members of the majority in some countries like Malaysia.

3 See Scott (1985) among many excellent studies on the effects of the Green Revolution in Malaysia.

4 An overwhelming majority of the people living in Kelantan are Malay Muslims, the dominant ethnic group in Malaysia, with a few Chinese mostly concentrated in the state capital, Kota Baru.

5 Following the official name of the resettlement, I referred to people as 'Jahai Negritos' then. This ethnic label is inappropriate for the whole resettlement as I will discuss later. There were many people in the resettlement that were not 'Jahai Negritos' but belonged to other 'Negrito' groups.

2 Social and cultural milieu

1 Skeat and Blagden (1906) and Schebesta (1926) named the three groups in their classificatory scheme as Semang, Sakai, and Jakun. This scheme is still adhered to in official categorization today with some changes to ethnic nomenclature; the three groups are referred to as Negritos, Senoi, and Melayu Asli (Aboriginal Malays). However, the detailed allocation of specific ethno-linguistic populations to these categories have varied from author to author, and from time to time.

2 A label used in reference to the Malays since the 1960s. While the term, derived from Sanskrit, literally means 'Princes (*Putera*) of the Soil (*Bumi*)', in its general usage in Malaysia it implies indigeneity and subsequently became a reference term for all indigenous peoples in Malaysia, including the native or tribal peoples of Sabah and Sarawak. An implicit meaning of *Bumiputera* in the Malaysian context is the political supremacy of the Malays over the other citizens (mainly Chinese and Indians) who are simply referred to as 'Non-Bumiputeras'.

3 Statistics obtained from various sources including JHEOA population figures provided at the Head Office in Kuala Lumpur and reports by the Malaysian Department of Statistics.

4 Benjamin (1976: 45–8) lists these subgroups as Kensiu, Kintaq Bong, Jehai, Mendriq, Bateg Deq, Mintil, Bateg Nong, Semnam, Sabum, Lanoh Yir, and Lanoh Jengjeng. Benjamin (personal communication) notes that 'Strictly, this is a classification of speech-varieties, not ethnic groups.'

5 Kirk Endicott (1979a: 3–5) lists them as Batek Dè', Batek 'Iga', Batek Nòng, Batek Teh, and Batek Tè'.

6 The layers are usually light red and white in colours resembling the colours of the Malaysian national flag with the topmost layer in a dark red colour.

7 It is important to consider Benjamin's clarification of his tabulation: 'I have given the ethnic categorization mainly in terms of the official JHEOA labels, which absorbs some smaller groups into neighbouring populations . . . The Semelai figure probably includes that for the very small Temoq population. There are a few smaller groups such as the Mintils (or Batek Tanum), and the various populations (such as Semnams and Sabüms) lumped together under "Lanoh", whose distinctiveness has never been recognized by the JHEOA, probably they are too small to make any notable statistical difference. The Besisis are referred to as Mah Meri by the JHEOA, who also employ certain spellings that are not found in the scholarly literature' (2002: 22–3).

8 See Nagata (2006) for an elaborate and comprehensive discussion on Menraq (in Malaysia and Thailand) ethnonyms.

9 The Malaysian Constitution defines Malay as someone who is a Muslim, habitually speaks the Malay language, and follows Malay custom or *adat* (see, for example, Nagata 1974).

10 In a recent personal communication, Endicott asserts that he now uses the term 'Semang' rather than 'Negrito', following criticisms of his usage of the label 'Negrito' in his early publications.

11 The word appears to be a Malay loan word meaning 'clan', group, or party.

12 I shall elaborate on Menraq sharing practices in Chapter 6.

13 However, Endicott (1974: 223) notes, 'For the Batek, marriages are easily made and just as easily dissolved.'

14 Batek use the term *kemam* for conjugal family (Endicott, personal communication). *Kemam* appears to be a derivative of the term *kelamin*.

15 Kirk Endicott (personal communication) notes that Batek women do speak for themselves in camp-wide discussions.

16 'Penghulu' usually refers to a government-appointed and salaried position as compared to 'Ketua' which means 'Head' in Malay. In Malay villages (*kampong*), one may find a Penghulu and a Ketua Kampong, the former a civil servant or representative of the government responsible for the village administration and the latter playing a more traditional role of village leader or headman.

17 See Shuichi Nagata (2004) for an extended discussion of the implications of government policy on leadership in a 'Semang' resettlement in Kedah.

18 In his essay on headhunting in Southeast Asia, McKinley (1976: 105) described what he considers a common Southeast Asian tribal cosmology. He has referred to the cosmological centre as the 'known world' which he delineates as 'the earth and its inhabitants who are one's own fellow villagers'.

19 Sellato (1994: 210–11) uses this term to refer to the habitus (after Bourdieu) which he defines as 'a system of lasting and transferable patterns of thought and behavior that regulates social and economic activities and is passed on from generation to generation through all the vicissitudes of history and changes in the "external culture"'.

3 Modernity, development, and tribal communities

1 Academic literature on development theories and practices is vast. Some of the recently published key texts which provide a comprehensive survey of the field of development, mainly from an anthropological perspective, include Edelman and Haugerud (2005), Olivier de Sardan (2005), Schech and Haggis (2000), and Willis (2005). For a brief overview of the various theories of development, see Gomes (2002).

2 http://www.un.org/millennium/declaration/ares552e.htm, accessed 25 September 2006.

3 http://www.mca.gov/about_us/overview/index.shtml, accessed 25 September 2006.

4 In the early years of British colonialism, control over the various states was by no means uniform. The Malay Peninsula was divided politically into three regions: Straits Settlements (Penang, Singapore, and Melaka), Federated Malay States (Selangor, Perak, Negri Sembilan, and Pahang) and the Unfederated Malay States (Kedah, Perlis, Kelantan, Trengganu, and Johor). As Andaya and Andaya (1982: 205) have indicated, 'The Straits Settlements and the Federated Malay States (FMS) had been under British influence longest, and consequently their various institutions were more closely co-ordinated than those in the Unfederated Malay States (UMS).'

5 Since the 1940s, research scientists, particularly from the International Maize and Wheat Improvement Centre based in Mexico and the International Rice Research Institute (IRRI) in Los Banos in the Philippines, have undertaken to create varieties of wheat and rice, respectively, which are fast-growing and high-yielding. The rapid adoption of high-yielding rice and wheat varieties prompted commentators and policy-makers to refer to the attendant changes in farming technology and the accompanying social, economic, and ecological transformations as a 'revolution'. Thus the Green Revolution gained momentum in the late 1960s and during the 1970s spread globally.

6 See, for example, Howitt *et al.* (1996), Kingsbury (1995), Miller (2003), and Niezen (2003).

7 While Malays consider themselves as indigenous and are undoubtedly 'native' to the country, by being politically and demographically dominant they do not strictly fulfil the defining criteria for indigenous peoples or communities as promulgated in international conventions (UN and ILO). As the following discussion underlines, an important criterion in the identification of indigenous communities is minority status. In conventional anthropological parlance, minority or marginalized status is implicit in the terms 'indigenous communities' or 'indigenous peoples', making the label 'indigenous minorities' tautological. In the Malaysian context, however, it would be politically necessary to use the term 'indigenous minorities' in reference to people like the Orang Asli to differentiate them from the 'indigenous' Malays.

8 The effects of modernization and modernity on tribal communities in various parts of the world have received much scholarly attention. See, for example, Bodley 1988, 1990, Burger 1987, Howitt 2001, and Maybury-Lewis 2002. A few recent publications including Barnes *et al.* (1995), Duncan (2004), Nicholas and Singh (1996) complement an earlier Cultural Survival publication (1987) on the impact of capitalism and the nation-state on Asian tribal minorities. With respect to Malaysia, Appell (1985), Ave and King (1986), Colchester (1999), Dentan *et al.* (1997), Gomes (2004), Hong (1987), Lim and Gomes (1990), Nicholas (1994, 2000), Razha (1995), and Winzeler (1997) contain significant insights on how modernity has affected tribal communities in the country.

9 I will elaborate on the implications of Orang Asli resettlement carried out during this period of communist insurgency in Chapter 4.

10 I have used the work of such postcolonial critics of development as Crush (1995), Escobar (1995), Ferguson (1990), Gupta (1998), and Sachs (1992) as a model.

4 Rual Resettlement

1 Regroupment is a euphemism in Malaysian government rhetoric for resettlement. It is, however, a slightly more accurate term than resettlement, as such schemes involve the amalgamation of several villages to form a composite village located in the vicinity of the original settlements.
2 It should, however, be noted that the terminology used in the 1930s at the time Noone wrote this report may not carry the same connotations as current usage, especially with regard to 'propaganda'.
3 This plan was initially developed to deny the communists support from Chinese villagers and in some cases, Malay villagers. Resembling Noone's 'controlled reservations', the Briggs Plan involved the forcible removal of rural Chinese suspected of aiding communist insurgents. However, unlike Noone's proposal, which allowed people free movement, the Briggs Plan put the inhabitants of these 'new villages' behind fences and subjected them to curfew and regular searches. Tinned food, for example, had to be opened on purchase to prevent it being smuggled to jungle hideouts.
4 Although the forests in the traditional territory were made available for timber extraction from the mid-1970s, the perilous security situation arising from communist activity in the region deterred logging companies from working in the area. In the late 1990s, an area of 10,000 hectares was leased to a timber company, Perak Integrated Timber Complex (PITC), which claimed to operate its concession on the basis of the Malaysian Forest Stewardship Council (FSC) standards, among which includes consideration for the rights of indigenous communities. To meet such standards, PITC declared it would employ Orang Asli to make up 50 per cent of its workforce at the forestry camp and recognize and respect the rights and knowledge of the indigenous communities. In May 2003 the company had six Menraq on its payroll. They were hired to carry out manual work such as road construction and maintenance for a salary of RM30 per day (Meyer 2003).
5 As mentioned in Chapter 2, bands are referred to by the names of their respective headmen.
6 PPRT stands for Program Pembangunan Rakyat Termiskin (Development Programme for the Hardcore Poor), a development initiative introduced in Malaysia in the 1990s as part of the New Development Policy (1990–2000). The provision for better housing is one of the main aspects of PPRT, and the standard houses developed for this purpose were accordingly referred to as PPRT houses. In the 1980s the Government allocated RM6,000 for the construction of each PPRT house and this allocation was increased to RM10,370 per house in the 8th Malaysian Plan (2001–2005).
7 *Sepak takraw* is a popular traditional Malay/Thai ball game involving three players on each side of the court. The ball (*takraw*, a Thai word for ball) is woven out of rattan or hard plastic. With rules similar to volleyball, players kick (*sepak* in Malay) or head the ball across a net. Unlike volleyball, players cannot touch the ball with their hands in the process of play.
8 On the other hand, toilets built in 1996 alongside the houses were in disrepair and fell out of use soon afterwards.
9 I have estimated the figures for 1998 from the census I carried out in 1999. To do this I added the net population gain or loss since April 1998 to the 1999 census figure. I have done this to standardize the inter-census interval to 10 years to facilitate comparative analysis.

10 The data presented here is based on my own demographic surveys of the Rual population. The population figure for 2006 mentioned above was obtained from a JHEOA census which does not provide the sort of details needed for the analysis I conduct here. I should indicate that it was difficult determining the ages of people as Menraq are not concerned with calendar ages and usually categorize individuals as old, middle-aged or young. I used a combination of three methods or sources: ages on identity cards, relative age ranking, and event calendar. The age of a respondent on his or her ID card was used as the basis of the enquiry. This figure itself is an estimate made by another person, usually the registration officer. I then asked the respondents whether they were younger or older than people whose ages I had already determined. On the basis of this I formed a schedule with the relative age ranking of individuals in the population. To check the age of a person, I used the method of event calendar. This method consists of making a chronological list of memorable events which can be absolutely dated from written records – wars, natural disasters, visits of royalty, etc. – and then attempting to find out whether individuals were born before or after each of these. The events I used in my study were limited to only a few dateable events: 1926 Great Flood, 1942–45 Japanese Occupation, 1946–60 Emergency (*Masa Dzarurat*), 1957 Independence (*Merdeka*), 1967 Floods, 1969 13 May Riots. The ages were checked several times to ensure against over or under estimation or misreporting of age.

11 Number of children aged 0–4 divided by the number of women aged 15–44 per 1,000 population.

12 The mean number of live births per living woman over age 45.

13 The average number of live births per woman.

14 The total number of births per 1,000 population.

15 While the child–woman ratio and crude birth rates are generally useful as fertility indicators, they tend to be somewhat unreliable measures of fertility in small populations. Since they are both strongly affected by mortality patterns, a high incidence of mortality among children below the age of 5 in a small population like the Menraq population is likely to produce considerable statistical aberration. To obtain a more accurate and reliable depiction of the level of fertility, it makes sense to focus on the TMR and MR.

16 It was difficult to talk about their dead relatives. It is even a taboo to call out the names of deceased people. Menraq even sometimes have trouble remembering the names of their dead relatives. For fear of attack from malevolent spirits of the dead, Menraq refer to dead people using necronyms (cf. Kirk Endicott 1974: 203).

5 Menraq as foragers

1 My description is drawn partly from ethnographic observations of Rual in the late 1970s and from the writings of Dallos (2003), Endicott (1974, 1984), Lye (1997), and Nagata (1997a, 1997b, 2004) and, from an earlier generation of ethnographers, the still useful accounts by Evans (1937) and Schebesta (1928, 1954). Endicott's study is particularly useful as it focuses on the traditional economy of the Batek, a Menraq subgroup who live about 100 kilometres south of Rual.

2 Examples of such critiques are Bailey *et al.* (1989), Headland and Reid (1989), Schrire (1984), and Wilmsen (1989).

3 These 'breaks' in the tropical forests are what ecologists call ecotone areas, the transitional zone between two or more distinct biotic communities where resources tend to be particularly diverse and abundant (Rambo 1979).

4 The number of varieties obtained was not as extensive as that reported in earlier studies. Schebesta (1954: 54–5) listed seventeen varieties of edible wild yams

(*Dioscorea*) gathered by Menraq. He also noted that they harvested eleven types of rattan (*Calamus*) roots gathered for food. Endicott (1974) reported that one of his Batek informants was able to identify twenty-four edible wild tubers.

5 The local currency was referred to as the Malaysian dollar in the 1970s. It is now commonly known as *ringgit* and denoted as 'RM'. In the 1970s, the exchange rate was roughly RM2.50 to one US dollar. It was pegged at RM3.80 to a US dollar from 1997 to 2005.

6 *Durian* collecting is a lucrative cash earning activity in many Orang Asli villages. Orang Asli are renowned as suppliers of tasty *durians* that are highly sought after, particularly by Malaysian Chinese who regard *durian* as a delicacy and are willing to pay handsomely for it.

6 From foragers to commodity producers

1 It takes rubber trees about five years to produce reasonable quantities of latex.

2 Soils in tropical forest areas tend to be poor. The rich nutrients normally found in soil are absorbed by the lush forest vegetation. Hence, the removal of this vegetation leaves behind nutrient-poor soils. Furthermore, the loss of vegetation also exposes the soils to leaching by rainwater.

3 In the 1970s and 1980s Malaysia was the world's leading producer of tropical hardwoods. Commenting on timber trade in Malaysia, Jomo *et al.* (2004) indicate:

> timber has generally been a major source of export earnings for Malaysia. Indeed, timber has been Malaysia's second largest net export earner, after petroleum, since the early 1980s, greatly exceeding palm oil . . . and rubber. In 1990, for instance, timber export earnings and timber products amounted to RM8.9 billion, or 11.3 per cent of total export proceeds, compared to RM10.6 billion for petroleum, RM4.4 billion for palm oil and RM3.0 billion for rubber. In 1995, the contribution of timber exports to export earnings from primary commodities still accounted for some 20.4 per cent, although it declined, as expected, to 5.5 per cent by 2000.

4 It is possible to consider these changes in the light of my study on the Semai, who were once subsistence-oriented swiddeners but are now simple commodity producers like the Menraq (Gomes 1986, 2004). In that research I found that the Semai people were deeply involved in commodity production. On the basis of a year-long time allocation study in the early 1980s, I observed that Semai spent about treble the amount of time on commodity production, namely fruit production and forest collecting for the market, than on subsistence production such as swiddening, hunting, fishing, and gathering. From an analysis on how people worked out their productive time allocation, it was apparent that their decisions on labour allocation were predominantly made on the basis of their estimations of cash returns for labour expended. One of the main reasons for their preference for cash-oriented work is simply because the Semai are heavily dependent on the market for their subsistence requirements. I do not, however, have the same detailed and precise data on the Menraq economy as I do for the Semai.

7 Social and cultural change

1 Similarly, in his study of a Semang resettlement, Kampung Lebuk Legong in Kedah, Nagata (1995: 98) reports: 'The only and perhaps most serious apprehension parents expressed is that school teaches Orang Asli children to become Muslims. This fear is acutely felt by all the Orang Asli parents of the village.'

2 See Nagata (1984) for an excellent record of this development in Malaysian Islam.

3 Known as the Torrens System, this land code was established during the British colonial administration and has continued to be in force, with some amendments, in post-colonial Malaysia.

4 The official was a former anthropology class-mate of mine and it appears that the anthropology we had learnt, particularly in respect of the follies of ethnocentrism, seems to have been lost on him.

5 For an overview of the Malaysian government's health and medical programme for the Orang Asli, see Carey (1976) and Abdul Halin (1990).

6 I have estimated the reported cases of malaria from JHEOA figures provided online: http://www.jheoa.gov.my/e-medical.htm, accessed 24 August 2004.

7 http://www.aliran.com/monthly/2000/05f.html, accessed 24 August 2004.

8 My data on the cause of deaths is somewhat sketchy and the records I have obtained from the JHEOA death registers do not provide precise information on the cause of deaths.

9 For a detailed discussion of the findings of these studies, see Baer (1999a) and Chee (1995).

10 See Chee (1995) for a review of studies of how worsening material conditions resulting from development have adversely affected health status in several indigenous communities in Africa and Latin America.

8 Conclusion

1 See, for example, Panter-Brick, Layton, and Rowley-Conwy (2001), Peterson and Matsuyama (1991), Schweitzer, Biesele, and Hitchcock (2000), Wilmsen (1989).

2 See Li (1999) for a discussion on the concept of marginalization.

3 Indigenous peoples' political mobilization has attracted considerable scholarly attention in recent years. See, for example, Blaser *et al.* (2004), Hendry (2005), Miller (2003), Niezen (2003), Sissons (2005), and Stewart-Harawira (2005) for detailed discussions of the nature, range and political efficacy of indigenous activism internationally and in a number of different countries.

Bibliography

Briefly annotated list of key references

In recent years, the literature on the Orang Asli has been extended considerably. Lye's (2001) comprehensive bibliography lists more than 1,700 references. Baer (1999), Carey (1976), Dentan *et al.* (1997), and Nicholas (2000) are important general surveys on Orang Asli societies and cultures, with the later publications focusing on the pressing issues related to development, health, and social change. Benjamin and Chou (2003), Lim and Gomes (1990), Rahza and Karim (2001), and Winzeler (1997) are collections of recent research papers. Major published ethnographies of particular Orang Asli groups include Couillard (1980) on the Jah Hut people, Dentan (1979) on the Semai, Endicott (1979) on the Batek, Gianno (1990) on the Semelai, Gomes (2004) on the Semai, Howell (1989) on the Chewong, Karim (1981) on the Ma' Betisek (Mah Meri), Jennings (1995) on the Temiar, Nicholas (1994) on the Semai, and Roseman (1991) on the Temiar. Many of these ethnographies focus on religion and ritual.

Abdul Halin Hamid (1990) 'Health among the Orang Asli in Peninsular Malaysia: an overview', in Victor T. King and Michael J. G. Parnwell (eds) *Margins and Minorities: The Peripheral Areas and Peoples of Malaysia*, Hull, Hull University Press, pp. 77–93.

Alias Mohd. Ali (1977) 'Aktiviti "memburu-menhimpun" (hunting-gathering) di kalangan Orang Jahai Negrito di kawasan penempatan semula Orang-orang Asli di Pos Sungai Rual, Tanah Merah, Kelantan' [Hunting and gathering activities among the Jahai Negrito at Pos Sungai Rual Orang Asli Resettlement Area], unpublished BA graduation exercise, Department of Anthropology and Sociology, University of Malaya.

Amran Kasimin (1991) *Religion and Social Change among the Indigenous People of the Malay Peninsula*, Kuala Lumpur, Dewan Bahasa dan Pustaka.

Andaya, Barbara Watson and Andaya, Leonard Y. (1982) *A History of Malaysia*, London, Macmillan Press.

Anderson, Benedict (1987) 'Introduction', in *Southeast Asian Tribal Groups and Ethnic Minorities: Prospects for the Eighties and Beyond*, Cambridge, Mass., Cultural Survival, pp. 1–15.

Appadurai, Arjun (1996) *Modernity at Large: Cultural Dimensions of Globalization*, Minneapolis, Minn., University of Minnesota Press.

Appell, George (ed.) (1985) *Modernization and the Emergence of a Landless Peasantry: Essays on the Integration of Peripheries to Socio-economic Centers*, Studies in Third World Societies Publication No. 23, Williamsburg, College of William and Mary.

Ave, Jan B. and King, Victor T. (1986) *People of the Weeping Forest: Tradition and Change in Borneo*, Leiden, The National Museum of Ethnology.

Baer, Adela (1999a) *Health, Disease and Survival: A Biomedical and Genetic Analysis of the Orang Asli of Malaysia*, Subang Jaya, Selangor, Centre for Orang Asli Concerns.

—— (1999b) 'Rainforest malaria, mosquitoes and people', *Malayan Nature Journal*, 53: 299–305.

Bailey, R. C., Head, G., Jenike, M., Owen, B., Rechtman, R., and Zechenter, E. (1989) 'Hunting and gathering in tropical rain forest: is it possible?', *American Anthropologist*, 92: 59–82.

Barnes, R. H., Gray, Andrew, and Kingsbury, Benedict (eds) (1995) *Indigenous Peoples of Asia*, Ann Arbor, Mich., Association for Asian Studies, Monographs of the Association for Asian Studies No. 48.

Bellwood, Peter (1997) *Prehistory of the Indo-Malaysian Archipelago*, rev. edn, Honolulu, University of Hawai'i Press.

—— (1999) 'Archaeology of Southeast Asian hunters and gatherers', in Richard B. Lee and Richard Daly (eds) *The Cambridge Encyclopedia of Hunters and Gatherers*, Cambridge, Cambridge University Press, pp. 284–8.

Bengwayan, Michael A. (2003) *Intellectual and Cultural Property Rights of Indigenous and Tribal Peoples in Asia*, London, Minority Rights Group International.

Benjamin, Geoffrey (1966) 'Temiar social groupings', *Federation Museums Journal*, 11: 1–25.

—— (1967) 'Temiar religion', unpublished PhD thesis, Cambridge University.

—— (1973) 'Introduction', in Paul Schebesta, *Among the Forest Dwarfs*, London, Oxford University Press, pp. v–xiv. Originally published 1929, Hutchinsons.

—— (1976) 'Austroasiatic subgroupings and prehistory in the Malay Peninsula', in Philip N. Jenner, Laurence C. Thompson, and Stanley Starosta (eds) *Austroasiatic Studies*, Honolulu, University of Hawai'i Press, pp. 37–128.

—— (1979) 'Indigenous religious systems of the Malay Peninsula', in Aram Yengoyan and Alton L. Becker (eds) *The Imagination of Reality: Essays in Southeast Asian Coherence Systems*, Norwood, NJ, Ablex Publishing Corporation, pp. 9–27.

—— (1985) 'In the long term: three themes in Malayan cultural ecology', in Karl L. Hutterer, A. Terry Rambo, and George Lovelace (eds) *Cultural Values and Human Ecology in Southeast Asia*, Ann Arbor, Mich., Center for South and Southeast Asian Studies, University of Michigan, pp. 219–78.

—— (2001a) 'Orang Asli languages: from heritage to death?', in Razha Rashid and Wazir Jahan Karim (eds) *Minority Cultures of Peninsular Malaysia: Survivals of Indigenous Heritage*, Penang, Malaysia, Academy of Social Sciences (AKASS), pp. 101–22.

—— (2001b) 'Process and structure in Temiar social organisation', in Razha Rashid and Wazir Jahan Karim (eds) *Minority Cultures of Peninsular Malaysia: Survivals of Indigenous Heritage*, Penang, Malaysia, Academy of Social Sciences (AKASS), pp. 125–49.

—— (2002) 'On being tribal in the Malay world', in Geoffrey Benjamin and Cynthia Chou (eds) *Tribal Communities in the Malay World: Historical, Social and Cultural Perspectives*, Leiden, IIAS, Singapore, ISEAS, pp. 7–76.

—— and Chou, Cynthia (eds) (2002) *Tribal Communities in the Malay World: Historical, Social and Cultural Perspectives*, Leiden, IIAS, Singapore, ISEAS.

Berman, Marshall (1988) *All That is Solid Melts into Air: The Experience of Modernity*, New York, Viking Penguin.

Bernstein, Henry (1979) 'African peasantries: a theoretical framework', *Journal of Peasant Studies*, 6 (4): 421–43.

Blaser, Mario, Feit, Harvey, and McRae, Glenn (2004) *In the Way of Development: Indigenous Peoples, Life Projects and Globalization*, London and New York, Zed Books, in association with International Development Research Centre.

Bodley, John H. (1988) *Tribal Peoples and Development Issues: A Global Overview*, Mountain View, Calif., Mayfield.

—— (1990) *Victims of Progress*, 3rd edn, Mountain View, Calif., Mayfield.

Brandt, John H. (1961) 'The Negrito of Peninsular Thailand', *The Journal of the Siam Society*, 49 (20): 123–60.

Bulbeck, David (2003) 'Hunter-gatherer occupation of the Malay Peninsula from the Ice Age to the Iron Age', in Julio Mercader (ed.) *Under the Canopy: The Archaeology of Tropical Rain Forests*, New Brunswick, NJ, Rutgers University Press, pp. 119–60.

—— (2004) 'Indigenous traditions and exogenous influences in the early history of Peninsular Malaysia', in Ian Glover and Peter Bellwood (eds) *Southeast Asia: From Prehistory to History*, London and New York, RoutledgeCurzon, pp. 314–36.

Burenhult, Niclas (2001) 'Linguistic aspects of the Semang' in Razha Rashid and Wazir Jahan Karim (eds) *Minority Cultures of Peninsular Malaysia: Survivals of Indigenous Heritage*, Penang, Malaysia, Academy of Social Sciences (AKASS), pp. 75–82.

Burger, Julian (1987) *Report from the Frontier: The State of the World's Indigenous Peoples*, London, Zed.

Carey, Iskandar (1976) *Orang Asli: The Aboriginal Tribes of Peninsular Malaysia*, Kuala Lumpur, Oxford University Press.

Chee, Heng Leng (1995) 'Health and nutrition of the Orang Asli: the need for primary heath care amidst economic transformation', in Razha Rashid (ed.) *Indigenous Minorities of Peninsular Malaysia: Selected Issues and Ethnographies*, Kuala Lumpur, Intersocietal and Scientific Sdn. Bhd. (INAS), pp. 48–71.

COAC (2002) 'Victory for Orang Asli in land rights' case', *Aliran Monthly*, http://www.malaysia.net/aliran/monthly/2002/4d.html

Colchester, Marcus (1994) 'Sustaining the forests: the community-based approach in South and South-east Asia', *Development and Change*, 25: 69–100.

—— (1999) 'Introduction', in Minority Rights Group (ed.) *Forests and Indigenous Peoples of Asia*, London, Minority Rights Group International, pp. 4–8.

Conway, Gordon R. and Barbier, Edward B. (1990) *After the Green Revolution: Sustainable Agriculture for Development*, London, Earthscan.

Couillard, Marie-Andree (1980) *Tradition in Tension: Carving in a Jah Hut Community*, Penang, Malaysia, Penerbit Universiti Sains Malaysia.

Crush, Jonathan (ed.) (1995) *Power of Development*, London, Routledge.

Cultural Survival (1987) *Southeast Asian Tribal Groups and Ethnic Minorities: Prospects for the Eighties and Beyond*, Cambridge, Mass., Cultural Survival.

Dallos, Csilla (2003) 'Identity and opportunity: asymmetrical household integration among the Lanoh, newly sedentary hunter-gatherers and forest collectors of Peninsular Malaysia', unpublished PhD dissertation, McGill University.

Dentan, Robert Knox (1964) 'Senoi-Semang', in Frank M. Lebar, G. C. Hickey, and J. K. Musgrave (eds) *Ethnic Groups of Mainland Southeast Asia*, New Haven, Conn., Human Relations Area Files Press, pp. 176–86.

—— (1975) 'If there were no Malays, who would the Semai be', in Judith Nagata (ed.) *Pluralism in Malaysia: Myth and Reality*, Leiden, E. J. Brill, pp. 50–64.

—— (1979) *The Semai: A Non-Violent People of Malaya*, New York, Holt, Rinehart and Winston.

—— (1997) 'The persistence of received truth: how ruling class Malays construct Orang Asli identity', in Robert L. Winzeler (ed.) *Indigenous Peoples and the State: Politics, Land, and Ethnicity in the Malayan Peninsula and Borneo*, New Haven, Conn., Yale University Southeast Asia Studies Monograph 46, pp. 98–134.

—— Endicott, Kirk, Gomes, Alberto, and Hooker, Barry (1997), *Malaysia and the Original People: A Case Study of the Impact of Development on Indigenous Peoples*, Needham Heights, Mass, Allyn and Bacon.

Diffloth, Gerard (1979) 'Aslian languages and Southeast Asian prehistory', *Federation Museums Journal*, (N.S.), 24: 2–16.

Draper, Patricia (1975) '!Kung women: contrasts in sexual egalitarianism in foraging and sedentary contexts', in Rayna R. Reiter (ed.) *Toward an Anthropology of Women*, New York, Monthly Review Press, pp. 77–109.

Duncan, Christopher R. (ed.) (2004) *Civilizing the Margins: Southeast Asian Government Policies for the Development of Minorities*, Ithaca, Cornell University Press.

Dunn, Frederick L. (1968) 'Epidemiological factors: health and disease in hunters-gatherers', in Richard Lee and Irven DeVore (eds) *Man the Hunter*, Aldine, Chicago University Press, pp. 221–8.

—— (1975) *Rain-forest Collectors and Traders: A Study of Resource Utilisation in Modern and Ancient Malaya*, Kuala Lumpur, Monographs of the Malaysian Branch of the Royal Asiatic Society, No. 5.

Early, John D. and Headland, Thomas N. (1998) *Population Dynamics of a Philippine Rain Forest People: The San Ildefonso Agta*, Gainesville, University Press of Florida.

Edelman, Marc and Haugerud, Angelique (eds) (2005) *The Anthropology of Development and Globalization: From Classical Political Economy to Contemporary Neoliberalism*, Malden, Mass., Oxford, and Carlton, Victoria, Australia, Blackwell Publishing.

Endicott, Karen Lampell (1979) 'Batek Negrito sex roles', unpublished MA thesis, Australian National University.

—— (1981) 'The conditions of egalitarian male–female relationships in foraging societies', *Canberra Anthropology*, 4: 1–10.

—— (1999) 'Gender relations in hunter-gatherer societies', in Richard B. Lee and Richard Daly (eds) *The Cambridge Encyclopedia of Hunters and Gatherers*, Cambridge, Cambridge University Press, pp. 411–18.

Endicott, Kirk Michael (1974) 'Batek Negrito economy and social organization', unpublished PhD dissertation, Harvard University.

—— (1979a) *Batek Negrito Religion: The World-view and Rituals of a Hunting and Gathering People of Peninsular Malaysia*, Oxford, Clarendon Press.

—— (1979b) 'The impact of economic modernization on the Orang Asli (aborigines) of Northern Peninsular Malaysia', in James C. Jackson and Martin Rudner (eds) *Issues in Malayan Development*, Singapore, Heinemann, pp. 167–204.

—— (1983) 'The effects of slave raiding on the aborigines of the Malay Peninsula', in Anthony Reid (ed.) *Slavery, Bondage, and Dependency in Southeast Asia*, Brisbane, University of Queensland Press, pp. 216–45.

—— (1984) 'The economy of the Batek of Malaysia: annual and historical perspectives', in Barry L. Isaac (ed.) *Research in Economic Anthropology*, Vol. 6, Greenwich, Conn., JAI Press, pp. 29–52.

—— (1988) 'Property, power and conflict among the Batek of Malaysia', in Tim Ingold, David Riches, and James Woodburn (eds) *Hunters and Gatherer*, Vol. 2: *Property, Power and Ideology*, Oxford, Berg, pp. 110–27.

—— (1997) 'Batek history, interethnic relations, and subgroup dynamics', in Robert L. Winzeler (ed.) *Indigenous Peoples and the State: Politics, Land, and Ethnicity in the Malayan Peninsula and Borneo*, New Haven, Conn., Yale University Southeast Asia Studies Monograph 46, pp. 30–50.

—— (2002) 'The significance of trade in immediate-return societies', unpublished paper presented at Ninth Conference of Hunting and Gathering Societies in Edinburgh.

—— (n.d.) 'The Batek revisited: 1990: New conditions, new responses', unpublished manuscript.

—— and Dentan, Robert Knox (2004) 'Into the mainstream or into the backwater? Malaysian assimilation of Orang Asli', in Christopher R. Duncan (ed.) *Civilizing the Margins: Southeast Asian Government Policies for the Development of Minorities*, Ithaca, Cornell University Press, pp. 24–55.

Escobar, Arturo (1995) *Encountering Development: The Making and Unmaking of the Third World*, Princeton, NJ, Princeton University Press.

Evans, Ivor H. N. (1937) *The Negritos of Malaya*, Cambridge, Cambridge University Press.

Evrard, Olivier and Goudineau, Yves (2004) 'Planned resettlement, unexpected migrations and cultural trauma in Laos', *Development and Change*, 35: 937–62.

Ferguson, James (1990) *The AntiPolitics Machine: Development, Depoliticization and Bureaucratic Power in Lesotho*, Cambridge, Cambridge University Press.

Fix, Alan G. (1977) *The Demography of the Semai Senoi*, Ann Arbor, Mich., University of Michigan Museum of Anthropology.

—— (2002) 'Foragers, farmers, and traders in the Malayan Peninsula: origins of cultural and biological diversity', in Kathleen D. Morrison and Laura L. Junker (eds) *Forager-Traders in South and Southeast Asia: Long-term Histories*, Cambridge, Cambridge University Press.

Forde, Daryll C. (1971) *Habitat, Economy and Society: A Geographical Introduction to Ethnology*, 5th edn. First published 1934, London, Methuen.

Fratkin, Elliot M., Roth, Eric Abela, and Nathan, Martha A. (1999) 'When nomads settle: the effects of commoditization, nutritional change, and formal education on Ariaal and Rendille pastoralists', *Current Anthropology*, 40: 729–35.

Geertz, Clifford (1963) *Agricultural Involution: The Processes of Ecological Change in Indonesia*, Berkeley and Los Angeles, University of California Press.

Gianno, Rosemary (1990) *Semelai Culture and Resin Technology*, New Haven, Conn., The Connecticut Academy of Arts and Sciences.

Gibbons, David S., de Koninck, Rodolphe, and Ibrahim Hasan (1979) *Agricultural Modernization, Poverty and Inequality: The Distributional Impact of the Green Revolution in Regions of Malaysia and Indonesia*, Farnborough, Hants, Saxon House.

Giddens, Anthony (1990) *The Consequences of Modernity*, Cambridge, Polity.

Gomes, Alberto G. (1979) 'Ecological adaptation and population change: a comparative study of Semang foragers and Temuan horticulturalists', unpublished MA thesis, University of Malaya.

—— (1982) 'Ecological adaptation and population change: Semang foragers and Temuan horticulturalists in West Malaysia', Research Report No. 12, Honolulu, HI, Environment and Policy Institute, East-West Center.

—— (1983) 'Demography and environmental adaptation: a comparative study of two aboriginal populations in West Malaysia', in Wilfredo F. Arce and Gabriel F. Alvarez (eds) *Population Change in Southeast Asia*, Singapore, Institute of Southeast Asian Studies, pp. 391–477.

—— (1990) 'Demographic implications of villagisation among the Semang of Malaysia', in Betty Meehan and Neville White (eds) *Hunter-gatherer Demography: Past and Present*, Sydney, Oceania Publications.

—— (1994a) 'Introduction', in Alberto G. Gomes (ed.) *Modernity and Identity: Asian Illustrations*, Bundoora, Victoria, La Trobe University Press, pp. 1–22.

—— (1994b) 'Modernity and Semai ethnogenesis', in Alberto G. Gomes (ed.) *Modernity and Identity: Asian Illustrations*, Bundoora, Victoria, La Trobe University Press, pp. 176–91.

—— (1999a) 'Peoples and cultures', in Amarjit Kaur and Ian Bedford (eds) *The Shaping of Malaysia*, London, Macmillan, New York, St. Martin's Press, pp. 78–98.

—— (1999b) 'Modernity and indigenous minorities in Malaysia and Indonesia', *Review of Indonesian and Malaysian Affairs (RIMA)*, 33: 1–15.

—— (2002) 'Development', in Peter Beilharz and Trevor Hogan (eds) *Social Selves, Global Culture*, Melbourne, Oxford University Press, pp. 225–34.

—— (2004) *Looking for Money: Capitalism and Modernity in an Orang Asli Village*, Subang Jaya, Malaysia and Melbourne, Center for Orang Asli Concerns and Trans Pacific Press.

Gomez, Edmund Terence and Jomo, K. S. (1997) *Malaysia's Political Economy: Politics, Patronage and Profits*, Cambridge, Cambridge University Press.

Government of Malaysia (1961) 'Statement of policy regarding the administration of the Orang Asli of Peninsular Malaysia'.

Griffin, Bion P. (1991) 'Philippine Agta forager-serfs: commodities and exploitation', in Nicholas Peterson and Toshio Matsuyama (eds) *Cash, Commoditisation, and Changing Foragers*, Senri Ethnological Studies No. 30, Osaka, National Museum of Ethnology, pp. 199–222.

Gupta, Akhil (1998) *Postcolonial Developments: Agriculture in the Making of Modern India*, Durham, NC, Duke University Press.

Halim Salleh (1999) 'Development and the politics of social stability in Malaysia', *Southeast Asian Affairs 1999*, Singapore, Institute of Southeast Asian Studies, pp. 185–204.

Hamilton, Annette (2001) 'State's margins, people's centre: space and history in the Southern Thai jungles', *Nomadic Peoples*, 5: 89–103.

Harrell, Stevan (1995) 'Introduction: civilizing projects and the reaction to them', in Stevan Harrell (ed.) *Cultural Encounters on China's Ethnic Frontiers*, Seattle, University of Washington Press, pp. 3–36.

Headland, Thomas and Reid, Lawrence (1989) 'Hunter-gatherers and their neighbours from prehistory to the present', *Current Anthropology*, 30: 43–66.

Hendry, Joy (2005) *Reclaiming Culture: Indigenous People and Self-Representation*, New York and Basingstoke, Palgrave Macmillan.

Hong, Evelyne (1987) *Natives of Sarawak: Survival in Borneo's Vanishing Forests*, Penang, Institut Masyarakat.

Hood Mohd. Salleh (1978) 'Semelai rituals of curing', unpublished D.Phil. thesis, Oxford University.

Hooker, Barry M. (1976) *The Personal Laws of Malaysia: An Introduction*, Kuala Lumpur, Oxford University Press.

Howell, Signe (1983) 'Chewong women in transition: the effect of monetisation on a hunter-gatherer society of Malaysia', Occasional Paper 1 (Women and Development in Southeast Asia), Canterbury, University of Kent.

—— (1989) *Society and Cosmos*: *Chewong of Peninsular Malaysia*, Chicago, University of Chicago Press.

Howitt, Richard (2001) *Rethinking Resource Management: Justice, Sustainability and Indigenous Peoples*, New York, Routledge.

——, Connell, John and Hirsch, Philip (eds) (1996) *Resources, Nations and Indigenous Peoples: Case Studies from Australasia, Melanesia and Southeast Asia*, Melbourne, Oxford University Press.

Jennings, Sue (1995) *Theatre, Ritual and Transformation: The Senoi Temiars*, London, Routledge.

JHEOA (1993) *Programme Summary*, Kuala Lumpur, Jabatan Hal Ehwal Orang Asli.

Jimin Idris (1983) 'Planning and administration of development programmes from tribal peoples (the Malaysia Setting)', Kuala Lumpur, Center on Integrated Rural Development for Asia and the Pacific.

Jomo, K. S., Chang, Y. T. , and Khoo, K. J. (2004) *Deforesting Malaysia: The Political Economy and Social Ecology of Agricultural Expansion and Commercial Logging*, London, Zed Books in association with United Nations Research Institute for Social Development.

Jones, Alun (1968) 'The Orang Asli: an outline of their progress in modern Malaya', *Journal of Southeast Asian History*, 9 (2): 286–305.

Kahn, Joel S. (2001) 'Anthropology and modernity', *Current Anthropology*, 42: 651–80.

Karim, Wazir Jahan (1981) *Ma' Betisek Concepts of Living Things*, London, Athlone Press, London School of Economics Monographs on Social Anthropology No. 54.

—— (1995) 'Transformations in Ma' Betise' economics and ideology: recurrent themes of nomadism', in Razha Rashid (ed.) *Indigenous Minorities of Peninsular Malaysia: Selected Issues and Ethnographies*, Kuala Lumpur, Intersocietal and Scientific Sdn. Bhd. (INAS), pp. 109–27.

Kent, Susan (1995) 'Does sedentarization promote gender inequality? A case study from the Kalahari', *Journal of the Royal Anthropological Institute*, (N.S.), 1: 513–36.

Khor Geok Lin (1994) 'Resettlement and nutritional implications: the case of Orang Asli in regroupment schemes', *Pertanika (Journal of the Society for Science and Humanities)*, 2 (2): 123–32.

King, Victor T. and Wilder, W. D. (2003) *The Modern Anthropology of South-East Asia: An Introduction*, London, RoutledgeCurzon.

Kingsbury, Benedict (1995) ' "Indigenous peoples" as an international legal concept', in R. H. Barnes, Andrew Gray, and Benedict Kingsbury (eds) *Indigenous Peoples of Asia*, Ann Arbor, Mich., Association for Asian Studies, Monographs of the Association for Asian Studies No. 48.

Knauft, Bruce M. (ed.) (2002a) *Critically Modern: Alternatives, Alterities, Anthropologies*, Bloomington, Indiana University Press.

—— (2002b) *Exchanging the Past: A Rainforest World of Before and After*, Chicago, University of Chicago Press.

Laird, Peter (1978) 'Temoq shamanism and affliction: a preliminary investigation', unpublished PhD thesis, Monash University.

Leacock, Eleanor (1954) *The Montagnais 'Hunting Territory' and the Fur Trade*, American Anthropological Association, Memoir No. 78.

—— (1987) 'Women in egalitarian societies', in Renate Bridenthal, Claudia Koonz, and Susan Stuard (eds) *Becoming Visible: Women in European History*, Boston, Houghton Mifflin, pp. 15–38.

—— and Lee, Richard B. (eds) (1982) *Politics and History in Band Societies*, Cambridge, Cambridge University Press.

Lee, Richard B. (1979) *The !Kung San: Men, Women, and Work in a Foraging Society*, Cambridge, Cambridge University Press.

—— and Daly, Richard (eds) (1999) *The Cambridge Encyclopedia of Hunters and Gatherers*, Cambridge, Cambridge University Press.

Li, Tania (ed.) (1999) *Transforming the Indonesian Uplands: Marginality, Power and Production*, Amsterdam, Harwood Academic Publishers.

—— (2001) 'Masyarakat adat, difference, and the limits of recognition in Indonesia's forest zone', *Modern Asian Studies*, 35 (3): 645–76.

Lim, Teck Ghee and Gomes, Alberto G. (eds) (1990) *Tribal Peoples and Development in Southeast Asia*, Special issue of the Journal *Manusia dan Masyarakat* (Humans and Soceity), Kuala Lumpur, Department of Anthropology, University of Malaya.

Lopez-Gonzaga, V. (1983) *Peasants in the Hills: A Study of the Dynamics of Social Change Among the Buhid Swidden Cultivators in the Philippines*, Diliman, Quezon City, University of the Philippines Press.

Lye, Tuck Po (1997) 'Knowledge, forest, and hunter-gatherer movement: the Batek of Pahang, Malaysia', unpublished PhD dissertation, University of Hawai'i.

—— (ed.) (2001) *Orang Asli of Peninsular Malaysia: A Comprehensive and Annotated Bibliography*, Center for Southeast Asian Studies (CSEAS) Research Report Series No. 88, Kyoto, Japan, Kyoto University.

—— (2003) 'Forest peoples, conservation boundaries, and the problem of "modernity" in Malaysia', in Geoffrey Benjamin and Cynthia Chou (eds) *Tribal Communities in the Malay World: Historical, Social and Cultural Perspectives*, Leiden, IIAS, Singapore, ISEAS, pp. 160–84.

McKinley, Robert (1976) 'Human and proud of it! A structural treatment of headhunting rites and the social definition of enemies', in George N. Appell (ed.) *Studies in Borneo Societies: Social Process and Anthropological Explanation*, De Kalb, Ill., Center for Southeast Asian Studies, Northern Illinois University, pp. 92–126.

Mahathir Mohamad (1970) *The Malay Dilemma*, Singapore, Donald Moore for Asia Pacific Press.

—— (1984) 'Malaysia incorporated and privatisation: its rationale and purpose', in Mohamed Nor Abdul Ghani *et al.* (eds) *Malaysia Incorporated and Privatization: Towards National Unity*, Petaling Jaya, Malaysia, Pelanduk Publications, pp. 1–7.

Maybury-Lewis, David (2002) *Indigenous Peoples, Ethnic Groups, and the State*, 2nd edn, Boston, Allyn and Bacon.

Meyer, Christoph (2003) 'Good on the ground: indigenous Orang Asli at the FSC-certified PITC-concession in Peninsular Malaysia', http://www.tropicalforesttrust.com/reports-docs/GoodontheGround.pdf

Miller, Bruce Granville (2003) *Invisible Indigenes: The Politics of Nonrecognition*, Lincoln and London, University of Nebraska Press.

Mohd. Tap Salleh (1990) 'An examination of development planning among the rural Orang Asli of West Malaysia', unpublished PhD thesis, University of Bath.

Murdock, George P. (1934) *Our Primitive Contemporaries*, New York, The Macmillan Co.

Murphy, Robert F. and Steward, Julian H. (1956) 'Tappers and trappers: parallel process in acculturation', *Economic Development and Cultural Change*, 4: 335–55.

Nagata, Judith (1974) 'What is a Malay? Situational selection of ethnic identity in a plural society', *American Ethnologist*, 1: 331–50.

—— (1981) 'In defense of ethnic boundaries: the changing myths and charters of Malay Identity', in Charles Keyes (ed.) *Ethnic Change*, Seattle, University of Washington Press.

—— (1984) *The Reflowering of Malaysian Islam: Modern Religious Radicals and Their Roots*, Vancouver, University of British Columbia Press.

Nagata, Shuichi (1995) 'Education and socialisation in a Semang resettlement community of Kedah, Malaysia: the case of the Kensiu, the Kintak Bogn and the Kintak Nakil', in Razha Rashid (ed.) *Indigenous Minorities of Peninsular Malaysia: Selected Issues and Ethnographies*, Kuala Lumpur, Intersocietal and Scientific Sdn. Bhd. (INAS), pp. 86–108.

—— (1997a) 'The origin of an Orang Asli reserve in Kedah', in Robert L. Winzeler (ed.) *Indigenous Peoples and the State: Politics, Land, and Ethnicity in the Malayan Peninsula and Borneo*, New Haven, Conn., Yale University Southeast Asia Studies Monograph 46, pp. 84–97.

—— (1997b) 'Working for money among the Orang Asli in Kedah, Malaysia', *Contributions to Southeast Asian Ethnography*, 11: 13–31.

—— (2004) 'Leadership in a resettlement village of the Orang Asli in Kedah, Malaysia', *Contributions to Southeast Asian Ethnography*, 12: 95–126.

—— (2006) 'Subgroup "names" of the Sakai (Thailand) and the Semang (Malaysia): a literature survey', *Anthropological Science*, 114: 45–57.

Nash, June (2001) *Mayan Visions: The Quest for Autonomy in an Age of Globalization*, New York and London, Routledge.

Needham, Rodney (1964) 'Blood, thunder, and mockery of animals', *Sociologus*, 14 (2): 136–49.

Nicholas, Colin (1990) 'In the name of the Semai? The State and Semai society in Peninsular Malaysia', in Lim Teck Ghee and Alberto G. Gomes (eds) *Tribal Peoples and Development in Southeast Asia*, Special issue of the Journal *Manusia dan Masyarakat* (Humans and Soceity), Kuala Lumpur, Department of Anthropology and Sociology, University of Malaya, pp. 68–88.

—— (1994) *Pathway to Dependence: Commodity Relations and the Dissolution of Semai Society*, Clayton, Victoria, Australia, Monash University Centre of Southeast Asian Studies, Monash Papers on Southeast Asia No. 33.

—— (2000) *The Orang Asli and the Contest for Resources: Indigenous Politics, Development and Identity in Peninsular Malaysia*, Copenhagen, International Work Group for Indigenous Affairs, Subang Jaya, Malaysia, Centre for Orang Asli Concerns.

—— and Singh, Raajen (eds) (1996) *Indigenous Peoples of Asia: Many Peoples, One Struggle*, Bangkok, Thailand, Asian Indigenous Peoples Pact.

Nietschmann, Bernard Q. (1973) *Between Land and Water: The Subsistence Ecology of the Miskito Indians, Eastern Nicaragua*, New York, Seminar Press.

Niezen, Ronald (2003) *The Origins of Indigenism: Human Rights and the Politics of Identity*, Berkeley, Los Angeles and London, University of California Press.

Noone, H. D. (1936) 'Report on the settlements and welfare of the Ple-Temiar Senoi of the Perak-Kelantan watershed', *Journal of Federated Malay States Museums*, 19: 1–85.

Nowak, Barbara S. (1986) 'Marriage and household: Btsisi' response to a changing world', unpublished PhD dissertation, State University of New York, Buffalo.

Olivier de Sardan, Jean-Pierre (2005) *Anthropology and Development: Understanding Contemporary Social Change*, London and New York, Zed Books.

Panter-Brick, Catherine, Layton, Robert H., and Rowley-Conwy, Peter (eds) (2001) *Hunter-gatherers: An Interdisciplinary Perspective*, Cambridge, Cambridge University Press.

Pennington, Renee (2001) 'Hunter-gatherer demography', in Catherine Panter-Brick, Robert H. Layton, and Peter Rowley-Conwy (eds) *Hunter-gatherers: An Interdisciplinary Perspective*, Cambridge, Cambridge University Press, pp. 170–204.

Perry, Richard J. (1996) . . . *From Time Immemorial: Indigenous Peoples and State Systems*, Austin, University of Texas Press.

Peterson, Nicholas (1991) 'Introduction: cash, commoditisation and changing foragers', in Nicholas Peterson and Toshio Matsuyama (eds) *Cash, Commoditisation, and Changing Foragers*, Senri Ethnological Studies No. 30, Osaka, National Museum of Ethnology, pp. 1–16.

—— (1993) 'Demand sharing: reciprocity and the pressure for generosity among foragers', *American Anthropologist*, 95 (4): 860–74.

—— and Matsuyama, Toshio (eds) (1991) *Cash, Commoditisation, and Changing Foragers*, Senri Ethnological Studies No. 30, Osaka, National Museum of Ethnology.

Polunin, Ivan (1953) 'The medical natural history of Malayan Aborigines', *The Medical Journal of Malaya*, 8 (1): 55–174.

Porath, Nathan (2001) 'Foraging Thai culture: a performing tribe of South Thailand', in D. G. Anderson and K. Ikeya (eds) *Parks, Property, and Power: Managing Hunting Practice and Identity within State Policy Regimes*, Senri Ethnological Studies No. 59, Osaka, National Museum of Ethnology.

Pred, Allan and Watts, Michael (1992) *Reworking Modernity: Capitalisms and Symbolic Discontent*, New Brunswick, NJ, Rutgers University Press.

Rambo, A. Terry (1978) 'Bows, blowpipes and blunderbusses: ecological implications of weapons change among the Malaysian Negritos', *Malayan Nature Journal*, 32: 206–16.

—— (1979) 'Primitive man's impact on genetic resources of the Malaysian tropical rain forest', *Malaysian Applied Biology*, 8 (1): 59–65.

—— (1985) *Primitive Polluters: Semang Impact on the Malaysian Tropical Rain Forest Ecosystem*, Ann Arbor, Mich., University of Michigan Museum of Anthropology, Anthropological Papers No. 76.

Razha Rashid (ed.) (1995) *Indigenous Minorities of Peninsular Malaysia: Selected Issues and Ethnographies*, Kuala Lumpur, Intersocietal and Scientific Sdn. Bhd. (INAS).

—— and Wazir Jahan Karim (eds) (2001) *Minority Cultures of Peninsular Malaysia: Survivals of Indigenous Heritage*, Penang, Malaysia, Academy of Social Sciences (AKASS).

Robarchek, Clayton (1977) 'Semai non-violence: a systems approach to understanding', unpublished PhD dissertation, University of California at Riverside.

Robinson, Herbert C. and Kloss, C. Boden (1913) 'Additional notes on the Semang Paya of Ijok, Selama, Perak', *Journal of Federated Malay States Museums*, 5 (4): 187–91.

Rokeman Abdul Jalil (1988) 'Rancangan pembangunan dan Orang Asli: Satu ethnografi terhadap Orang Jahai di Sungai Rual, Kelantan' [Development planning and Orang Asli: an ethnographic study of the Jahai of Sungai Rual, Kelantan], unpublished BA graduation exercise, Department of Anthropology and Sociology, University of Malaya.

Rosaldo, Renato (1980) *Ilongot Headhunting, 1883–1974: A Study in Society and History*, Stanford, Calif., Stanford University Press.

Roseman, Marina (1991) *Healing Sounds from the Rainforest: Temiar Music and Medicine*, Berkeley, University of California Press.

Rostow, Walt W. (1960) *The Stages of Economic Growth: A Non-Communist Manifesto*, Cambridge, Cambridge University Press.

Sachs, Wolfgang (ed.) (1992) *The Development Dictionary: A Guide to Knowledge as Power*, London, Zed Books.

Sacks, Karen (1974) 'Engels revisited: women, the organization of production, and private property', in Michelle Z. Rosaldo and Louise Lamphere (eds) *Woman, Culture, and Society*, Stanford, Calif., Stanford University Press, pp. 207–22.

Sahlins, Marshall (1972) *Stone Age Economics*, Chicago, Aldine.

Schebesta, Paul (1926) 'The jungle tribes of the Malay Peninsula', *Bulletin of the School of Oriental and Asian Studies*, 4: 269–78.

—— (1928) *Among the Forest Dwarfs of Malaya*, London, Hutchinsons. Reprinted 1973, London, Oxford University Press.

—— (1954) *Die Negrito Asiens: Wirtschaft and Soziologie*, St. Gabriel-Verlag, Vienna-Modling, Studia Instituti Anthropos, Vol. 12. Partially translated by Frieda Schutze, Human Relations Area Files, 1962.

—— and V. Lebzelter (1928) 'Anthropological measurements on Semangs and Sakais in Malaya', *Anthropologie (Praque)*, 6: 183–251.

Schech, Susanne and Jane Haggis (2000) *Culture and Development: A Critical Introduction*, Oxford and Malden, Mass., Blackwell Publishers.

Schrire, Carmel (ed.) (1984) *Past and Present in Hunter-Gatherer Studies*, Orlando, Fla., Academic Press.

Schweitzer, Peter P., Biesele, Megan, and Hitchcock, Robert K. (eds) (2000) *Hunters and Gatherers in the Modern World: Conflict, Resistance, and Self-Determination*, New York and Oxford, Berghahn Books.

Scott, James C. (1976) *The Moral Economy of the Peasant: Rebellion and Subsistence in Southeast Asia*, New Haven, Conn., and London, Yale University Press.

—— (1985) *Weapons of the Weak: Everyday Forms of Peasant Resistance*, New Haven, Conn., and London, Yale University Press.

—— (1998) *Seeing Like a State: How Certain Schemes to Improve the Human Condition Have Failed*, New Haven, Conn., Yale University Press.

Searle, Peter (1999) *The Riddle of Malaysian Capitalism: Rent-seekers or Real Capitalists?*, St Leonards, NSW, Allen and Unwin.

Sellato, Bernard (1994) *Nomads of the Borneo Rainforest: The Economics, Politics, and Ideology of Settling Down*, trans. Stephanie Morgan, Honolulu, University of Hawai'i Press.

Shiva, Vandana (1991) *The Violence of the Green Revolution: Third World Agriculture, Ecology, and Politics*, Penang, Malaysia, Third World Network.

Sissons, Jeffrey (2005) *First Peoples: Indigenous Cultures and their Futures*, London, Reaktion Books.

Skeat, Walter William and Blagden, Charles Otto (1906) *Pagan Races of the Malay Peninsula*, London, Macmillan, 2 vols. Reprinted 1966, London, Frank Cass.

Sloane, Patricia (1999) *Islam, Modernity and Entrepreneurship among the Malays*, London, Macmillan and New York, St. Martin's Press.

Stewart-Harawira, Makere (2005) *The New Imperial Order: Indigenous Responses to Globalization*, London, New York, and Wellington (New Zealand), Zed Books and Huia Publishers.

Talalla, Rohini (1985) 'Ethnodevelopment and the Orang Asli of Malaysia: a case study of the Betau Settlement for Semai-Senoi', *Antipode*, 16: 27–32.

Thambiah, Shanti (1999) 'Orang Asli women and men in transition', in Jomo Kwame Sundram (ed.) *Rethinking Malaysia*, Hong Kong, Asia 2000, pp. 267–92.

Tsing, Anna Lowenhaupt (1993) *In the Realm of the Diamond Queen: Marginality in an Out-of-the-Way Place*, Princeton, NJ, Princeton University Press.

Van der Sluys, Cornelia (1999) 'The Jahai of northern Peninsular Malaysia', in Richard B. Lee and Richard Daly (eds) *The Cambridge Encyclopedia of Hunters and Gatherers*, Cambridge, Cambridge University Press, pp. 307–11.

—— (2000) 'Gifts from the immortal ancestors: cosmology and ideology of Jahai Semang', in Peter P. Schweitzer, Megan Biesele, and Robert K. Hitchcock (eds) *Hunters and Gatherers in the Modern World: Conflict, Resistance, and Self-Determination*, New York and Oxford, Berghahn Books, pp. 427–54.

Wilkinson, Richard James (1910) *Papers on Malay Subjects*, Kuala Lumpur, Federated Malay States Government Press.

—— (n.d.) *A Malay–English Dictionary*, Tokyo, Armed Forces.

Williams-Hunt, Peter D. R. (1952) *An Introduction to the Malayan Aborigines*, Kuala Lumpur, Government Press.

Willis, Katie (2005) *Theories and Practices of Development*, London and New York, Routledge.

Wilmer, Franke (1993) *Indigenous Voice in World Politics*, Newbury Park, Calif., Sage Publications.

Wilmsen, Edwin N. (1989) *A Land Filled with Flies: A Political Economy of the Kalahari*, Cambridge, Cambridge University Press.

Winzeler, Robert L. (1997) *Indigenous Peoples and the State: Politics, Land, and Ethnicity in the Malayan Peninsula and Borneo*, New Haven, Conn., Yale University, Southeast Asia Studies Monograph 46.

Wolf, Eric R. (1982) *Europe and the People Without History*, Berkeley, University of California Press.

Woodburn, James (1980) 'Hunters and gatherers today and reconstruction of the past', in Ernest Gellner (ed.) *Soviet and Western Anthropology*, London, Duckworth, pp. 95–117.

—— (1982) 'Egalitarian societies', *Man*, 17: 431–51.

World Bank (1990) 'Indigenous peoples in Bank-financed projects', Operational Directive 4.40, Washington, DC, The World Bank.

Zalina Mohd Zain (2000) 'Sejarah perkembangan masyarakat Orang Asli Kampung Sungai Rual Jeli, Kelantan' [History of societal development of Sungai Rual Jeli Orang Asli village, Kelantan], unpublished BA graduation exercise, History Department, University of Malaya.

Zulkifli, A., Khairul Anuar A., and Atiya, A. S. (1999) 'The nutritional status of children in resettlement villages in Kelantan', *Southeast Asian Journal of Tropical Medicine and Public Health*, 30 (1): 122–8.

Index

Page numbers in *Italics* represent Tables and page numbers in **Bold** represent Figures. Page numbers followed by {n} are endnotes.

Printed in the United States
by Baker & Taylor Publisher Services